UNIVERSITY RELIGION SERIES

UNIVERSITY RELIGION SERIES

Theology for the Layman

The Christian Virtues
CHARLES E. SHEEDY, C.S.C.

Evidence for Our Faith
JOSEPH H. CAVANAUGH, C.S.C.

God and the World of Man
THEODORE M. HESBURGH, C.S.C.

Redemptive Incarnation
ALBERT L. SCHLITZER, C.S.C.

EVIDENCE FOR
OUR FAITH

by Joseph H. Cavanaugh, C.S.C.

UNIVERSITY OF NOTRE DAME PRESS

Notre Dame, Indiana

Imprimi Potest: Theodore J. Mehling, C.S.C., Provincial

Nihil Obstat: Roland G. Simonitsch, C.S.C., Censor Deputatus

Imprimatur: Leo A. Pursley, D.D., Ll.D.,
Bishop of Fort Wayne

June 19, 1959

Third Edition 1959

First Printing 1959
Second Printing 1960

Library of Congress Catalog Card Number 59-10456

© Copyright, 1949, 1952, 1959
University of Notre Dame Press
Notre Dame, Indiana

Preface to the Third Edition

THIS textbook was first published in 1948. Despite other heavy and time-consuming responsibilities, the author prepared a second, revised edition which appeared in 1952. The work on a third revision was interrupted by his untimely death in 1953.

The present textbook incorporates some of the changes planned by the author. It is the work of a committee appointed by the head of the Religion Department, Rev. Roland Simonitsch, C.S.C. The committee was made up of Rev. George Bernard, C.S.C., Rev. F. G. Connolly, Rev. Joseph Haley, C.S.C., Rev. James Maguire, and Rev. Robert Pelton, C.S.C.

The attention of the committee was focused primarily upon the general makeup of the textbook in accordance with the demands of an undergraduate course. It was deemed advisable to draw a sharper line of demarcation between the general discussion of the Church's authority to teach, govern, and sanctify all mankind and the special discussion of the teaching authority of the Church than had been done in the preceding editions. This was accomplished by making them into two parts of the textbook. To these was added a third part in which the two primary sources of the Church's doctrines, Holy Scripture and Tradition, are briefly examined. Time will tell whether and to what extent this third part should be further expanded.

Two principal changes have been made in the first part of the textbook which deals with the general authority of the Church, namely, the authority to teach, govern, and sanctify all mankind.

First of all, the chapters on the philosophical presuppositions to the course were made into an appendix and transferred to the end of the book. Secondly, at the urging of a number of teachers who use the textbook, two new chapters were added. In the first, the present-day "world" religions are briefly described. In the second, a general picture of the background of Christ's claims is drawn.

In the second part, which deals with the teaching authority of the Church, a chapter has been introduced on the infallible teaching authority in action. In it the twofold magisterium of the Church, ordinary and solemn, and the twofold manner in which the solemn magisterium is exercised, are examined.

The members of the committee have willingly sacrificed much time and effort in order to continue the work of the author, Rev. Joseph Cavanaugh, C.S.C. They did so in tribute to a kindly, unassuming and devoted priest. This third edition is dedicated to his memory.

F. G. Connolly
Chairman of the Revision Committee

Notre Dame, Indiana
May 4, 1959

Preface to the Previous Edition

THIS textbook is the product of many classes in Apologetics at the University of Notre Dame. It was written to explain how reasonable it is to believe what the Catholic Church teaches. In other words, it is an attempt to present the case for Catholicism. The difficulty has been, not to find sufficient evidence for the case, but to select the best evidence and to present it convincingly in such a little book. If a student thinks the evidence for any point is insufficient or the explanation unsatisfactory, he can consult the books mentioned in the bibliography, for the more he searches through the evidence, the more reasons he will discover for accepting the Catholic faith. Indeed, the Church welcomes critical research that is sincere.

In this book, the appeal is not to the emotions and prejudices of the student, but to his intelligence. It is a statement of facts and reasons and not an expression of feelings. Though I have tried to avoid the controversial note, I have not hesitated to state the reasons why Catholic scholars regard their church as the only true church. Just as a good scientist attempts to present to his students in a fair and objective manner the facts and reasons for a scientific conclusion, so I have tried to state fairly and objectively the historical facts and reasons that establish the claim of the Catholic Church to be the one society founded by Christ and assured of his divine assistance even to the consummation of the world.

May this book, written in honor of our Blessed Mother at the University she has blessed so abundantly, bring the reader to a greater knowledge and love of our Lord Jesus Christ and of his Mystical Body, the Church.

Joseph H. Cavanaugh, c.s.c.

University of Notre Dame

Acknowledgments

THE author wishes to thank the following publishers for their kind permission to reprint selections from their publications.

The Atlantic Monthly: "What About Church Unity?," by Bernard Iddings Bell. Geoffrey Bles Ltd.: *Miracles*, by C. S. Lewis. The Bruce Publishing Company: *The Question and the Answer*, by Hilaire Belloc. Burns, Oates, and Washbourne, Ltd.: *The Early Papacy*, by Adrian Fortescue. The Dial Press: *Why Rome*, by Selden Peabody Delany. Eyre and Spottiswoode: *Difficulties*, by Ronald A. Knox and Arnold Lunn. Fathers of the Church Inc. for some translations. Harper and Brothers: *Our Bible and the Ancient Manuscripts*, by Sir Frederic Kenyon; *The Belief of Catholics*, by Ronald A. Knox; *Can Protestantism Win America*, by Charles Clayton Morrison; *Christian Apologetics*, by Alan Richardson. B. Herder Book Company: *The Believer's Christ*, by Ludwig Koesters; *Reason to Revelation*, by Daniel J. Saunders; *The Disciplinary Decrees of the General Councils*, by H. J. Schroeder. The John Hopkins Press: *From the Stone Age to Christianity*, by William Foxwell Albright. Longmans, Green and Company: *He Who Is*, by E. L. Mascall. The Macmillan Company: *Does God Exist?*, by A. E. Taylor; *The Catholic Church and History*, and *Survivals and New Arrivals*, by Hilaire Belloc; *Towards Reunion*, edited by Alexander Carlyle; *The Case for Christianity*, by C. S. Lewis; *Jesus of Nazareth*, by Joseph Klausner; *The Church on Earth*, by Ronald A. Knox; *The Theology of Albert Schweitzer*, by E. N. Mozley; *Truths Men Live By*, by John A. O'Brien; *The*

Catholic Church and the Appeal to Reason, by Leo P. Ward. The Newman Press: *The Third Day,* by Arnold Lunn. G. P. Putnam's Sons: *Luke the Physician, The Date of the Acts and of the Synoptic Gospels,* and *What Is Christianity?,* by Adolf Harnack. Sheed and Ward: *Religions of Mankind,* by Otto Karrer; *Broadcast Minds,* by Ronald A. Knox; *Now I see* and *Within That City,* by Arnold Lunn; *Catholic Evidence Outlines,* by Maisie Ward and F. J. Sheed; *Pascal,* by Jacques Chevalier. Time magazine for part of a story about "Mother Cabrini." Williams and Norgate: *History of Dogma,* by Adolf Harnack. These selections are copyrighted (at the dates indicated in the footnotes) and may be reprinted only with permission of the publishers.

Contents

Preface to the Third Edition vii

Preface to the Previous Edition ix

Acknowledgments xi

Introduction 1

Part I. THE CHURCH'S AUTHORITY 5

I. *The Religions of Mankind* 7
    I. HINDUISM 7
    II. BUDDHISM 8
    III. TAOISM, CONFUCIANISM AND SHINTOISM . . . 9
    IV. ISLAM 11
    V. ATHEISTIC COMMUNISM 12
    VI. CONCLUSION 14

II. *Christ's Background* 15
    I. FROM ADAM TO ABRAHAM 16
    II. FROM ABRAHAM TO CHRIST 16

III. *Christ's Claims* 26
    I. CHRIST'S LIFE AND DEATH 26
    II. IN THE BEGINNING HIS CLAIMS WERE OBSCURE . 27
    III. IMPLICIT CLAIMS 30
        A. He Perfects the Law of Moses 30
        B. He Is Superior to Prophets and Kings . . 31

C. He Claims Utter Allegiance 31
D. He Will Judge All Men 32
E. He Demands the Same Reverence as His Father
Receives 32
F. He Alone Knows God's Mind and God Alone
Knows His 33
G. He Forgives Sins 34
H. He Works Miracles 34
IV. EXPLICIT CLAIMS 35
A. He Has Pre-Existed with the Father . . 35
B. He Is Equal to the Father 35
C. St. Peter's Confession 36
D. The Transfiguration 37
E. The Parable of the Wicked Husbandmen . . 38
F. His Trial Before Caiphas 39
G. Confirmation 40
V. CONCLUSION 41
READING: The Question Concerning Christ . 41

IV. *The Historicity of the Gospels* 44
I. THE GOSPEL CRITICS 44
II. PROOF OF THE HISTORICITY OF A DOCUMENT . 49
A. Tests of Historicity 49
B. Evidence 50
III. THE HISTORICITY OF THE GOSPELS . . . 51
A. Evidence That the Gospels Are Genuine . . 51
B. Evidence That the Gospels Are Trustworthy . 55
C. Evidence That the Gospels Are Integral . 56
D. Conclusion 62
IV. ACTS OF THE APOSTLES AND EPISTLES OF ST. PAUL 62
V. APPENDIX: OTHER EARLY DOCUMENTS . . 63
READING: GOSPEL SCEPTICS 65

V. *Christ's Claims Are Credible* 71
I. THE PROMISED REDEEMER 71
II. THE SON OF GOD 74
A. The First Proof 74
B. The Second Proof 75
C. The Third Proof 87

D. Confirmations 97
E. Resurrections in Other Religions 100
III. CONCLUSION 103
READING: THE HALLUCINATION THEORY . . 104

VI. *The Testimony of History* 108
I. CATHOLIC AND PROTESTANT VIEWS . . . 110
A. The Catholic View 110
B. Protestant Views 111
II. THE EPISCOPAL AUTHORITY 113
A. Evidence from Scripture 113
B. Evidence from Tradition 119
1. The General Councils 119
2. The Fathers of the Church 122
III. PAPAL AUTHORITY 125
A. Evidence from Scripture 125
B. Evidence from Tradition 136
IV. CONCLUSION 146

VII. *The Stamp of God's Approval* 148
I. ITS MARVELLOUS GROWTH 149
II. ITS LOFTY HOLINESS 153
III. ITS INEXHAUSTIBLE FRUITFULNESS . . . 159
IV. ITS CATHOLIC UNITY 162
V. ITS UNCONQUERED STABILITY 165

VIII. *The Marks of the Church* 167
I. OUR LORD'S INTENTION 167
II. THE CHURCH AND THE MARKS 173
III. NO SALVATION OUTSIDE THE CHURCH . . 176

Part II. THE TEACHING AUTHORITY OF THE CHURCH 179

IX. *The Infallibility of the Pope* 181
I. THE INFALLIBILITY OF THE CHURCH . . . 183
A. Antecedent Probability 184
B. Proofs from Scripture and Tradition . . 185

  II. THE INFALLIBILITY OF THE POPE 188
       A. Scripture 189
       B. The Fathers and Councils 190
       C. The Infallible Church 195
       D. Alleged Failures 196
 III. CONCLUSION 200
       READING: THE WEIGHT OF EVIDENCE . . . 201

  X. *The Teaching Authority in Action* 204
   I. THE ORDINARY MAGISTERIUM 204
  II. THE SOLEMN MAGISTERIUM 206
       A. The Roman Pontiff 206
       B. The Ecumenical Council 208
 III. CONCLUSION 210

Part III. THE SOURCES 213

 XI. *Holy Scripture and Tradition* 215
   I. HOLY SCRIPTURE 215
  II. TRADITION 219
 III. THE DEVELOPMENT OF DOCTRINE 221

Appendix: PHILOSOPHICAL PRESUPPOSITIONS . . 225
   I. HUMAN REASON AND GOD 225
       A. God's Existence 225
       B. God's Nature and Attributes 229
       C. Common Objections 231
  II. REASON AND RELIGION 235
       A. Reason Tells Us Some Duties Towards God . 235
       B. The Reliability of Reason Alone as a Guide
           in Religion 237
       C. Evolution in Religion 240
       SUPPLEMENTARY READINGS 242
           The Existence of God 242
           Boys' Philosophies 244
           The Religion of the Primitive 246

Select Bibliography 250

Index 255

Introduction

YEARS ago, shortly after your birth, you were carried to your parish church for one of the most important events of your life. For there and then you became a member of the Roman Catholic Church through your reception of the sacrament of baptism at the hands of your parish priest or his official delegate. A few years later, when you had reached the age of reason and had become personally responsible before God for your conduct, you became a full-fledged member of the Church through your reception of the sacrament of confirmation at the hands of the bishop of your diocese or his official delegate. Since then you have learned much about the Church and her teachings. Now, as you are approaching maturity, the time has come when you should examine the foundations of your faith as a Roman Catholic. That is exactly what we intend to do in this course.[1]

Unfortunately, many young Catholic men and women do not see the necessity of making such an investigation. In many cases it stems from a failure to realize as yet how many-sided and bitter is the attack upon their faith in the world today. There is, first of all, the open and relentless opposition of atheistic communism to all religion and, especially, to the Catholic Church which it looks upon as the bulwark of religion. And, remember, this drive against religion and the Church is carried on with all the modern weapons of propaganda in the hands of an all-powerful State.

1. This course is called, in technical language, Fundamental Theology, that is to say, the study of the fundaments, the foundations, of our faith.

Another increasing challenge from outside Christianity comes from the growth of nationalism in the eastern world. This ferment has done much to revitalize the religions of eastern origin, Buddhism, Hinduism, Islam, and so on. Their new lease on life is manifesting itself more and more markedly in a growing opposition to Christianity, which is often considered as the religion of the "imperialistic" west, and in an increase of missionary activity even in the western world.

Besides these attacks from outside, there are other, more subtle and dangerous conflicts within Christianity itself. On the one hand, we are faced with a distortion of the Christian message by the Liberal Protestants because of their re-interpretation of that message in the light of an extreme rationalist and naturalist philosophy of life. On the other hand, we are confronted with the equally disastrous re-interpretation of that message by the Conservative Protestants in the light of their extreme irrationalist and supernaturalist philosophy of life.

Finally, there is the even more corrosive influence of religious indifferentism and of secularism to which all too many have already succumbed in the western world. In fact, it could well be argued that these insidious errors have done more harm to religion and to the Church than any of the more open and above-board attacks of their bitterest enemies.

All in all, it can be truthfully said that the faith of Roman Catholics has never been so sharply challenged and threatened since the foundation of the Church two thousand years ago. Such is the situation facing the young Catholic man or woman who is preparing to go out into the present-day world. From this challenge and this threat there is no escape. The only weapon of defense, if we do prize our faith as "the pearl of great price," is a careful and thorough-going examination of its foundations.

Such an investigation is carried out in three steps. First of all, there is the so-called "apologetic" problem,[2] which actually breaks down into two problems. The first is this: Why should I be a Christian, a follower of Jesus Christ? To one brought up in the western world and, especially, to one brought up in a thoroughly Christian environment, that may not seem, at first glance, to pose much of a problem. But think of it from the broader point of

2. An apology is a defense. This part of Fundamental Theology, in which we defend our position as Roman Catholics, is often called Apologetics.

view of a world that grows smaller and smaller as the years roll by. Many religions claim the allegiance of the peoples of the earth. Of its 2,600,000,000 inhabitants, only some 820,000,000, or less than a third, are Christians. Millions and millions of other men are just as confirmed followers of other great religious leaders of the past, of Buddha, Mohammed, Confucius, and so on. Why be a follower of Christ, not of one or the other of these leaders? And, by the way, some of these religions antedate the Christian religion by many centuries.

The second problem arises from the divisions within Christianity itself. Of the 820,000,000 Christians in the world today, some 485,000,000 are Roman Catholics; about 129,000,000 belong to the Separated Eastern Churches; [3] around 206,000,000 are Protestants. The second problem then is this: Why be a Roman Catholic? Why not be a Protestant or a member of one or other of the Separated Eastern Churches?

In order to defend our position as Christians we must establish the fact that Christ was not just another great religious leader who founded a world religion. We must show that he was sent by God himself to reveal to men what God expected of them and what they could expect of him. In order to defend our position as Roman Catholics we must establish the fact that Christ founded the Roman Catholic Church and gave it authority to teach, govern, and sanctify all men of all nations down to the end of the world.

The second part of the investigation of the foundations of our faith turns our attention to the *teaching* authority of the Church. Here two problems face us. One has to do with the quality of her teaching authority. Does the Church possess an *infallible* teaching authority so that she can interpret Christ's message to mankind without any possibility of error? If so, upon whom did Christ bestow this infallible teaching authority? Who exercises it in the name of the Church? As Roman Catholics we believe that Jesus Christ did bestow infallible teaching authority upon his church and that he granted this authority to St. Peter and his successors, the bishops of Rome. Here we have to examine our reasons for so believing.

Another problem is this: How does the Church actually exer-

3. Often called also the Dissident Oriental Churches or the Orthodox Churches.

cise her infallible teaching authority? As Roman Catholics we believe that she does so *ordinarily* through the bishops of the Church scattered throughout the length and breadth of the world, or *solemnly* through the declarations of the Pope or General Councils. Here we must examine the ways in which the ordinary and the solemn magisterium of the Church is actually exercised in the life of the Church.

Thirdly and finally, we meet up with the concluding problem in our examination of the foundations of our faith. What are the sources from which the Church derives her doctrines? As Roman Catholics we believe that there are two primary sources of the teachings of the Church, Holy Scripture and Tradition. Here, we must complete our examination of the foundations of our faith by a study of the sources of divine revelations to which the Church traces back her doctrines.

PART I

THE CHURCH'S AUTHORITY

As Roman Catholics we have been taught that Jesus Christ himself established the Roman Catholic Church, giving to it, and to it alone, authority to govern, teach, and sanctify all men down to the end of time. This sweeping claim to exclusive authority in the field of religion has aroused much resentment and, often enough, bitter resentment in those outside the Church. Here we intend to examine this claim. Is it justifiable before the bar of reason?

The problem is somewhat more complex than would appear at first glance. For in reality it contains within itself two problems. First of all, a Roman Catholic is a Christian. Here we have our first problem. Why should I be a Christian, a follower of Jesus Christ—not a follower of Buddha, of Mohammed, or of any other of the great religious leaders of mankind? Secondly, a Roman Catholic is a member of the Roman Catholic Church. This presents our second problem. Why should I be a member of the Roman Catholic Church—not a member of one or other of the hundreds of sects all laying claim to the Christian name? In this first part of the course we will discuss these two problems.[1]

1. There is a third, even more basic problem: Why should I be a theist or, more precisely, a monotheist? But the proofs for the existence of God pertain to philosophy. A review of the philosophical presuppositions to the course will be found in an appendix to the book.

CHAPTER I

The Religions of Mankind

OUR first problem is: Why should I be a Christian? We will begin the discussion with a study of the non-Christian religions. Apart from Christianity, five religions claim the allegiance of vast numbers of the human race. We will give a brief sketch of each.

I. HINDUISM

The religion of India is called Hinduism. It is based on the teachings of the Vedas which were written thousands of years ago by holy men who lived on the banks of the Indus and the Ganges. Hinduism has one God, Brahman, the eternal spirit. But it has likewise over three hundred million other gods. In fact, the Hindu supernatural world swarms with gods—some resembling men, others animals—and along with them a multitude of ghosts, demons, and heavenly dancing girls. While some Hindus consider these gods to be distinct, Hindu sages, past and present, hold that they are only different faces of the one infinite Brahman. There are dozens of sects within Hinduism, each with its own special god. The most important of the sects worship Brahma, the Creator, Vishnu, the Preserver, or Shiva, the Destroyer.

The world emanates from but remains rooted in Brahman. It has no reality apart from him. It will last millions of years and then be destroyed by fire or water. But it will be recreated by Brahman the Creator, for the endless cycle of life must go on.

The goal of human life is *moksha*, a state of peace and quiet within Brahman in which one escapes from the unreal world and becomes merged in the oneness of the Absolute. As this exalted condition cannot be achieved in one life, Hinduism teaches the doctrine of reincarnation. When the body dies the meritorious soul enjoys happiness and the wicked soul is punished. After these experiences it is once more reunited to a body and begins a new life, the character of which is determined by the merits of its past life on earth.

Hinduism claims the allegiance of over 300,000,000 people living in the vast subcontinent of India.

II. BUDDHISM

Buddhism is based on the teachings of a man named Siddhartha Gautama. The dates of his birth and death are uncertain but his life-span of eighty years covers the greater part of the fifth century, B.C. He was born at Kapilavatthu, the son of king Suddhodana. When he was 29 years old, he abandoned his wife and son and the princely luxury and splendor to which he had been accustomed and set out in search of an answer to the riddle of life. He became the disciple of five Hindu holy men but, dissatisfied, left them. Six long years of search came to a climax when, after 49 days of continuous meditation, he achieved the enlightenment for which he had sought. Thereafter he became known as the Buddha, the Enlightened or Awakened One.

Buddha made his way to the holy city of Benares, where the five Hindu holy men became his first disciples. For the remaining 45 years of his life Buddha travelled up and down northern India. His efforts were crowned with success, for he won from all classes an ever-increasing band of followers. Buddha retained many of the ideas he had held as a Hindu. He accepted the age-old idea that all living beings have to pass through a long cycle of births, deaths, and rebirths. Again, he taught that good conduct or bad is rewarded or punished in future reincarnations and that man can seek and attain freedom from suffering by taming all his worldly desires. But he rebelled against many of the time-honored religious and social beliefs of Hinduism, such as the infallibility of the Vedas, the caste system, and the Vedic sacrifices. Moreover, while Hinduism presented the soul's release from worldly desires as a goal to be achieved, it looked upon the world as God's creation, something to be enjoyed, and was therefore a religion filled with gay holydays, impressive temple ceremonies and colorful feasts. Disapproving of this side of Hinduism, Buddha put the emphasis on ethical conduct, on virtuous living.

During the Middle Ages Buddhism gradually declined in India, its place of origin, surviving only in Nepal, Sikhim, and Bhutan. But long before this it had spread eastward to Burma, Siam, Cambodia, Malaya, Sumatra, Java, and even into parts of Borneo and the Philippines. It had also moved northward into Tibet, China, Korea and Japan. Today Buddhism is divided into two great schools of thought: the Hinayana Buddhism of Ceylon and southern Asia, and the Mahayana Buddhism of Mongolia, Tibet, Korea, China, and Japan. In the Hinayana type the pantheistic trend is strong; the human character of Buddha is emphasized and he is represented as an austere manifestation of God. In the Mahayana type, which began to develop about the beginning of the Christian era, the trend is towards theism; Buddha's divine character is emphasized and he is presented as a god of infinite light and mercy who dwells in a heaven known as the "Great Western Paradise" or the "Pure Land" to which all good Buddhists will go.

Mahayan Buddhism is divided into numerous sects with considerable variations in doctrine. Two of these sects are strong in Japan. The Shinshu sects is the most powerful, having the greatest number of temples, monks and teachers. The second largest is Zen, a sect of stern discipline, having a closer resemblance to the austere Hinayana Buddhism than to the other Mahayana sects. It is estimated that there are more than 150,000,000 Buddhists in the world today.

III. TAOISM, CONFUCIANISM AND SHINTOISM

In prehistoric times the Chinese believed in a Supreme Being who rewarded the good and punished the wicked. He presided over a vast array of inferior gods, of benevolent spirits, *shen,* who could bring good fortune, and of evil spirits, *kwei,* who could dispense bad fortune. Much of the Chinese religion of these earlier days was concerned with soothsayers and with prescriptions for pleasing the good spirits and for driving away or, at least, placating the evil spirits. In the universe, it was said, there are two interacting forces, the *yang* and the *yin*. Everything in the universe possesses the qualities of both in varying degrees. The *yang* is the positive or masculine force; it is warm, bright, hard, dry, and stable. The *yin* is the negative or feminine force; it is cold, dark, soft, wet and unstable. When there is a state of imbalance between them, then there is disharmony and evil; when there is a state of balance between these forces, then there is harmony and good. How is this harmony to be achieved? Taoism and Confucianism do not agree on the answer to this problem.

Lao Tzu is credited with being the founder of Taoism and the author of its bible, *Tao Teh Ching*. He was born, according to tradition, on a farm in the Honan province of China in 604 B.C. After a long career at the court of the emperor, he is said to have become so disgusted with the corruption and constant warfare that he resigned his post and became a teacher. It was out of his teaching that Taoism developed.

Tao, which means a road or way, is a mighty power moving irresistibly on its course. Men are borne along by it like drops of water in a river so that all human striving is useless. Virtue consists in a quiet submission to the power of the Tao. Riches, fame, honor and power for which men strive only produce strife and warfare. A quiet yielding to the Absolute, the Tao, carries one eventually to one's destined place. The ideal is to retire to a life of simplicity and contemplation in some isolated corner of the world.

Confucius was born into a poor but aristocratic family in the Shantung province of China in 551 B.C. He wished to be a statesman but ended up as a teacher. He died in 479 B.C. Confucius agreed with Lao Tzu that the Tao represented the great law of life but he disagreed with him sharply as to how one should conduct oneself. To Confucius, following the true way did not mean a life of contemplative retirement but rather an active life of virtue. Accordingly, he set up practical rules for everyday living. He put the accent on statecraft and ethics. While he considered the worship of Heaven and of ancestors to be conducive to morality and social order and, therefore, approved of them, he would not even discuss the question of life after death. Again, he strongly opposed the age-old belief in good and bad spirits who could bring good or bad fortune to man, and the practices growing out of this belief.

For centuries his teachings were criticized and attacked, especially by the Taoists. It was not until around 200 B.C. that Confucian moralism began to gain favor. Then, with increasingly strong support from successive emperors, it became the supreme system in Chinese history. Taoism lost ground proportionately. Then Buddhism made its way into China and attracted to itself large numbers of the more enlightened Taoists. Taoism became more and more the religion of the masses and catered more and more to their superstitions. It is estimated that there are about 50,000,000 Taoists and around 300,000,000 Confucians in China today.

Shinto, which means the "Way of the Gods," is the native religion of Japan. It is approximately as old as Christianity. In modern Shinto there are two main streams: shrine Shinto, which was the state religion until disestablished in December, 1945, and sectarian Shinto, which exists in the form of thirteen officially recognized sects and numerous sub-sects. The deities honored in shrine Shinto include a number of primitive nature forces, the spirits of some of the emperors and of certain heros who gave their lives in the service of the nation and the emperor. The deities honored in sectarian Shinto include all the gods of shrine Shinto and others proper to each sect, notably the spirit of the founder of the sect. The beliefs and practices of the different sects vary greatly. Some emphasize a mountain worship mixed with primitive rites of spirit possession; others, ancient purification rites; others, faith healing. It is estimated that there are around 30,000,000 Shintoists in Japan.

IV. ISLAM

Islam [1] was founded by Mohammed. He was born at Mecca in Arabia in 570 A.D. At the time, Mecca was a prosperous city on the caravan route between India and Syria. Little is known with certainty of his early life. Mohammed was a deeply religious man, much given to prayer and fasting. He became particularly interested in Jewish and Christian doctrines and practices. At the age of forty he claimed to have had a revelation from God while at prayer in a cave outside Mecca and then presented himself to the people as the last and greatest of a long line of prophets from Abraham to Christ.

Doctrinally, he emphasized the unity of God (rejecting the divinity of Christ and the Christian doctrine of the Trinity), the last judgment, and God's predestination of good and evil. The religious practices obligatory on the Moslem believer are: the

1. Islam means submission or surrender to the will of God.

recital of the creed (There is no god but God and Mohammed is his apostle), the performance of divine worship five times a day, the fast in the month of Ramadan, almsgiving, and a pilgrimage to Mecca.

Mohammed's preaching was rejected at Mecca and he fled to Medina where he succeeded in making many converts and in organizing a small army. His talents as a leader enabled him to crush the warring factions in Arabia and to weld it into a formidable military state (630 A.D.). Within ten years of Mohammed's death, Islam had conquered the Persian Empire, Egypt, Palestine, and Syria. Fifty years later it overcame Roman Africa, Spain, and southern France. A decisive battle at Poitiers, France, stopped its westward advance. Another decisive battle at Constantinople stopped its advance into Europe from the East. The Golden Age of Islam was reached with the reign of Harun al-Rashid (786–809 A.D.). Soon after this, the Moslem Empire started to collapse. The final blow came when the Mongol hordes destroyed Baghdad, the capital. Fifty years later, the Mongols who had settled in Persia, embraced Islam. Later, a Mongol founded a great Moslem empire in India. From there Islam spread eastward into China and down into the islands of the Pacific.

The Moslem world has become divided into numerous sects, of which the largest—about nine-tenths of the total adherents—is the Sunni sect. Today Islam, at least 300,000,000 strong, constitutes around one seventh of the population of the globe.

V. ATHEISTIC COMMUNISM

In our own times there has emerged another great power over men's minds and wills, a religion which is at once the denial of all religion and itself the most potent secular religion ever to challenge the traditional religions of mankind. This is the atheistic communism that dominates Soviet Russia, Red China and some of the nations allied with them.

Its founder was Karl Marx (1818–1883). Marx was an atheist before he was a communist; in fact, his communism is deeply rooted in his atheism. For his first position was that matter is the only reality. Matter exists and the human mind reflects it. There is no God and no life after death. His second position is found in his interpretation of history. From the beginning of human history man's survival has depended on the production of such things as answer his needs. The particular form of production at any time determines the whole nature of society; the economic factor dominates everything, including religion. In the past the modes of production have been imperfect, leaving too many human needs unsatisfied. Man therefore built up for himself a God and a future life wherein all his needs would be satisfied. If and when a perfect mode of production is achieved religion will wither away. It is in this sense that Marx maintained that "religion is the opium of the people."

The third position is his explanation of the defects of man's productivity in the past. It was because men approached the problem as individuals. Production, to be perfect, must be a collective act, and the collective, therefore, is the unit to which the individual must be completely subordinated. His only value lies in the collectivity to which he belongs.

His fourth position determines how the human race moves inexorably towards the perfect mode of production. It is his theory of class war. At each stage of society, a particular class gains the upper hand and exploits the other classes for its own advantage. But each ruling class necessarily fosters the development of its opposite, the class which will eventually destroy it. Out of this conflict a new ruling class arises. But this process leads finally to a face-to-face conflict between the capitalists and the proletarians. To carry on the struggle successfully, a dictatorship of the proletariat has to be established. The inevitable result will be a society in which the capitalist class will be eliminated. Then the dictatorship of the proletariat will fade away, leaving a classless society, a society of free and equal men. And then heaven will be established on earth.

While many people still look upon Communism as merely a social, political and economic system different from our own, it is becoming more and more clearly recognized as a pseudo-religion. It demands a supreme allegiance to the State as to a quasi-God. It declares its gospel to be the one hope of all mankind. It has its own ceremonies, hymns and other ritual. It imposes an austere, even if perverted, morality of its own. It has, in a way, its own divinities: Marx, Lenin, Stalin—at present, at least, in disfavor—and another budding divinity, Khrushchev. The fervor of the communist devotee is a challenge to every other religion seeking world acceptance.

VI. CONCLUSION

Christianity is surrounded and outnumbered by several other world religions. Of these, the most inimical is, quite obviously, the atheistic communism of Marxism which already controls a major part of mankind and hopes and strives to extend its dominion over the whole world. The weak spot in our armor against its attack are the religious indifferentism and secularism which have made such deep inroads into the life and culture of the western world. The other world religions do not pose any great threat to Christianity—at least at the present time. It should be noted, however, that Islam, after centuries of slumber, is once more coming to life under the impetus of the growing Arab nationalism. Certain Buddhist sects have become quite active, sending out missionaries and extending their influence into the nations of the western world. In the rapidly-changing panorama of world affairs no one can predict what the future has in store for us.

CHAPTER II

Christ's Background

WHO was this man Jesus Christ? How did he capture the devotion and allegiance of a major part of the human race in the last two thousand years? What did he claim to be? Jesus Christ made two stupendous, breath-taking, almost incredible claims. Before we can begin to grasp their implications, we must get some idea of the background of his life. This means, since he was a Jew, that we must know something of the Jewish people. We will do it by turning to the first part of the Bible, the Old Testament as it is called.[1] The first five books of the Old Testament are the oldest literature of the Jews, having been written by Moses between 1460 and 1420 B.C.[2] They record the origin of the human race, the fall of man or, in other words, his loss of the friendship of God, and the establishment of God's plan for man's restoration to union with himself. The remaining books of the Old Testament tell us how God began to put his plan into execution through the instrumentality of the Jews, his chosen people. From these sources we will briefly sketch the history of the Jewish people down to the time of Christ.[3]

The history of the Jewish people falls into two major periods: I. From Adam to Abraham, and II. From Abraham to Christ.

1. The Old Testament, the first part of the Bible, is by far the larger part. It contains 45 books, whereas the New Testament has only 27.

2. These five books are called the Pentateuch. The word derives from the Greek. It simply means "Five Books."

3. The dates used are only approximate. They conform to the latest estimates of scholars.

I. FROM ADAM TO ABRAHAM

Little is known of the history of mankind during this period. We do not even know how long the human race has dwelt upon this earth. The conservative estimates proposed by scientists range up to a million years. The Book of Genesis, the first book of the Pentateuch, gives no details; it limits itself to basic facts. It records the creation of Adam and Eve, the first man and woman. It describes them as living in a state of perfect happiness and union with God. It pictures the trial by which God tested their fidelity to him and the act of disobedience, instigated by Satan, which destroyed the bond of friendship between God and man.[4]

In the very act of condemning Adam and Eve for severing the bond of union between himself and the human race, God promised to send a redeemer through whom the human race would have a chance to regain his friendship. "I will put enmities between thee (Satan) and the woman, and thy seed and her seed: she shall crush thy head, and thou shalt lie in wait for her heel" (Genesis 3, 15). But there is no indication as to the manner or the time of the fulfilment of this promise. The execution of God's plan for man's redemption begins centuries later with Abraham, the father of God's chosen people, from whom the redeemer was to come forth. And so the book of Genesis is only interested in tracing a line of descent from Adam to Abraham. It chooses Seth, one of Adam's sons, and lists his descendants down to Noah. After the deluge, it continues the line from Sem, Noah's oldest son, down to Abraham.[5]

II. FROM ABRAHAM TO CHRIST

With Abraham the long period of preparation for man's redemption begins to unfold. The probable date of his birth was 2200 B.C. His family, a branch of the Semites, was living in Ur of the Chaldees at the lower end of the Euphrates valley.[6] He it was whom God chose to found a separate people which was to be

4. All these aspects of man's relation to God will be studied in a later course.

5. For which reason the Jews are called "Semites." Most of the people who dwell in the Middle-East are of Semitic origin.

6. Present-day Iraq.

especially favored by God. At God's command Abraham and his family migrated to Chanaan (Palestine). There God made a covenant with him and his descendants. They were to worship him in a special manner and, in return, God promised to bestow special blessings, both spiritual and material, upon them. And God changed his name from Abram (high father) to Abraham (the father of a multitude). The mark of circumcision was to be the sign of the covenant between God and his chosen people. Later on God repeatedly made similar promises to Abraham and his seed.

After Abraham's death God renewed these promises to his son, Isaac. And when Isaac died, he again renewed the promises to one of Isaac's many sons, Jacob. When doing so God changed Jacob's name to Israel (he who wins God's favor).[7] Jacob or Israel had twelve sons. One of them, Joseph, was sold into slavery by his jealous brothers and was taken down into Egypt. There he found favor with the king of Egypt and became his prime minister. A famine broke out in Palestine and Jacob sent his sons down into Egypt to buy food. There they were reunited with Joseph. Then Jacob, at God's command, gathered together all his tribe and their possessions and journeyed to Egypt. Due to Joseph's influence with him, the king of Egypt gave them a section of the country as their own, and here they dwelt for about four hundred years. During this period they grew from a family of some two or three thousand to a large people estimated to number from six hundred thousand to two million souls. Moreover, they had been, when they first settled in Egypt, no more than a nomadic tribe, devoid of any literature, art or culture. Their stay in Egypt, one of the most powerful and cultured nations of antiquity, had schooled them in agriculture and irrigation, in cattle raising, in the arts, in architecture and mechanics, in weaving, dyeing, etc.

The prosperity which the Jews enjoyed in Egypt during the lifetime of Joseph continued after his death. How long it did so we do not know. We do know that their numbers, power and prosperity eventually aroused the fear of an Egyptian king and a period of bitter persecution set in. The king burdened them with excessive labor of the most exhausting kind. He gave orders to the Egyptian midwives to kill every male Jew at birth and, in

---

7. For which reason the Jews are also called "Israelites."

case some might escape this law, he ordered all his people to throw any such male child into the river Nile.[8]

God chose Moses and his brother, Aaron,[9] to free the Israelites from the bondage of the Egyptians. Under their leadership the Israelites crossed the Red Sea somewhere near the Suez Canal and advanced down the west coast of Sinai Peninsula. Three months later they came to Mount Sinai. There God renewed his covenant with them and gave them his law, a law whose precepts covered every aspect of their lives, civil, moral and religious.[10] The Israelites solemnly promised to abide by his law and the pact was sealed with a sacrifice. After a year of preparation spent at the foot of Mount Sinai, they began their advance towards the promised land of Chanaan, moving northward along the Gulf of Akabah. It was a rigorous journey and on several occasions the tribes almost broke out into open rebellion against the leadership of Moses. Arriving at Cades, near the northeastern end of Sinai Peninsula, a scouting party of twelve men, one from each of the tribes, was sent to investigate the situation in the land of Chanaan. On their return, all but two—despite God's promise to deliver the land to them as their own—maintained that it could not be conquered. It was proposed that Moses should be deposed as their leader and another man selected who would lead them back to Egypt. As the mutiny increased, God intervened, threatening to destroy the rebels with a pestilence. However, at Moses' entreaty, God announced that the chosen people would be preserved as such but that none of the present generation, excepting two of the twelve scouts, would enter the promised land of Chanaan. Then began thirty-eight years of wandering in the desert of the Sinai Peninsula at the end of which we find the Israelites again encamped at Cades at the southern border of the promised land. Moses decided against a direct advance into Chanaan. Instead, he

8. There is little doubt that this king of Egypt was Rameses II.

9. Aaron and Moses were of the tribe of Levi, the tribe later chosen by God to be his priests. Aaron was born before the edict of death for male infants. The birth of Moses was concealed by his parents; later, he was adopted by a daughter of the king of Egypt.

10. The tribe of Levi was selected by God for the service of his tabernacle. The sons of Aaron and their descendants, alone were the priests of God, the rest of the tribe and their descendants (called Levites) were their assistants. Aaron had the title and dignity of high priest. It was to be hereditary in his family.

led the Israelites down the river Arabah to the Gulf of Akabah, then northward towards Eastern Palestine, that is to say, that part of Palestine which was east of the Dead Sea and the river Jordan. During the journey Aaron died and was buried on Mount Hor. His son, Eleazar, succeeded him as high priest.

Sweeping northward the Israelites quickly conquered eastern Palestine and then prepared for the conquest of Chanaan. While encamped on the eastern shore of the river Jordan, Moses died and God chose Josue, a member of the tribe of Ephraim, to succeed him as the leader and judge of the chosen people. It was under his leadership that the Israelites crossed the river Jordan, conquered western Palestine, and divided up all Palestine among the twelve tribes, descendants of the twelve sons of Jacob (Israel). The Israelites had finally taken possession of the land which God had promised to them.

The subsequent history of the Jewish people down to the time of Christ falls into three periods: 1) the tribal period or the period of the judges, 2) the period of the monarchy, and 3) the period of subjection to foreign rule, a period which still endured when Christ appeared upon the scene.

1) The tribal period. Josue had not completed the conquest of Chanaan before his death so that, even within the territories assigned to the different tribes, there were to be found independent pagan tribes. The consequences were unfortunate but to be expected. Association with the heathens led to intermarriage and this in turn to a forgetfulness of their covenant with God and repeated falls into idolatry and immorality. Moreover, the settlement of the tribes, each in its own territory, and the death of Josue without any previously appointed successor, ended even the semblance of central power that had existed under Moses and Josue. This left the Israelites, to a great extent, at the mercy of the surrounding pagan tribes. And God, as a punishment for their repeated infidelities, allowed the different tribes to be repeatedly subjugated by their enemies.

From time to time individual tribal leaders were strong enough to exert some authority over all twelve tribes. Eight such leaders are recorded in the Book of Judges, of whom Samson is, without doubt, the most famous. Their appointment seems to have been by the free choice of the people, with the exception of two, Gedeon and Samson, who were selected by God for the office.

2) The period of the monarchy. After some years—the common opinion holds that the tribal period lasted upwards of 400 years—the Jews felt the need of a united kingdom because of the growing attacks and inroads of the Philistines from the west and the Ammonites from the east. They asked the prophet Samuel, the last of the Judges, to appoint a king. Acting under God's guidance, he chose Saul, who became the first of three famous Jewish kings—Saul, David, and Solomon. They ruled Israel for about a hundred years, 1050–950 B.C. It was under their leadership that the nation reached the highest point in its development.

After Solomon's death, his son Roboam became king. The northern tribes rebelled against him and two independent kingdoms were set up, the kingdom of Israel in northern Palestine, the kingdom of Juda in the south.

3) The period of subjection. In 721 B.C. the northern kingdom of Israel was conquered by the Assyrians and most of the people were killed or carried off into slavery in Assyria. They disappeared from history.[11] The conquerors sent colonists into the land and they, intermarrying with the remaining Jews, produced the Samaritans, a people of mixed blood, culture, and religion.

For another century and a half the southern kingdom of Juda maintained a precarious existence despite pressure from east and west. Then the Babylonians conquered their enemy to the east, the Assyrians, in 612 B.C. In self-defense the kingdom of Juda allied itself with their enemy from the east, the Egyptians. But the Babylonians swept into Palestine, destroyed the holy city of Jerusalem and carried off most of the Jews into Babylonia, leaving only the lower class to farm the land for their conquerors. About seventy years later, the Persians conquered the Babylonians. Their new masters allowed the Jews in Babylonia to return to Palestine. In 537 B.C., about 50,000 of them did so. Then they set to work to restore the nation and the temple, but under the rule of a civil governor appointed by the Persian king.

In 332 B.C. the Persians were in turn conquered by the Macedonians under Alexander the Great. His death, soon after this, precipitated a struggle for power among his generals. The kingdom of Juda fell under the sway of Ptolemy, king of Egypt. In 198 B.C. Antiochus III, king of Syria, defeated the Egyptians and took over control of Juda. Their new masters antagonized the Israelites

11. These are the so-called "lost" tribes of Israel.

so deeply that a full-scale rebellion broke out under the leadership of Matathias. It was continued by his son and successor, Judas Machabeus. Soon he, and his two brothers who succeeded him, Jonathan and Simon, had freed Palestine from Syrian rule. Under the successors of the Machabees, the kingdom was extended northward to embrace parts of the former kingdom of Israel. But the period of independence was short-lived. In 67 B.C. two brothers ruled the kingdom, Hyrcanus as the high priest, and Aristobulus as the head of the army. Hyrcanus, forced out by his brother, sought and gained the help of the Arabs. This gave Pompey, the leader of the Roman army, an excuse to intervene. He invaded Palestine and made it a part of the Roman province of Syria.

The Romans, as was their custom with conquered peoples, allowed the Jews to practice their own religion and to follow their own national customs. Thus, in effect, there were two rulers. The Sanhedrin or Council, the supreme religious and judicial tribunal of the Jews, had wide powers which it constantly sought to increase. It was composed of seventy-one members, all of whom had to be of pure Israelitic descent. They were of three classes: the high priests, the "ancients" (the aristocracy, both lay and priestly), and the scribes or lawyers or "rabbis." It was presided over by the high priest. At the time of Christ it had its own police force; [12] it could impose corporal punishment on offenders [13] and even inflict the death penalty with the consent of the Roman procurator.[14] The Romans even recognized its authority over all the Jewish communities scattered throughout the empire.[15]

Two parties or factions exercised an increasingly important part in the political and religious life of the Jews under Roman rule, the Sadducees and the Pharisees. It would be well to get an idea of their character before continuing the history of the Jewish people under Roman rule. The Pharisees were recruited from all classes, especially from the lower and middle classes and even some from the priestly class. They were the conservatives, men devoted to the Law, to its exact knowledge and observance. By their devotion they did help to keep the Jewish religion free from

12. Matt. 26, 7; Acts 4, 33; 5, 17.
13. Acts 5, 40; 2 Cor. 11, 24.
14. John 18, 30.
15. Acts 9, 2; 22, 5.

pagan influences but the party, as a whole, became notorious for two terrible failings. First of all, they were separatists in an extreme sense. They not only championed the separateness of the Jewish people from all other nations but, in the case of their own compatriots, they would only associate with those who observed the Law in its minutest detail. This position actually separated them from the multitude of the people. Why? The Law or Torah, as we have seen already, had been given to Moses by God about 1500 B.C. Since then the teachers and legislators of the Jews had applied its rules, civic, moral, and ceremonial, to the countless situations of everyday life. There grew up a body of rules known as "the tradition of the ancients." The Pharisees multiplied these regulations endlessly and, in many cases, to the point of absurdity. It became impossible for most Jews to know, let alone to observe, these minute regulations. But ignorance of the law was no excuse in the eyes of the Pharisees. Therefore they looked down on most of their compatriots as defiled and would not associate with them. This attitude engendered another terrible failing, their formalism. Religion became a purely external thing. Its practice consisted above all else in the minute observance of all the external rites or rules of conduct laid down in the Law and in "the tradition of the ancients." The internal spirit animating the faithful observance of the rules became of secondary or even less importance.

The Sadducees, on the other hand, were recruited especially from the priesthood, supported by the aristocracy and the wealthy landowners. They were the liberals, upholding the written Law of Moses but rejecting the Pharisaic "tradition of the ancients" as having a status equal to that of the Written Law. Yet, while they professed a due reverence for the Law, they were not, as a whole, religious men. In fact, they were tainted with rationalism and materialism; they denied the immortality of the soul, the resurrection of the body and future reward and punishment; they likewise rejected the existence of God's providence. Through the priests in their party they had control over the Sanhedrin and, since this body had control over the temple and the ritual of public worship, the Sadducees had a share in the enormous revenues that poured in from all the Jewish communities in the Empire. While the priests wished to maintain their position on the basis of the Mosaic law, they were quite willing to get rid of any customs or traditions which would have interfered with their worldly lives. And, unlike the Pharisees, they were quite willing to assimilate pagan thought and culture. Each party had its own group of scribes (lawyers, doctors of the Law, rabbis) to defend its ideas. And each party had its own particular impact upon the period that begins with the rule of the Roman Empire and ends with the disappearance of Israel as a nation.

Even though the Romans had given the Jews such an extensive area of independence in their own internal affairs, subjection to foreigners was a disgrace and a humiliation in the eyes of this proud and nationalistic people. Riots and rebellions broke out frequently and their violent suppression only deepened the hatred of the Jews for their Roman rulers. In 37 B.C., after about a quarter century of Roman rule, a man named Herod, an Idumaean by birth but a Jew by religion,[16] got himself appointed the tributary king of Palestine by the Roman Senate. To strengthen his own hand, Herod immediately changed the old constitution. The Sanhedrin or Council, previously the highest deliberative body in the land, was deprived of all executive or advisory power, becoming increasingly merely an academic and religious body. Everything possible was done to weaken the influence of the high priesthood. The occupant of the office was frequently changed, and Herod took over the custody of the sacred robes, the insignia of the office. When Herod died in 4 B.C. the kingdom was divided into three parts and given to three of his sons: Idumaea, Judea, and Samaria to Archelaus; Galilee and Perea to Herod Antipas; Itrurea and Trachonitis to Philip. Because of his savage excesses, Archelaus was soon deposed by the Roman Emperor and his territory was placed under a procurator or lieutenant-governor who was made responsible to the Imperial Legate of the Roman province of Syria. He set up his headquarters at Caesarea rather than at Jerusalem and it was from there that he ruled the nation.[17]

But the new arrangement did not bring peace to the land. Friction between the Jews and their rulers increased rather than diminished. Finally, in 66 A.D., they broke into open rebellion.

16. The Idumaeans had been conquered by the Jews and forcibly converted to Judaism in the days of the Machabees.

17. The fifth in the series of procurators, Pontius Pilate, who was appointed in 26 A.D., should be remembered; his name will come up later on.

The revolt was temporarily successful. But the Romans sent in reinforcements and slowly but surely regained control. In 70 A.D. Jerusalem, the last stronghold of the rebels, was besieged and finally taken. Jerusalem and the temple were completely destroyed.

The destruction of the temple at Jerusalem marked the beginning of the end of the Jews as a nation. With its destruction the priesthood itself came to an end and the Sadducees, whose whole life had been so closely bound up with the temple service, ceased to exist as a distinct party. The Pharisees were left masters of the field. The Rabbis, or teachers of the Law, who had long occupied a prominent place in the national life, now received the reverence formerly given to those of priestly rank. The Sanhedrin was reconstituted and eventually regained a semi-official status as representative of the Jews in their relationship with the Roman authorities. Courts for deciding legal cases in accordance with Jewish law were set up in every town with the Sanhedrin at Jamnia [18] acting as the supreme court. The local synagogue became the center of Jewish life.

For nearly a generation an uneasy peace reigned in Palestine. Then, in 132 A.D. another rebellion broke out. The Roman army moved in and laid waste to the country. The Palestinian Jews were almost wiped out of existence by the three years war and the wholesale enslavement which followed upon it. The end was near. When the Roman Empire became divided into two states during the fourth century A.D., Palestine became a part of the Eastern or Byzantine Empire. In 425 A.D. Theodosius II abolished the Sanhedrin. The last vestige of the ancient nation of Israel had disappeared from the pages of history.[19]

In the history of the Jewish people up to this point certain individuals stand out because of the very special office which they held. These were the prophets of Israel. The Jews were God's chosen people through whom salvation was to come to all mankind. With them God had made a covenant. The prophets were intermediaries between God and his chosen people. Their office was to make known God's will to the people—whether it concerned the future or the present. They strove to keep Israel loyal to its covenant with God and to the practice of its religion.

18. The Sanhedrin was later moved to Tiberias.
19. The nation of Israel was re-established in 1948.

They acted as authoritative interpreters of God's law. They rebuked the people for their repeated infidelities. Some of the great names among them were Moses, Elias, Eliseus, Isaias, Jeremias, and Daniel. The series began with Moses (1500 B.C.) and continued for about a thousand years down to Malachias (450 B.C.).

One of the functions of the prophets was to reveal, with increasing clarity as the centuries rolled by, what the future Messiah and his kingdom were to be like. Thus they gradually prophesied concerning his birth—that he would be of the tribe of Juda and a descendant of King David, that he was to be born of a virgin at Bethlehem. They foretold of his wonderful life, his sufferings and death, his resurrection and glorification in God's kingdom. At the time when Christ appeared on the scene, expectation was running high among the Jews; the kingdom of God was near at hand; the Messiah, "the One who is to come," would soon appear.

But what was the popular idea of God's kingdom and of the Messiah who was to establish it? The popular idea, while basically religious, was predominantly nationalistic and materialistic. It identified the kingdom of God with the kingdom of Israel. The Messiah was to be a Warrior-King who would not only free Israel from foreign domination but would conquer the world, bringing it into subjection to Israel and, through it, to the one true God. From Jerusalem this Warrior-King would come to rule the world. Thereupon a Golden Age of peace and unlimited prosperity would begin for the Jewish people. In this nationalistic and materialistic concept of the Messiah and his kingdom there was no room for a heavenly kingdom nor for a Messiah who would suffer and die a terrible death, for a Messiah-Priest who would offer up his life in atonement for the sins of mankind. Although this aspect of his coming was clearly contained in the prophecies concerning the redeemer who was to come and, above all, in the prophecies of Isaias,[20] it was completely ignored by his Jewish compatriots. This in brief was the popular idea of the approaching kingdom of God and of the Messiah who was to establish it. This idea had, as we shall see in a moment, a profound influence not only upon the reception that the Jews gave to Christ but even upon the way in which he presented himself to them as the promised Redeemer.

20. Cf. Isaias, chapter 53.

CHAPTER III

Christ's Claims

WHO was this man Jesus Christ? Who did he claim to be? What proofs did he present for his astounding claims? For an answer to these questions we turn to the New Testament. This, the second part of the Bible, is made up of twenty-seven "books." First of all, we have four Gospels, written by four of his followers; Matthew, Mark, Luke, and John; then comes an account of the activities of the apostles, the Acts of the Apostles; next we find twenty-one letters written by some of his apostles and disciples; and, finally, we have one prophetic book written by John, namely, the Apocalypse. Our attention is focussed primarily on the four Gospels. What do they have to say about Christ and his extraordinary claims? Let us examine their account of his life and death.

I. CHRIST'S LIFE AND DEATH

Jesus Christ was born into this world almost two thousand years ago at Bethlehem, a little town in Judea, five miles south of Jerusalem, the holy city of the Jews. He was, to all external appearances, the son of Joseph, the carpenter of Nazareth, and his wife, Mary.[1] Most of his life was passed in the quiet obscurity of Nazareth. But when he was just past thirty-one years of age, he came forth from Nazareth and began his public ministry. During two years and three months he journeyed back and forth through

1. Matth. 13, 55.

Palestine, bringing the good tidings, the "words of God," to mankind.[2]

Who did this man claim to be? He taught that he was the
Messiah, the redeemer promised to mankind by God. As such, he
laid claim to a threefold office; he was, he said, a king, a prophet
or teacher, and a priest.[3] He made an even more startling claim,
one so breath-taking in its sublimity as to be, humanly speaking,
incredible. He taught that in the unity of the Godhead there are
three Persons, Father, Son, and Holy Spirit, and that he himself
was the incarnate *Son* of God, who had come down on earth for
the redemption of the human race.

His Jewish compatriots, God's chosen people, rejected his
claims. Why? Several reasons can be offered. First of all, the
Jewish people at that time were, for the most part, morally corrupt. Josephus, the Jewish historian, says that, had not the Romans punished them, some other catastrophe would have struck
them down. Their evil minds were closed to the message of Christ.
Secondly, their leaders, the Scribes and Pharisees, hated Christ
vehemently. After he had condemned their pride, arrogance, and
hypocrisy, they bitterly opposed him in every possible way.
Finally, the Jews had misinterpreted some of the prophecies concerning the promised redeemer. Blinded by nationalism and materialism, they looked for a temporal, rather than a spiritual king,
for a warrior-king under whose leadership they would destroy
their enemies and conquer the world.

Not only did the Jews reject his claims but, for making them,
he suffered death as a blasphemer, a horrible and ignominious
death by crucifixion.

II. IN THE BEGINNING HIS CLAIMS WERE OBSCURE

The statement that Jesus claimed to be the promised redeemer
has to be qualified in one respect. Jesus did not clearly state that
he was the Messiah at the beginning of his ministry. As you know,
many of the Jews expected the Messiah to be a glorious, victorious
king. They looked for a Deliverer from the yoke of the Gentiles
rather than a Saviour from their sins. This error about the mission of the Messiah was due in great part to the apocryphal
literature that was widely disseminated during the two cen-

2. John 3, 34; 8, 47.
3. John 14, 6.

turies prior to the birth of Christ. Moreover, the intensely nationalistic Jews stressed those prophecies which foretold the
triumph of the Messiah and skipped over any reference to his
sufferings.

If Jesus had said that he was the Messiah at the beginning
of his ministry, the Jews would have misunderstood his claim. No
doubt, he would have caused an uproar for the Jews were ready
to make him king (John 6, 15). Thus before he made an explicit
claim, he made clear what sort of a Messiah he was claiming to be.

The progressive manifestation of his claim to be Messiah is evident in all the Gospels, especially in St. Matthew's. Note the
following texts: Matt. 3, 14; 4, 17; 7, 29; 9, 6; 9, 27; 10, 22; 11,
1–6; 13, 16–17; 13, 37; 15, 22; 16, 13–20; 17, 9; 17, 22; 19, 29; 20,
17; 21, 9; 23, 10; 24, 5. The proof that Jesus is the Messiah is not
essential to the progression of our argument. Harnack admits
Jesus claimed to be Messiah. He wrote: "To say nothing of anything else, such a story as that of Christ's entry into Jerusalem
would have to be simply expunged, if the theory is to be maintained that he did not consider himself the promised Messiah and
also desire to be accepted as such." [3a]

Similarly, the statement that Jesus claimed to be God has to
be qualified and indeed in two respects. First of all, he did not go
around loudly asserting that claim. On the contrary, he avoided
any clear statement for a long time (Matt. 16, 15; John 10, 24).
Secondly, he did not claim to be God only; he claimed also to be
man. Indeed, he insisted on that fact. Apparently, it was the only
reason why he told his Apostles of his temptations in the desert;
why he permitted them to witness his human weakness in the garden of Gethsemani. He seemed to fear that they would forget
about his humanity once they realized he was divine.

Why did Jesus avoid any clear statement of his divinity? The
reasons are obvious if you consider what would have resulted from
a premature assertion. Neither the Apostles nor the Jews would
have believed him. Sinners would have been frightened away.

The Apostles would not have been prepared for such a
surprising revelation. For centuries, the Jews had suffered cruel
persecutions rather than deny that God is one. They never
thought that God would become man. As good Jews, they were

3a. *What is Christianity?*, New York (Putnam's), 1908, pp. 140–141.

filled with profound respect and awe for the majesty of God. In
their minds, God meant the Supreme Being who had made the
world and who was infinitely different from anyone else. Imagine
their amazement if Jesus, who appeared to be only a man, had
asserted in the beginning that he was God. Without doubt, they
would have walked no more with him (John 6, 67). Indeed, their
slowness to believe, after three years of miraculous education, surprised even our Lord (Mark 8, 21).

The Jews would have killed him. Even after they had witnessed innumerable miracles, they refused to listen to his claims.
If he had stated clearly that he was God, they would have stoned
him. In fact, they were ready to do so on several occasions "because thou, who art a man, dost pretend to be God" (John 10,
33).

Finally, the sinners whom he came to save would have feared
him. Since the Jews pictured God as a stern and just Master,
they would have dreaded his approach. They had to learn that
God is loving and kind by experimental discovery that Jesus was
loving and kind. They had to learn Christ bit by bit, then bit by
bit realize that he was God.[4]

Jesus avoided any clear statements until the proper time would
come by closing the mouths of the witnesses and by using the
title "Son of Man." From the first he silenced the demoniacs
when they hailed him as the Son of God (Mark 1, 23; 3, 11; 5, 7).
This was a strong proof that he thought he was God, for you do
not silence speculation when you can dispose of it more easily
by a denial.

In like manner, he silenced his disciples when they began to
perceive his true nature. Thus, when Peter confessed his faith
at Caesarea Philippi, "he strictly charged them not to tell anyone about him" (Mark 8, 30; cf. Matt. 16, 20). After the Transfiguration, he again warned them, "do not tell anybody of what
you have seen, until the Son of Man has risen from the dead"
(Matt. 17, 9).

Publicly, Jesus often avoided any clear statement by referring
to himself as the "Son of Man." In the Gospels, he used this

4. Cf. Maisie Ward and F. J. Sheed, *Catholic Evidence Training Outlines,*
London (Sheed & Ward), 1939, p. 194; Sheed, *Theology and Sanity,* New
York (Sheed & Ward), 1946, pp. 54–60.

title eighty times. Since it aroused the curiosity of the Jews, it served a useful purpose. It led them to investigate further his claims. "Who is this Son of Man" (John 12, 34)? Although the prophet Daniel (Daniel 7, 14) had used this title in reference to the Messiah, the Jews were never sure what Jesus meant by it. Not until his trial did he bring out its full significance.[5]

While Jesus was refraining from any clear-cut claim, he was *carefully preparing* his disciples and the Jews for belief in him as God. At first he made implicit claims. They watched him doing things, and heard him saying things that only God has a right to do and say. As the truth slowly dawned upon them, he made his claims more clear, more explicit. Eventually, they realized that *his way of acting, speaking, thinking was quite natural if he was God but totally inexplicable, if he were only a man.*

III. IMPLICIT CLAIMS

Jesus claimed to be God by his actions and by his words. When the Jews suspect he is claiming to be God due to his actions, he often strengthens their suspicions by his words. He permits the truth to dawn slowly upon them so that they will have no excuse, if they reject him. When his disciples fail to grasp the full import of his actions, he instructs them by his words. After they are better prepared he makes his claim clearer. As a great teacher, he leads them gradually to the point where they perceive the truth. Ultimately, he publicly and explicitly states his divinity.

A. He Perfects the Law of Moses

In the Sermon on the Mount, Jesus perfects the moral law given by God to the Jews through Moses. "Do not think that I have come to set aside the law and the prophets; I have not come to set them aside but to bring them to perfection" (Matt. 5, 17). Unlike the prophets, he does not appeal to any divine commission. He speaks as one conscious of his own divine knowledge and authority. Thus he does not hesitate to perfect the law of Moses (Matt. 5). "You have heard that it was said, Thou shalt not commit adultery. But I tell you that he who casts his eyes on a woman so as to lust after her has already committed adultery with her in

5. Cf. M. J. Lagrange, *The Gospel of Jesus Christ*, Westminster (Newman), 1938, II, 127.

his heart. . . . You have heard that it was said, Thou shalt love thy neighbor and hate thy enemy. But I tell you, Love your enemies, do good to those who hate you . . . ." [6]

If we remember that in the Jewish mind Moses and the Law were inseparably linked with Jahve, it is difficult to explain the attitude of Jesus, save in the sense that he considered himself to be equal to Jahve.

B. He Is Superior to Prophets and Kings

Jesus is conscious that he is superior to the most exalted prophets and kings. "Then, turning to his own disciples, he said, Blessed are the eyes that see what you see; I tell you, there have been many prophets and kings who have longed to see what you see, and never saw it, to hear what you hear, and never heard it" (Luke 10, 23–24).

He declares that he is greater than Jonah and Solomon whom the Jews venerated (Matt. 12, 41–42). Indeed, he is the Lord of the angels whom he calls his servants and whom he surpasses in knowledge (Matt. 13, 14). Often he implies that he is Son of God. When he teaches the disciples to pray, for example, he tells them: "When you pray, you are to say, our Father . . ." (Luke 11, 2). But nowhere else in the Gospels do we find these words. Instead he always distinguishes between "my Father" and "your Father." Evidently, he thought of himself as Son of God in a special sense, not even shared by the apostles themselves.[7]

C. He Claims Utter Allegiance

Without a doubt, Jesus claimed a devotion which no mere man can demand. A person must be ready to give up father and mother, brother and sister, for his sake (Matt. 10, 37–39). Indeed, a person must be willing to give up life itself; to take up the cross and follow him (Luke 9, 24). Love of him wins forgiveness of sins (Luke 7, 41–49). Towards him, men cannot be neutral. "He who is not with me, is against me; and he who does not gather his store with me, scatters it abroad" (Matt. 12, 30).

He accepts the adoration of men as something perfectly normal

---

6. Note the repeated emphatic form of address "But I tell you . . ."

7. Cf. Matt. 7, 21; 10, 32; 11, 27; 12, 50; 15, 13; 16, 17; 18, 10; 20, 23; 24, 36; 26, 29; Mark 8, 38; 13, 32; 14, 36; Luke 2, 49; 9, 26; 10, 22; 22, 29; 24, 49.

and natural. "And the ship's crew came and said, falling at his feet, Thou art indeed the Son of God" (Matt. 14, 33; cf. Matt. 8, 2; 15, 25).

D. He Will Judge All Men

God alone can judge fairly the thoughts, words, and deeds of billions of men. Christ declares that he will do this. "The Son of Man will come hereafter . . . and he will recompense every-one, then, according to his works" (Matt. 16, 27). He will reward men according to what they have done for him (Matt. 25, 34–46). The final judgment for all men will be either "come to me" or "depart from me" (Matt. 25, 31–46). Although these assertions may seem ordinary to us, for we are accustomed to think of Christ as God, it is easy to imagine how they amazed the Jews of his time. According to Jewish tradition, God alone would judge the world.

While he warns men of the judgment, he offers them his as-sistance. "Come to me, all you that labour and are burdened; I will give you rest. Take my yoke upon yourselves, and learn from me; I am gentle and humble of heart; and you shall find rest for your souls. For my yoke is easy, and my burden is light" (Matt. 11, 28–30).

E. He Demands the Same Reverence as His Father Receives

As the months passed, Jesus revealed more clearly the intimate relationship that existed between the Father and the Son. It was a revelation which prepared the way for the declaration of identity of nature in Father and Son. On one occasion, for ex-ample, when the Jews were displeased because he cured a man on the Sabbath, Jesus declares: "My Father has never ceased working and I too must be at work" (John 5, 17). Although he does not state explicitly his equality with God, for the proper time had not yet come, his reasoning takes it for granted. The Jews real-ized this, for they accused him of blasphemy. "He not only broke the Sabbath, but spoke of God as his own Father, thereby treating himself as equal to God."

In reply, Jesus urges them to believe that the Father loves the Son, and discloses to him all that he himself does. "And . . . just as the Father bids the dead rise up and gives them life, so the Son gives life to whomsoever he will. So it is with judgment; the Father, instead of passing judgment on any man himself, has left all judgment to the Son, so that *all may reverence the Son just as they reverence the Father . . ."* (John 5, 21–23).

Jesus goes on to point out the *reasons* why they should believe in him. First of all, he recalls the *testimony of John the Baptist* to whom the Jews are now favorably disposed. He reminds them how John had borne witness to the truth by pointing him out as the one who was to come after him.

Jesus, however, does not depend on human testimony, though the testimony of this last of the prophets should not be over-looked. There was a further testimony of a more conclusive character, namely, the *testimony of miracles* by which men might recognize that a person was sent by God. Thus Moses and the prophets had convinced their forefathers. Now the Jews should know and believe as a result of his miracles that his Father had sent him.

Finally, Jesus *appeals to the Scriptures,* which the Jews studied so diligently, for they bear witness to him. Because they were more interested in obtaining a reputation for learning than in the truth, Jesus concludes that Moses, the very man in whom the Jews put their trust, will be their accuser before his Father.[8] "If you believed Moses, you would believe me; it is of me that he wrote."

F. He Alone Knows God's Mind and God Alone Knows His

When the seventy-two disciples returned from their first mission, Jesus thanks his Father for opening their eyes to the truth.

At this time, Jesus was filled with gladness by the Holy Spirit, and said, O Father, who art Lord of heaven and earth, I give thee praise that thou hast hidden all this from the wise and prudent, and revealed it to little children. Be it so, Lord, since this finds favour in thy sight. My Father has entrusted everything into my hands; none knows what the Son is, except the Father, and none knows what the Father is, except the Son, and those to whom it is the Son's good pleasure to reveal him (Luke 10, 21–22; cf. Matt. 11, 25–27; John 10, 15).

In these simple words there is hidden a wealth of meaning. Jesus alone perfectly knows the Father because he is the Son of

8. Cf. Lagrange, *op. cit.,* I, 240–243.

God. Like the Father, he is omniscient. The Son is perfectly known by the Father alone for he is as incomprehensible as the Father. All created beings are shut off from his knowledge proper to God himself—except in so far as the Son communicates it to them. Because this passage evidently testifies to his divinity, rationalists have endeavored to throw doubt upon it. Fortunately, "it is so well attested by manuscript tradition and by the versions that not a single editor of the gospels has ever dared to alter it." [9]

G. He Forgives Sins

Note how Christ forgives sins, not by calling upon God, but by his own authority. The scribes quickly perceive the fact that he assumes the role of God, for sin is an offense against God himself.

And at this, some of the scribes said to themselves, He is talking blasphemously. Jesus read their minds, and said, Why do you cherish wicked thoughts in your hearts? Tell me, which command is more lightly given, to say to a man, Thy sins are forgiven, or to say, Rise up, and walk? And now, to convince you that the Son of Man has authority to forgive sins while he is on earth (here he spoke to the palsied man), Rise up, take thy bed with thee, and go home. And he rose up, and went back to his house, so that the multitudes were filled with awe at seeing it . . . (Matt. 9, 3–8).

On another occasion, Jesus forgives the sins of Mary Magdalen. The Pharisee, Simon, was shocked because Jesus permitted a public sinner to approach him and kiss his feet. Jesus reads his thoughts. He contrasts Magdalen's love for him with Simon's want of love. Because she loves Jesus, her sins are forgiven. "Then he said to her, Thy sins are forgiven. And his fellow-guests thereupon thought to themselves, Who is this, that he even forgives sins?" (Luke 7, 48–50).

H. He Works Miracles

In the next chapter we shall discuss his miracles at greater length. Here we merely wish to note his manner of working them. Unlike the prophets and saints of the Old Testament, Jesus never prays for a miracle. Always the actual word which heals is his own *ipse dixit*. On every occasion he gives the impression that this

9. Cf. Lagrange, *op. cit.*, II, 8.

miraculous power is proper to him and that he can use it when he pleases. In fact, he grants the disciples power to work miracles in his name (Luke 10, 17–19).

Obviously, some of these implicit claims, which we have been considering, are clearer than others. But they all indicate that Jesus' way of acting and speaking was quite natural if he was God but totally inexplicable, if he were only a man. By means of the implicit claims, Jesus gradually prepared his disciples for the more explicit claims.

IV. EXPLICIT CLAIMS

When the disciples were disposed to believe that he was the Son of God, Jesus made his claim more explicit.[10] Eventually, his claim was so clear that no Jew could plead ignorance of it. In fact, Jesus warns the Jews on several occasions: "If you were children of God, you would welcome me gladly; it was from God I took my origin, from him I have come" (John 8, 42).

A. He Has Pre-Existed with the Father

When Jesus tells the Jews that a man who is true to his word will never see death, the Jews ask him: "Art thou greater than our father Abraham? He is dead, and the prophets are dead. What dost thou claim to be?" (John 8, 53).

In reply, Jesus is almost forced to assert his rightful rank. If he did not do so, he would lead them into error. Thus he confesses that he is greater than Abraham. In fact, Abraham rejoiced to see his day. When the astounded Jews asked him: "Hast thou seen Abraham, thou, who are not yet fifty years old? And Jesus said to them, Believe me, before ever Abraham came to be, I am" (John 8, 57–58).

Since Abraham had lived over a thousand years before, the Jews realized that Jesus was claiming to be divine. "Whereupon they took up stones to throw at him; but Jesus hid himself, and went out of the temple."

B. He is Equal to the Father

On another occasion the Jews asked him if he was the Messiah (cf. John 10, 22–39). Jesus refused to answer by a simple affirma-

10. Evidently this division between implicit and explicit claims is somewhat arbitrary.

tion. Since the Jews had a false notion of the Messiah, it was a dangerous confession to make. Moreover, it would be only a partial truth, for he was much more than that.

So he reminds them again of his miracles which prove that the Father loves him. He promises them eternal life if they will put their trust in him. Simply he states the greatest truth of all, "My Father and I are one."

Previously, he had called himself God's Son who has the same knowledge and same power as the Father (Luke 10, 22; cf. Matt. 11, 27; John 5, 17–20). Here he distinguishes himself from the Father. They are two distinct persons, yet in some mysterious way they are one. The Jews are sure he is blaspheming—making himself equal to God. They pick up stones to kill him.

But the Master calms their minds by professing his respect for Scripture and still more for him who gave the Scriptures. Thus he gives them time for reflection though he has no intention of withdrawing his declaration. They should know that he does not wish to diminish the worship due his Father, much less take his place. Again, he appeals to his actions. From them the Jews should learn to believe that *"the Father is in me, and I in him."* Thus he reasserts his first statement in all its fullness. The infuriated Jews tried to lay hold of him but he escaped.

C. St. Peter's Confession

Although St. Peter's confession had occurred before the mission of the seventy-two disciples, we purposely delayed its consideration, for it was a revelation limited to a few who were requested not to divulge it until the Son of Man had risen from the dead (Matt. 16, 13–17). Prior to his confession, the disciples had followed Jesus for over two years. They had seen him doing things and heard him saying things that only God has a right to say and do.

Often, they reflected upon what they had seen and heard, "And they were overcome with awe; Why, who is this, they said to one another, who is obeyed even by the winds and the sea?" (Mark 4, 40; cf. Luke 8, 49). Slowly, they began to surmise who he was: "And the ship's crew came and said, falling at his feet, Thou art indeed the Son of God" (Matt. 15, 33). As a great teacher, Jesus did not tell them who he was; but he led them to the point where they told him.

When he knew they were prepared, he questioned them about what men said concerning him. Thus he paved the way for the expression of their own thoughts. His life and works had been so marvelous that no person could take him for an ordinary man. So the disciples replied that some thought he was John the Baptist, others Elias, still others Jeremias, or one of the prophets. "Jesus said to them, And what of you? Who do you say that I am? Then Simon Peter answered, Thou art the Christ, the Son of the living God."

Had Jesus not been the Son of God, he would have shown a holy indignation at Peter's bold utterance. At all events, he was obliged to make some answer. The answer he made still resounds in our ears, day by day and age after age. "Blessed art thou, Simon son of Jona; it is not flesh and blood, it is my Father in heaven who has revealed this to thee."

So certain and spontaneous is Peter's perception of his divine nature that Jesus knows it is due to a revelation from God the Father. Jesus, therefore, in the name of his Father confirms what Peter had said of him. He is truly the Son of God. His subsequent words and deeds will strengthen their incipient faith.[11]

Then Jesus foretells the future role of Simon in his church. As a sign of his future position, Jesus gives him a new name "Cephas," the Aramaic word for rock. In Greek the word for rock is "petros" from which we get the name "Peter." Later we will consider the words of Christ in this regard. At present we are concerned only with his claim to be the Son of God.

D. The Transfiguration

Six days after Peter's confession, a most extraordinary event in the life of Jesus, the Transfiguration, took place [12] (cf. Matt. 17, 1–8; Mark 9, 2–8; Luke 9, 28–36). The Evangelists note the exact time between the two events because the Transfiguration was a miraculous confirmation of the faith Peter confessed.[13] As wit-

11. Cf. Lagrange, *op. cit.*, I, 257–263.
12. Cf. Lagrange, *op. cit.*, I, 268.
13. Relying upon internal evidence alone, Albert Schweitzer concludes that the Evangelists were wrong in placing Peter's confession before the Transfiguration. Moreover, he says: "What we call the Transfiguration is in reality nothing else but the revelation of the secret of messiahship to the Three." Most Christians would prefer the testimony of the Evangelists who lived with Christ to the opinion of Schweitzer. This is a good example of how the so-

nesses Jesus selected Peter who was the appointed head of the Apostles, John who was the beloved disciple, and his brother James who would be the first Apostle to shed his blood for the gospel.

Jesus had told the Jews: "If you believed Moses, you would believe me; it was of me that he wrote." Here Moses comes from heaven to bear witness to him. Elias also is present. Thus the greatest representatives of Israel's past pay homage to Christ and forewarn the Apostles of his approaching death.

For the first time the Apostles see Jesus in the glory that properly belongs to him. At Peter's confession, Jesus had accepted the title of Son of God. "And now, there was a voice which said to them out of the cloud, This is my beloved Son, in whom I am well pleased; to him, then listen." This voice could only be the voice of the Father.

Imagine the tremendous impact this miracle must have had upon the Apostles. Before their very eyes Jesus was transfigured—his face shining like the sun and his garments becoming white as snow. From a shining cloud, they heard the voice of the Father acknowledging Jesus as his beloved Son. No doubt they wished to spread the news immediately throughout Israel. But Jesus warned them to tell no man until the Son of Man had risen from the dead.

E. The Parable of the Wicked Husbandmen

The parable of the Wicked Husbandmen drew back still more the veil from his Divinity. At the same time it served as a terrible warning to the Jews. The parable presents no difficulty.

And now he took occasion to tell the people this parable; There was a man who planted a vineyard, and let it out to some vine-dressers, while he went away to spend a long time abroad. And when the season came, he sent one of his servants on an errand to the vine-dressers, bidding them pay his share of the vineyard's revenues. Whereupon the vine-dressers beat him, and sent him away empty-handed. Then he sent another servant; and him too they sent away empty-handed, beating him first, and insulting him. Then he sent a third; and they drove him away wounded, like the others. So the owner of the vineyard said, What am I to do? I will send my well-beloved son; perhaps they will have reverence

called critics of the Gospel do not let historical facts interfere with their suppositions. Cf. Mozley, *The Theology of Albert Schweitzer*, New York (Macmillan), 1951, p. 36.

for him. But the vine-dressers, on seeing him, debated thus among themselves; This is the heir, let us kill him, so that his inheritance may pass into our hands. And they thrust him out of the vineyard and killed him. And now, what will the owner of the vineyard do to them? He will come and make an end of those vine-dressers, and give his vineyard to others. God forbid, they said, when they heard that (Luke 20, 9–19).

It was an unforgettable warning given to men who were obstinately denying his mission and rights. Their forefathers had persecuted the prophets. Now they were ready to murder his Son.

F. His Trial before Caiphas

The night before he died Jesus testified under oath before all the leaders and priests of Judea that he was the Son of God. Gradually, Christ had built up to this dramatic moment. At first, he aroused the curiosity of the Jews by his life, his wisdom and his works. Then he made them wonder still more by his implicit claims to be God and by a number of astounding miracles. When the Jews accused him time after time of claiming to be equal to God, he never denied it. In fact, he continued to say and do things that only God has a right to say and do. Finally, he made his claim so clear that all the Jews could understand it.

The case of Christ became the question of the hour in Judea. The common people loved and admired him. But the leaders and priests, filled with envy and hatred, were determined to put him to death. They tried to convict him by false witnesses. But since they could not agree, Caiphas, the high priest, was finally forced to ask the crucial question.

Then the high priest stood up, and asked Jesus, Hast thou no answer to make to the accusations these men bring against thee? He still was silent, still did not answer; and the high priest questioned him again, Art thou the Christ, the Son of the Blessed God? Jesus said to him, I am. And you will see the Son of Man sitting at the right hand of God's power, and coming with the clouds of heaven. At this, the high priest tore his garments, and said, What further need have we of witnesses? You have heard his blasphemy for yourselves; what is your finding? And they all pronounced against him a sentence of death (Mark 14, 60–64; cf. Matt. 26, 62–67; Luke 22, 66–71).

Thus before all the leaders and priests of Judea, Jesus openly asserts his Divinity. In the future, no one could be justifiably ignorant of his claim.

In reply to Caiphas' question Jesus, first of all, *admits* that *he is the Christ* (Messiah) foretold by all the prophets. Since the Messiah was expected to come to earth in great glory, Jesus explains his answer. In effect, he said: "I am the Christ but it is not now but hereafter that you will see me come on the clouds of heaven seated at the right hand of my Father."

Secondly, Jesus *asserts* that *he is truly the Son of God.* He who always had been careful to make distinctions answers the high priest's question without any qualification. He realized that the Jews understood by these words that he was making himself equal to God. Unless he qualified his statement, he knew that he would be put to death. Evidently, his words stated exactly what he meant. In testimony to their truth he laid down his life.

In the eyes of the Sanhedrin his reply was blasphemy. He made himself equal to God. To express his horror and reprobation of it, the high priest tore his garments. "What further need have we of witnesses?" he cried. "You have heard his blasphemy for yourselves; what is your finding?" It only remained to take the vote. Jesus was condemned to death for blasphemy (cf. Deut. 13, 2–6). As Ronald A. Knox says:

> The force of the foregoing arguments is perhaps best realized if the reader will put to himself the following question: 'If Jesus of Nazareth did not claim to be God, what *did* he claim to be?' Is it credible that he did what he did, said what he said, hinted what he hinted, kept silence where he kept silence, and finally answered the challenge of Caiphas without a word of qualification, of explanation, or of self-defence, if all the time he belonged; and was conscious of belonging to any order of Being less than divine? [14]

G. *Confirmation*

Finally, there is no reasonable explanation for the firm belief of the apostles and first Christians in the divinity of Christ, except the fact that Christ had claimed to be God. It is unbelievable that the first Jewish Christians would have adored Jesus as God unless he had convinced them of his divinity. This faith of the first Christians in the divinity of Christ was so strong that they suffered scourgings and death itself rather than deny it. It is evident in all their writings.

The *Acts of the Apostles,* for example, written by St. Luke

14. Ronald A. Knox, *The Belief of Catholics,* New York (Sheed & Ward), 1940, pp. 111–112.

before the year 65, shows this faith. God and Jesus are indiscriminately called "the Lord." Jesus is regarded as the "author of life," that is, God (Acts 3, 15). He is worshipped as God (Acts 7, 55, 59; 9, 14, 21; 22, 18). In his name, the apostles work countless miracles (Acts 3, 6; 9, 34). The first martyr, Stephen, sees Jesus, the Lord of all, ready to welcome him. "Lord Jesus, he said, receive my spirit; and then, kneeling down, he cried aloud, Lord, do not count this sin against them" (Acts 7, 58–59).

St. Peter begins his Second Epistle with the words: "Simon Peter, a servant and apostle of Jesus Christ, to those who share with me the common privilege of faith, justified as we are by our God and Saviour Jesus Christ . . ." St. Peter reminds his readers that he witnessed Jesus' divine glory at the transfiguration and heard the voice of God the Father saying: "This is my beloved Son, in whom I am well pleased; to him, then, listen" (2 Peter, 1, 17).

V. CONCLUSION

Our conviction that Christ claimed to be God is founded on ample and clear evidence found in proven historical documents. As we have seen, Jesus gradually revealed his divinity to his disciples by his actions and by his words. Eventually, they realized that his way of acting and speaking was quite natural if he was God but totally inexplicable, if he were only a man. When they were properly disposed to believe, Jesus stated his claim explicitly. Before all the leaders and priests of Judea, he asserts under oath that he is truly the Son of God. Though he faced death, he refused to qualify this claim. In testimony of its truth, he laid down his life. And the first Christians were willing to suffer persecution and death rather than deny his divinity.

THE QUESTION CONCERNING CHRIST

Supplementary reading from Ludwig Koesters, *The Believer's Christ*, St. Louis (Herder), 1939, pp. 1–4.

This question has aroused the most intense interest in the past and continues to do so today; no other problem has given rise to so much speculation or produced so extensive a literature. And

small wonder. The question about Christ is not only one of the
most interesting and difficult problems for the psychologist, the
historian, and the student of religions; it is much more a question
of conscience for millions, a question that engages the earnest
attention of every thoughtful person. Three hundred and eighty-
two million Catholics profess as an article of faith, that is, they
are firmly convinced, that Jesus Christ is true God, because he has
been announced and confirmed by the Almighty Himself as the
consubstantial Son of God and, therefore, as true God himself.
This faith in the divinity of Christ has for its object the historical
Christ who was "born of the Virgin Mary" in "Bethlehem, the
city of David," under the "Roman Emperor Caesar Augustus"
and "Cyrinus, the governor of Syria"; he "suffered under Pontius
Pilate," the historically known procurator of Judea, was "crucified, died and was buried." The Church's faith in Christ recognizes
no distinction between the "Christ of history" and the "Christ of
faith." Of the three hundred and fifty-one million Christians who
are not part of the Roman Catholic Church, the great majority
have preserved faith in the divinity of Christ as a sacred inheritance from their fathers.

Faith in Christ, acceptance of his divinity, is a fact. The individual, faced with the question about Christ, has only one of two
choices. Either he embraces this faith or he rejects it. There is no
middle ground. Either Jesus Christ is the consubstantial Son of
God or he is not. But if he is really the Son of God, then Christianity is the only true religion, the religion revealed by God;
then Christianity is of strict obligation for every man; then
Christ's word is the highest norm, and all contrary points of view
must give way before it; then the Christian's faith and the Christian's hope for time and for eternity are built upon a strong and
solid foundation.

Or Christ is not true God. In that case, he is merely a man like
any other. In that case, his words and precepts may indeed be
interesting and worth knowing, but they are not of obligation;
for then Christianity is merely one of the many systems which the
history of religions tells of, systems that succeed and supplant one
another, systems that we study but do not profess. Then anyone
is entitled to explain and recast Christianity according to his own
pleasure. But then, also, faith in Christ is a false doctrine, the
deification of a man, not conceived as the caprice of a polytheistic

mythology, but in all earnestness as the monotheistic adoration of the one, eternal God—hence a blasphemy, a terrible mistake or a shocking deception, whether the blame for this error or deception lies with Jesus himself or with Christianity. Even though we choose a vaguer and less severe term, the fact remains. Whoever admits a contradiction between the objective truth concerning Christ and the traditional faith in Christ no longer has the right to call himself a Christian in the sense in which uncounted millions of those faithful to Christ have used and continue to use this designation. . . .

There is no other way out; no compromise is possible. The decisive question demands an unconditional Yes or No for an answer. When many call Christ the greatest and wisest of men, they are not answering the question.

CHAPTER IV

The Historicity of the Gospels

CHRIST claimed to be the promised redeemer. He made a far greater claim than this, namely, to be the incarnate Son of God. These claims were rejected by the chosen people. Since that day many men have sought, by every conceivable subterfuge, to deny that Christ even made the claims attributed to him. One of the most drastic of these attacks was made within two hundred years after the Protestant Reformation. It was made by the Rationalists and by their converts within Christianity itself, namely, the Liberal Protestants. The original, or what is now called the Conservative, Protestants had placed the Bible on a lofty pedestal as the inspired word of God; it was the one and only rule of faith.[1] Now the pendulum swings in the opposite direction, and a new brand of Protestantism comes into being. The Liberal Protestants, succumbing to the attacks of the eighteenth century Rationalists, rejected the historical value of the New Testament and, in particular, of the four Gospels. That is why we must defend their historicity before we examine the proofs that Christ offered in justification of his claims.

I. THE GOSPEL CRITICS

The roots of the Liberal Protestant attitude towards the Gospels may be traced back to the Renaissance and the Reformation.

1. Why Protestants believe the Bible is inspired is a mystery. There is nothing in the text itself to prove it is.

The student who is interested may study this historical background in the first volume of Carleton J. Hayes' splendid work, *Political and Cultural History of Modern Europe*.[2] Without doubt, the Renaissance brought about a change in man's point of view. In the Middle Ages, men were conscious of this all-important truth that material creation is subordinate to man and man is subordinate to God. The Renaissance dimmed this consciousness by centering man's attention upon himself through the art forms of pagan culture. The beauty of the art and the fine literary forms made men unaware of the errors which they clothed. Without directly opposing the faith, the Renaissance promoted a growing spirit of pride and individualism. In the sixteenth century, the Protestant revolt from the Church fostered this spirit. After Luther rejected the authority of the Church, subsequent reformers denied the authority of Luther and ultimately all authority.

The eighteenth century Rationalists [3] presumed as true the hypothesis that any supernatural intervention of God is impossible. They spoke as if they knew exactly what God can and cannot do; as if God were unable to change in any way the world he had created. Eventually, innumerable attempts were made to bring the traditional faith in Christ into harmony with this false hypothesis. In other words, the first attacks on the Gospels, after seventeen hundred years of universal acceptance, did not spring from a scientific and historical examination of them but from philosophical prejudices. These futile attacks agreed only in so

2. Carleton J. Hayes, *Political and Cultural History of Modern Europe*, New York (Macmillan), 1932, Vol. I.

3. They are usually referred to as "deists." Deism is a theological term with two accepted meanings. In a technical sense, Deism refers to a philosophy that limits divine activity to the creation of the world. It is popularly called "the doctrine of an absentee-God," for it rejects the idea of divine providence. In a broad sense, Deism means a trend of negative theological thought that relies upon reason alone. In other words, it is a form of rationalism consisting primarily in the criticism and denial of the divine inspiration of Scripture, of miracles and of mysteries. The author of the article on "Deism" in the *Encyclopedia Britannica* characterizes the Deists as neither scholars nor thinkers of more than mediocre ability. Among the leading Deists were John Toland who wrote *Christianity Not Mysterious* (1696) and Matthew Tindale who wrote *Christianity as Old as the Creation; or, the Gospel a Republication of the Religion of Nature* (1730). Cf. "Deism," *The Encyclopedia Britannica* (14th ed.), VII, 144–145.

far as they denied the supernatural character of Christ. Often they were contradictory and cancelled one another out. This is evident if you glance at a few of them.

Hermann Reimarus and Gotthold Lessius, for example, proposed a "deception theory." According to them, Christ was merely a man. The Gospels were deliberate falsifications of Christ's life written by Christians in the second century.[4] Some years later David Strauss [5] changed this theory. According to him, the authors of the Gospels actually believed what they wrote for the followers of Christ had unconsciously accepted more and more myths about him. Because it would take a long time for these myths to grow and be accepted as true, Strauss concluded the Gospels were written in the second or third century. He admitted, however, that his hypothesis would collapse if any Gospel was proved to belong to the first century. Today all scholars agree that at least the first three Gospels were written in the first century.[6]

Some moderns who follow in the footsteps of Strauss make Christ the product of Oriental, Babylonian, Egyptian, Syrian, or Greek myths. Needless to say, no two of them agree. Another group of "critics" attempted to find a natural explanation for everything supernatural in the life of Christ.[7] The miracle at Cana, for example, was described as a wedding prank. When Jesus seemed to be walking on the water, he was really walking on a rock just beneath the surface. Countless cures were due to fortunate coincidences following mistaken medical analysis. When Christ fed five thousand men, he merely hypnotized them into believing they ate and were filled. Even when men permitted them to alter the Gospel text, it required unlimited faith to accept their far-fetched suppositions.

4. Reimarus was a high school teacher in Hamburg. After his death, Lessing, who was a playwright, published (1774–1778) some of Reimarus' writings under the title of the *Wolfenbüttel Fragments*. Although Liberal Protestants today reject this theory, the Communists still repeat it.

5. Strauss was professor of theology at Tubingen. Probably, *The Life of Jesus* (1835) is his best-known work.

6. Cf. Albright, *From the Stone Age to Christianity*, Baltimore (John Hopkins), 1946, p. 292.

7. Cf. Heinrich Paulus, *Das Leben Jesu*, Heidelburg (Winter), 1828.

Cf. Albright, *From the Stone Age to Christianity*, Baltimore (John Hopkins), 1946, p. 292.

Even in recent years, many Liberal Protestants have tried to explain away everything supernatural about Christ by distinguishing between the Christ of faith and the Christ of history.[8] The latter was merely a man; he did not even claim to be divine. The Christ of faith is the product of the imaginations of the early Christians who clothed the human Christ with supernatural qualities. Though the Christ of faith never existed, he is the dynamic source of the Christian life.

The so-called Critical School aimed to prove by means of literary and historical criticism that all miracles and mysteries recorded in the Gospels were not genuine or were interpolations.[9] Most of its members judged the historical value of the Gospels from internal evidence alone.[10] But like their predecessors, they endeavored to make the Gospel picture of Christ fit into their preconceived notions.[11] In the beginning their show of scholarship confused and almost routed the conservative Protestants.

8. The best known exponents of this theory were Loisy and Tyrell. They were called "modernists."

9. A leader in the early Critical School was Henrich J. Holtzmann, a professor at Strasbourg, who wrote a series on the New Testament, *Handkommentar zum Neuen Testament* (1889–1890). The leader of the later Critical School was Adolf von Harnack (1851–1930), who was a professor at Berlin. In this book, we often refer to his works.

10. In the past, it has been vitiated under the guise of "higher criticism" as Pope Leo XIII pointed out in his Encyclical, *Providentissimus Deus.* "There has arisen, to the great detriment of religion, an inept method, dignified by the name of 'higher criticism,' which pretends to judge the origin, integrity and authority of each book from internal indications alone. It is clear, on the other hand, that in historical questions such as the origin and handing down of writings, the witness of history is of primary importance, and that historical investigation should be made with the utmost care; and that in this matter internal evidence is seldom of great value, except as confirmation. To look upon it in other light will be to open the door to many evil consequences. . . . It will not throw on the Scriptures the light which is sought, or prove of any advantage to doctrine; it will only give rise to disagreement and dissension, those sure notes of error which the critics in question so plentifully exhibit in their own persons; and seeing that most of them are tainted with false philosophy and Rationalism, it must lead to the elimination from the sacred writings of all prophecy and miracle, and of everything else that is outside of the natural order."

11. In many places Harnack noted how the so-called Critics followed their preconceived ideas. In regard to the Gospel of St. Matthew, he wrote: "Critics may call this narrative (story of the infancy in St. Matthew) late, but in saying this they only express the fact that they find themselves out of sympathy

All the critics believed the hypothesis that nothing exists outside of the natural order. This dogma of their "faith" compelled
them to deny the possibility of miracles and the divinity of
Christ. Since the New Testament contains miracles, many critics
decided it was not genuine. Others declared the miracles and mysteries were interpolations. No two critics agreed on the authors
and dates of the Gospels.

Their scholarship, however, led them towards the truth. Gradually they were forced to set back the date of the composition of
the Gospels until their "high priest," Adolf Harnack, practically
agreed with the dates assigned by Catholic scholars.[12] It is interesting to note the gradual change in Liberal Protestant ideas.

	Matthew	Mark	Luke
Strauss (1835)	No earlier than the year 150		
Baur (1847)	130–134	150	150
Renan (1877)	84	76	a.94
Harnack (1911)	a.70	a.65	b.63

Indeed, Harnack admitted that the Synoptic Gospels (Matthew,
Mark, and Luke) are historical; that they represent Christ as
claiming to be God. He also admitted that St. John wrote the
fourth Gospel. In his opinion, it does not possess the historical
value of the Synoptics. He conceded:

'St John' is also a Jew, and indeed, like 'St. Matthew,' a Jew of Palestine. If we have called St. John a glorified St. Matthew, because his aim
also is didactic and apologetic, we may with equal justice call him a
glorified St. Mark and St. Luke, for he shares in the aims which domi-
nate both the evangelists. By means of the historic narrative he strives,
like St. Mark, to show that Jesus is the Son of God, and, like St. Luke,
to prove that He is the Saviour of the world, in opposition to the unbelieving Jews and the disciples of St. John the Baptist. Thus the leading
ideas of the synoptists are found in combination in St. John.[13]

These were amazing concessions on the part of a Liberal Protestant. Since his death (1930) most Liberal Protestants have made

with it; and to be in sympathy with a narrative of this kind is especially
difficult for us Westerns of the nineteenth and twentieth centuries!" Harnack,
The Date of the Acts and of the Synoptic Gospels, New York (Putnam's Sons),
1911, p. 142. Cf. Albright, *op. cit.,* p. 293.

12. Cf. *ibid.,* pp. 124, 162.

13. Harnack, *Luke the Physician,* New York (Putnam's), 1911, p. 168, note.

similar admissions [14] though they continue to deny that anything supernatural belonged to the primitive Gospels. In regard to the Gospel of St. John, recent discoveries have forced the Liberals to admit that it was written in the first century.[15]

Thus, the Liberal Protestant scholars, contrary to their original intention, have made the Catholic position stronger than ever before. Unfortunately these Gospel critics destroyed the faith of hundreds of thousands in the process. This tragedy has been due largely to the countless books and pamphlets which popularized their disbeliefs. Since the conclusions of scholars like Harnack were not sensational, they were seldom publicized. And ordinary people rarely questioned the assumptions or noted the contradictions of the earlier critics.

II. PROOF OF THE HISTORICITY OF A DOCUMENT

A. Tests of Historicity

Before good historians accept any document as historical, they examine it to see if it is *genuine, trustworthy,* and *integral.*

A document is genuine if it was written by the author whose

14. Sir Frederic Kenyon says: "Since the publication of Harnack's *Chronologie der altchristlichen Litteratur* in 1897 it has been generally admitted that, with very few exceptions, the traditional dates of the New Testament books may be accepted as approximately correct. The doctrines of the school of Baur, which regarded the earliest Christian books as a tissue of falsifications of the second century have been exploded. 'That time,' says Harnack, 'is over. It was an episode, during which science learnt much, and after which it must forget much.' Recent discoveries have only confirmed this conclusion." *Our Bible and the Ancient Manuscripts,* New York (Harper and Brothers), 1948, p. 98, note.

15. As Albright says: "In view of the extremely late date to which it (the Gospel of John), has often been assigned, Torrey's demonstration that it rests on an Aramaic substratum has been peculiarly resented by many New Testament scholars, though it has been enthusiastically accepted in principle by men of the standing of J. de Zwaan (1938). Meanwhile the sensational publication of a fragment of the Gospel from the early second century (C. H. Roberts, 1935) and of a roughly contemporary fragment of an apocryphal gospel dependent on John (H. I. Bell, 1935) has dealt the *coup de grace* to all radically late dating of John and has proved that the Gospel cannot be later than the first century A.D. . . . Moreover, the objections to the authenticity of the Book because of its alleged ignorance of history and geography have been considerably reduced in recent years." *Ibid.,* pp. 298–299.

name it bears. A document is trustworthy if the author knew the facts and told the truth. A document is integral, or complete, if it is substantially the same today as when it was written. In other words, nothing very much has been added or taken away.

Needless to say, a document that has been accepted as genuine, integral and trustworthy by the contemporaries of the author should be accorded the same value by succeeding generations unless sufficient evidence is discovered for rejecting the document. Moreover, according to the principles of historical criticism, no part of a genuine, trustworthy and integral document can be rejected unless it is proven erroneous.

B. Evidence

To make these tests of the historical value of a document, we must have evidence. This evidence may be *external* or *internal.*

External evidence is obtained from contemporary or later writers who testify to the historical value of a document. It is *most valuable* in establishing the historicity of a document. Eyewitness accounts, like Caesar's *Gallic Wars* or St. Matthew's *Gospel,* are called *primary sources* because they relate evidence gathered on the spot. Histories written from a study of these documents are called *secondary sources.* Strange to say, these *may* be more valuable *if* the author is a good historian who checks, correlates, and compares the evidence. Part of St. Luke's *Gospel* is an example, for he diligently questioned those who were "eyewitnesses from the beginning."

Internal evidence is derived from the study of the document itself. Often scholars can determine the author, approximate date, etc., from the persons and events mentioned, the language used, the idioms and figures of speech employed, and the style of writing. This involves an examination of meter, parallels, doublets, as well as correspondence to or divergence from related documents. From this study they may also ascertain any changes in the original document. Ordinarily internal evidence is used merely to *confirm* conclusions reached by means of external evidence. It is not used to establish the authenticity of a document unless external evidence is lacking. Unfortunately, internal evidence may be easily vitiated.

III. THE HISTORICITY OF THE GOSPELS

We have just seen how the historical value of a document is established. Now we must apply the three tests to the Gospels to determine their historical value. Are they genuine? In other words, were they actually written by Matthew, Mark, Luke and John? Are they trustworthy? In other words, did their authors, Matthew, Mark, Luke, and John, know the facts and were they truthful men? Are they integral? In other words, have their writings come down to us substantially unchanged?

A. Evidence That the Gospels Are Genuine

Now we ask the question, who wrote the Gospels? If they were written by Matthew, Mark, Luke, and John, they are genuine. The best evidence to answer this question is found in documents written by Christians and non-Christians in the first and second centuries. These men, from whom we shall quote, were much nearer to the facts than we are. Many of them either knew the Evangelists or their immediate successors. Doubt might creep into our minds if there were any evidence of dispute about this question among them. But there is none. Evidently, everyone was convinced that Matthew, Mark, Luke, and John wrote the four Gospels.[16]

1. TESTIMONY BY CHRISTIANS

Pope St. Clement, for example, wrote a letter to the Corinthians (96) to settle a dispute there. In the letter he quotes the Gospels of Matthew and Luke as authoritative. And he states: "The Apostles received the Gospel for us from the Lord Jesus Christ." [17]

In regard to Pope St. Clement, St. Irenaeus (125–202) writes:

The blessed Apostles (Peter and Paul) having founded and built up the Church (at Rome), bestowed the episcopal office of administering the Church on Linus. Paul mentions this Linus in his Epistles to Timothy.

16. In this regard, there is a striking difference between the four Gospels and the apocryphal gospels. While the latter were attributed by their authors to St. Peter and other apostles, they were never accepted anywhere as genuine. Even in the second century, St. Irenaeus points out that there are only four Gospels, written by Matthew, Mark, Luke, and John. Cf. *Against Heretics,* III, 1, 1.

17. *Letter to the Corinthians,* 42.

Anacletus succeeded him and after Anacletus, in the third place from the apostles, Clement received the bishopric. Since he saw the Apostles and conversed with them, he would have the preaching of the Apostles resounding (in his ears), and their Tradition before his eyes. Nor was he alone in this for there were still many living then who had been instructed by the Apostles.[18]

Papias (65–130) was a bishop in Phyrgia. Although his works were lost, Eusebius has preserved several valuable quotations from them. In his *History of the Church*, he quotes Papias as follows:

The Presbyter also said this: Mark, the interpreter of Peter, wrote down carefully what he remembered, both the sayings and the deeds of Christ, but not in chronological order. . . . So Matthew composed his discourses in Hebrew and everyone interpreted them to the best of his ability.[19]

St. Justin (100–164) was a Greek philosopher before his conversion. In his books he quoted from the Gospels over two hundred and fifty times. Although he does not give the names of the Evangelists, he speaks of the "commentaries of the apostles which are called Gospels," [20] and of "the commentaries which I say were written by his apostles and their disciples." [21]

St. Irenaeus (125–202) was a pupil of St. Polycarp who was taught by St. John the Apostle. Irenaeus states:

Matthew wrote a version of the Gospels for the Hebrews in their own tongue at the time that Peter and Paul were preaching the Gospel and founding the Church at Rome. After their death, Mark, the disciple and interpreter of Peter, also handed down to us the things which were preached by Peter. Luke also, the companion of Paul, wrote down in a book the Gospel that was preached by him. Finally, John, the disciple of the Lord who had reclined on his breast, published his Gospel while he was residing in Ephesus. . . . Nor are there more than these, nor again can you find fewer than these Gospels.[22]

In his treatise against the heretic Marcion (a. 208), Tertullian of Africa asserts that the Gospels were written by Matthew, Mark, Luke, and John. He writes:

18. St. Irenaeus, *Against Heretics,* III, 3, 3. Transl. mine.

19. Eusebius, *Hist. Eccl.* III, 39.

20. *Apology,* I, 66.

21. *Dialogue with Trypho,* 103.

22. *Op. cit.,* III, 1, 1. What a difference between the authority of St. Irenaeus who dates Matthew's Gospel before 64 A.D. and some rationalists like Strauss who said (1835) someone else wrote it after 150 A.D.

Of the apostles, John and Matthew impart to us the faith; of the disciples Luke and Mark renew it. . . . Mark's Gospel is called that of Peter whose interpreter he was, just as Luke's Gospel is often ascribed to Paul.[23]

In respect to the Gospels, the historian, Eusebius, quotes from the *Sixth Hypotyposis* of Clement of Alexandria (150–216) the following passage:

Again, in the same work, Clement also gives the tradition respecting the order of the Gospels. . . . He says that those which contain the genealogies were written first; and that the Gospel of Mark was occasioned in the following manner: 'When Peter had preached the word publicly at Rome . . . a great number of people requested Mark who was the companion of Peter and remembered well what he said, to put down these things in writing.' After Mark completed the task, he gave it to those who requested it. . . . But John, last of all, thinking that the references in the other Gospels to the body of Christ were sufficiently detailed, put in writing, under the guidance of the Holy Spirit, a spiritual Gospel.[24]

2. Testimony by Non-Christians

According to Harnack, the sources force us to admit that the heretic Marcion (92–153) considered the Gospels of Matthew and John to be apostolic.[25] Basilides (62–133), another heretic, wrote

23. *Against Marcion*, IV, 5.

24. Eusebius, *op. cit.*, VI, 14. Daniel J. Saunders points out: "Ironically enough, Wellhausen, Loisy, Case, and others, who disregard the documents of the second century, have attempted to make a case against the genuineness of the Fourth Gospel by appealing to the testimony of Georgius Harmartolus (ninth century) and Philip of Side (fifth century), both of whom hold an early martyrdom for John the apostle. How worthless this testimony is may be judged from the fact that the document of Georgius which contains the quotation about the early martyrdom also has the tradition about the long life of John. Secondly, it is by no means clear that Georgius and Philip are independent witnesses. Thirdly, the latter is well known as a very poor historian. Fourthly, it is most unlikely that the Church of Asia Minor would have kept complete silence concerning the glory of John's martyrdom if he had given up his life for the faith. Finally, there is no evidence of such a story before the time of Philip; it seems to have been unknown to such serious investigators as Irenaeus, Eusebius, Tertullian, Origen, and all the other ecclesiastical writers of the first three centuries." *Reason to Revelation*, St. Louis (Herder), 1949, p. 63.

25. Cf. Harnack, "Neue Studien zu Marcion," *Texte und Unterschungen*, XLIV, 4, 1923, p. 22, n. 1.

a commentary on the four Gospels. Although he misinterpreted them, he acknowledged them to be genuine.

In the second century, Celsus, a pagan philosopher, bitterly attacked Christianity. But he never questioned the fact that the Gospels were written by the Evangelists. If there were any reason to doubt this point, Celsus certainly would have brought it up.

3. RESUMÉ

Even from the evidence we have mentioned, we may conclude the Gospels are genuine. First of all, these authors living in the first and second centuries either *name* the *four Evangelists* as the authors of the four Gospels *or presuppose* that *everyone knows* who they are. The fact that they presuppose this knowledge, even at this early date, is a strong proof of their genuinity. We presuppose, for example, that everyone knows who wrote the Gettysburg Address, for the evidence is so clear that no one questions it. Similarly, no one in the first two centuries questioned the fact that the Evangelists wrote the Gospels. Even the pagans and heretics accepted it, for the evidence was clear and convincing.

Secondly, the fact that the Gospels were *held in veneration* and regarded as *genuine* in *all churches, while* the contemporaries of the Apostles were still alive, is conclusive proof of their genuineness. Surely, the friends and contemporaries of the Apostles would never have permitted forgeries to be palmed off as the authentic works of the Apostles without violent protests. But there were never any protests. On the contrary, official teachers like Pope St. Clement "who had conferred with the Apostles" quote the Gospels as authoritative. Moreover, why should anyone doubt the words of St. Irenaeus, who was taught by St. John's disciple, when he explicitly names the authors of the four Gospels?

Thirdly, the Jewish converts would never have accepted them as equal to the books of the Old Testament if there were *any* doubt about their authors. And many of the Gentile converts, like St. Justin, were highly educated men. Naturally, they carefully investigated the written sources of the Christian religion.

The contrary notion that the Gospels were forgeries can never be demonstrated. In fact, there is no shred of evidence to indicate it. Any suggestion of this falsehood implies that the immediate successors of the Apostles were foolishly deceived by impious frauds or else they fabricated these diabolical frauds and cleverly deceived millions of Christians and non-Christians. And what did they stand to gain except persecution and death?

Finally, the internal evidence confirms these conclusions reached from external evidence, for a study of the Gospels themselves brings to light many facts about their authors.[26] Since the Gospels (except St. Matthew's) were written in the colloquial Greek of the first century, their authors were apparently men of that period. Moreover, although the authors were ignorant of Greek literature and philosophy, they knew the religion, customs, and practices of the Jews. Indeed, they portray accurately the political, social, and religious conditions in Palestine at the time of Christ. They were familiar with Herod's position, with the topography of Palestine, with the dissensions and antagonisms of the Pharisees, the Sadducees, and the doctors of the Law, with the complicated coinage systems of the Romans, the Greeks, and the Jews. Since these conditions were complicated and transient, some modern scholars have concluded from this evidence alone that the Gospels were written by contemporaries of Christ. Indeed, since many non-Catholic scholars like Harnack, who admitted the Gospels were genuine, relied primarily on this sort of evidence we may surmise how strong it is. Thus a study of the internal evidence tends to confirm the conclusions reached from external evidence. Matthew, Mark, Luke, and John wrote the four Gospels. They are *genuine*.

B. Evidence That the Gospels Are Trustworthy

The Gospels are trustworthy if the authors *knew the facts* and *told the truth*.

Obviously the Evangelists knew the facts. Matthew and John were Apostles who were constantly with Christ. Luke, the best historian of all, was a disciple who diligently questioned those "who from the beginning were eyewitnesses and ministers of the word" (Luke 1, 2). Mark was a disciple and a companion of St. Peter whose words he records in his Gospel.

They told the truth. "No one lies in serious matter without a reason." There was no reason why the Evangelists should lie. Cer-

26. For a more detailed treatment of this point see Leonce De Grandmaison, *Jesus Christ*, London (Sheed & Ward), 1930, I, 56–189. We have omitted any consideration of the Synoptic problem. If a student is interested, he may consult *ibid.*, pp. 91–116; Saunders, *op. cit.*, pp. 94–105.

tainly, they had nothing to gain. As is clear from the *Acts,* all they could expect was persecution and martyrdom. Ultimately, they sealed their testimony with their own blood.

Moreover, they could not have lied even if they wanted to. Most of Christ's words and actions were public, seen or heard by many, and easy to recall. The contemporaries of Christ, who knew what he did and said, would have exposed them. And the Jewish leaders who hated them would certainly have refuted them. But although the Jews persecuted them, they never denied the facts that the Apostles preached. Indeed, Peter appeals to the crowd to corroborate his statements (Acts 10, 34–43).

The fact that they differ on accidentals is additional proof of their sincerity. Each Evangelist relates the facts exactly as he recalls them. Evidently they never got together and said: "What shall our story be?" Writing independently they agree on all important facts although they differ about accidentals as we might expect. They disagree, for example, about the number and location of the angels at the tomb on the first Easter morn. And yet every one is certain about the fact of the resurrection. Their minor differences may be easily explained.[27]

The effects of their preaching proves their trustworthiness. Within a few years, hundreds of thousands entered the Church. Among these converts were educated men and many of the (Jewish) priests (Acts 6, 7). Surely, they would not have given up everything before they investigated the claims of the Apostles. And they lived at a time when the facts could *easily be verified.*

C. The Gospels Are Integral

The fact that the Gospels were known and reverenced *as divine revelation* by Christian communities throughout the world is strong guarantee of their integrity even before we examine the actual evidence. Surely no good Christian would deliberately change the words of God.[28] And in those days, Christians knew

27. Cf. Koesters, *op. cit.,* pp. 301–307; Adam, *The Son of God,* New York (Sheed & Ward), 1934, pp. 227–232.

28. The great reverence Christians had for the words of God is evident from a letter Irenaeus sent to a boyhood friend who had become a heretic. The bishop of Lyons wrote: "These opinions, Florinus, to speak mildly, are not those of sound doctrine. They do not agree with (the teaching of) the Church. . . . These opinions are not in the tradition of our predecessors who were disciples of the apostles. While I was still a youth enjoying the com-

the Bible much better than we do. Even minor changes in wording caused difficulties. Thus St. Augustine feared to use St. Jerome's new Latin translation.[29] In a letter to Jerome, he said:

We have come to this that a brother Bishop (of Oea), having ordered your translation to be read in the church to which he was accredited, people were disturbed because you had rendered a passage from the prophet Jonas in a very different manner from that which had grown old in all their memories and which so many generations had repeated. All the people were in an uproar; the Greeks especially, passionately accusing you of having falsified the text. . . . Our Bishop found himself obliged to rectify the passage as being erroneous in order to retain his people who were on the verge of abandoning him.[30]

If the early Christians were so disturbed by a new wording of a passage from the Old Testament, how would they react to a substantial change in the New Testament? Since many of them knew the Gospels by heart, any change was practically impossible. Moreover, the official teachers were anxious to teach all that Jesus taught and nothing more. No doubt, they often recalled the words of St. Paul: "If anyone preach to you a gospel, besides that which you have received, let him be anathema" (Gal. 1, 9).

But let us examine the actual evidence for the integrity of the Gospels. At present we possess approximately thirteen thousand manuscripts of the Bible.[31] Of these, more than four thousand are in Greek and Hebrew. The rest are Syriac, Latin, Coptic, Armenian, Georgian, Ethiopian, Arabic, and Gothic translations.

---

pany of Polycarp, in Asia Minor, I saw you trying to win his esteem when you were at the imperial court. . . . So well do I remember it all that I could tell the place where the blessed Polycarp sat while teaching and his manner of entering and of going out, . . . the familiar conversation which he had with John and with the others who had seen the Lord, as he has related and has recalled their words. And what he heard from them concerning the Lord, his miracles, his teaching, the details concerning those who had seen with their eyes the Word of Life, as Polycarp related it, and all in conformity with the Scriptures . . . I listened carefully, and I engraved it, not on papyrus, but in my heart and forever. By the grace of God, I remember it exactly." Eusebius, *History of the Church,* V, 20, 4.

29. The Old Latin versions had been used in Africa for several hundred years.

30. St. Augustine, *Ep.,* 71, 5.

31. Manuscript comes from the Latin *manu-scriptum* which means "written by hand."

Needless to say, we do not possess the original manuscripts of the Gospels. Although some fragments containing parts of the Gospels date back to the second century, the earliest complete manuscripts of the New Testament come from the fourth century.

This is not surprising, for the oldest manuscript of Horace dates from the eighth or ninth century. The manuscripts of Plato, Cicero, and Seneca are from the ninth century; those of Thucydides, Herodotus, Aeschylus, and Sophocles date from the tenth and eleventh centuries. The oldest complete manuscript of Homer belongs to the thirteenth century. Yet no one doubts these manuscripts are substantially the same as the originals. Therefore they have less reason to doubt that the Gospel manuscripts are substantially the same as the originals. Indeed, no other book can compare, even remotely, with the Scriptures in the number and antiquity of its extant copies.

The Gospels were probably written on papyrus, the common writing material at that time. Papyrus has about the same consistency as paper. Since it was not durable, papyrus manuscripts have been found only in the dry sands of Egypt.[32] Since the original Gospel manuscripts were probably written on papyrus, scholars do not expect to discover them. In the fourth century, vellum (or parchment) which is made from the skins of cattle, sheep, goats, and sometimes deer, became the common material used in books. Because vellum is quite durable, many manuscripts written on it have been discovered. The *Codex Vaticanus* and the *Codex Sinaiticus,* for example, which are the primary sources of modern texts of the Greek Bible, were written on vellum in the fourth century.

The Gospel manuscripts have been studied much more carefully by far more scholars than the manuscripts of any other work. Above all, scholars have scrutinized the "various readings" found in different manuscripts. The phrase, "various readings," means

32. Recently some papyrus rolls which contain portions of the Bible have been found in Egypt. These are very important for textual criticism, for the antiquity of many of them place them beyond all rivals in value. The fragment of the fourth Gospel (John 16, 14–30), for example, published in *Oxryhynchus Papyri* (Part XV) by Grenfell and Hunt, London, 1922, belonging to the same manuscript as the fragment previously published in Part II of the same collection (John 1, 23–40; 20, 11–25), dates back to the end of the third century, and is consequently earlier than many of the oldest.

that the same passage may read differently in diverse manuscripts. While several manuscripts, for example, give the last words of St. Luke's Gospel as "blessing God," two versions have "praising God." Still other manuscripts give the words "praising and blessing God." To understand how these "various readings" came about, you must know something about the history of the Bible.[33]

Before the invention of printing, each separate copy of a book had to be written by hand. Now no person can copy a long book without making errors. No doubt, many copies of the Bible, especial during persecutions, were made hurriedly and without careful revision. Mistakes were bound to occur.[34] These mistakes were multiplied whenever fresh copies of the faulty manuscripts were made. If we had the original manuscripts, the errors of later copies could be easily corrected. But since we do not have the originals, scholars (textual critics) have to try to determine the exact text of the original manuscripts by a comparison of later copies.

The task of the textual critic of the Gospels, however, is not too difficult because we possess so many ancient manuscripts. Although some mistakes may be found in every manuscript, few mistakes, if any, will be common to all the manuscripts. Where all the manuscripts read the same, scholars regard the text as certain. Where the manuscripts have various readings, scholars have to decide which reading is correct. Obviously, some manuscripts are better than others. Today most scholars agree on the dates and trustworthiness of the important manuscripts. The research of

33. Cf. Sir Frederick Kenyon, *Our Bible and the Ancient Manuscripts,* New York (Harper and Brothers), 1948, Fourth Edition. This is an excellent book by the former Director and Principal Librarian of the British Museum.

34. The mistakes of copyists were of many kinds and of varying importance. Sometimes they confused words of similar sound, as in English, we sometimes write *here* for *hear* or *assent* for *ascent.* Sometimes they passed over a word or even lines of a manuscript. Besides such errors of hand and eye, there were errors of the mind. If the copyist's mind wandered a little, he could write down words which came mechanically into his head, just as we do sometimes when we are distracted. Some copyists may have even deliberately altered a few passages. Fortunately, the great veneration in which the Bible has always been held, protected it against most of these intentional alterations. Moreover, since many people knew the Bible or major parts of it by heart, any important change would be immediately detected. Cf. *ibid.,* pp. 19–21.

scholars, of course, is not limited to the four thousand manuscripts in Greek and Hebrew which are the languages in which the Bible was written.

Besides these Greek and Hebrew manuscripts, scholars have nine thousand manuscripts in seven other languages. Although these are translations (or versions, as they are called), some of them are older than the Greek manuscripts. While the oldest Greek manuscripts of the Bible were written about 200 A.D., the earliest Latin and Syriac translations date back to 150 A.D. From these translations scholars are usually able to determine which Greek words the authors were translating. Consequently, the versions serve as another source of evidence for determining exactly the original text of the Gospels. Though the versions have errors peculiar to themselves, they were unaffected by the mistakes that later crept into the Greek. In other words, scholars compare the various versions with the Greek manuscripts to arrive at a more perfect text. Note that any addition or omission made in one version would be immediately evident from another version.

Still another storehouse of evidence used to establish the original text of the Gospels is the works of the Fathers of the Church. These early Fathers were the successors of the Apostles, the bishops and official teachers in the primitive church. In their many works which we still possess, they quote from the Gospels countless times. From these quotations, scholars can reconstruct the Gospels which they used. In other words, scholars know, for example, the important passages of the Gospels which St. Ignatius used in the year 107.[35] Or they can reconstruct all the important parts of the Gospels which St. Justin and St. Irenaeus used later in the second century.[36] Recently, copies of the *Diatessaron,* a

---

35. Dr. Streeter says: "Ignatius and the author of the *Didache* stand to Matthew as the preacher to his text." *The Four Gospels,* New York (Macmillan), 1925, p. 511. And C. F. Burney writes: "The fact which principally concerns us is Ignatius's knowledge of the Fourth Gospel, which seems to be proved by demonstration. The manner in which he utilizes its teaching shows further than his acquaintance with it was not merely superficial, but that he has assimilated it through a familiarity extending over many years." *The Aramaic Origin of the Fourth Gospel,* Oxford, 1922, p. 191.

36. In his three extant works, St. Justin (100–164) quotes the four Gospels over two hundred and fifty times. In like manner, St. Irenaeus (125–202) quotes the Gospels over three hundred times. And Tertullian of Africa (160–230) gives over nine thousand quotations from the New Testament.

harmony of the Gospels, composed about 120 by Tatian, a Syrian, have been found.[37] From this work, scholars can reconstruct the Gospels used by the Syrians in the first part of the second century.

Obviously, scholars have a vast amount of evidence—four thousand Greek and Hebrew manuscripts, nine thousand versions in half a dozen languages, and all the writings of the Fathers. Countless scholars, especially in the last century, have devoted their lives to the study of them.

Today all textual critics agree that no doctrine of the Christian faith rests on a passage of Scripture that is questionable.[38] Indeed, passages still disputed constitute an infinitesimal part of the whole Bible and have no bearing on our faith. A noted British scholar, Sir Frederic Kenyon, writes:

It is true (and it cannot be too emphatically stated) that none of the fundamental truths of Christianity rests on passages of which the genuineness is doubtful. . . . It cannot be too strongly asserted that in substance the text of the Bible is certain. Especially is this the case with the New Testament.[39]

After many years of painstaking research (1882), Westcott and Hort, two of the leading non-Catholic scholars in textual criticism, computed that only one-sixtieth part of the Gospels needs critical examination if questions merely concerned with orthography are left out. Moreover, according to Hort, if we omit all the

---

37. Cf. Kenyon, *op. cit.*, pp. 156–160.

38. "On the basis of our critical editions of the New Testament (Cf. Tischendorf (1869–1872); Westcott and Hort (1881); B. Weiss (1902); Nestle (1927); H. V. Soden (1913); Vogels, Greek-Latin (1922); Merk, Greek-Latin (1935)), we can determine in each instance whether other readings must be considered and, if a well-founded doubt is present, we can refrain from making scientific use of a passage that is in any way doubtful. For the rest, as far as contents are concerned, only four passages of the Gospels are disputed: the concluding verses of St. Mark's Gospel (Mark 16, 9ff.), the passage about the agony in the garden (Luke 22, 43ff.), the passage about the angel at the Pool of Bethsaida (John 5, 4), and the pericope about the adulteress (John 8, 1–11). All these passages, however, are of no importance at all in our historical demonstration of the truth and, moreover, they are acknowledged by every unbiased critic to be of great antiquity." As Koesters mentions, this is true especially of the disputed section of St. Mark's Gospel. Some noted scholars maintain that St. Mark himself added this fitting conclusion to his Gospel some time after he finished the first edition. Cf. Koesters, *The Believer's Christ*, St. Louis (Herder), 1939, p. 171.

39. *Op. cit.*, pp. 18, 23.

variations that are insignificant in themselves, such as the inter-
change of pronouns and proper names, the transposition of words,
and other differences that do not affect the meaning in the slight-
est, then only a thousandth part of the text remains disputed.[40]
No other ancient work is so authentic. Even the manuscripts of
Shakespeare are less integral. In other words, after one hundred
years of critical examination, the vast majority of scholars conclude that the Gospels today are substantially the same as when
they were written. All the recently discovered manuscripts confirm this conclusion.

D. Conclusion

All the evidence at our disposal leads us to the conclusion that
the Gospels are genuine, trustworthy, and integral. As we have
said, no other book can compare, even remotely, with the New
Testament, in the number and antiquity of its extant manuscripts.
No document has ever been studied so carefully by so many
scholars. After more than a century of critical examination, the
vast majority of scholars agree that the Gospel manuscripts we
possess are substantially the same as the originals. This conclusion
is the fruit of the study of thirteen thousand manuscripts as well
as thousands of direct quotations found in the works of the Fathers
of the Church.

Similarly, the Gospels are almost universally recognized as genuine today. This conclusion is founded primarily on the testimony
of the early Fathers of the Church who lived in the first and second centuries. It is confirmed by non-Christian writers of that
period, by the later Fathers of the Church, and by the respect paid
to the Gospels from the beginning. While some Liberal Protestants are still reluctant to admit that St. John's Gospel is authentic,
recent discoveries have weakened their opposition. If the Gospels
are genuine, they are evidently trustworthy. The authors knew
the facts and told the truth. Thus all the evidence leads us to the
conclusion that the Gospels are reliable historical documents.

IV. ACTS OF THE APOSTLES AND EPISTLES
OF ST. PAUL

It is possible to prove the historicity of the Acts and the Epistles
of St. Paul in the same manner. But it seems unnecessary. Because

40. Cf. Hort, *The New Testament in the Original Greek*, London, 1882,
II, 2.

the evidence is so clear and convincing many Rationalists and Liberal Protestants admit they are historical documents.[41] No one else has ever doubted it.

In regard to the Acts, they acknowledge Luke as their author. Harnack, for example, held that opinion. Even the sceptic, Renan, said: "A thing beyond all doubt is the Acts have the same author as the third Gospel and are a continuation of it."

In regard to the Epistles of St. Paul, all modern scholars admit that the Epistles to the Romans, Corinthians, Galatians, Philippians, Colossians, I Thessalonians, and Philemon are genuine. Since these are amply sufficient for our purposes we need not discuss the others in Apologetics.

V. APPENDIX: OTHER EARLY DOCUMENTS REFERRING TO CHRIST

A. Apocryphal Gospels

Among other early documents referring to Christ there are a number of spurious or apocryphal Gospels ascribed to Sts. James, Thomas, Peter, and others. They were "never" accepted as authentic by the Church. Even in the second century St. Irenaeus points out: "Nor are there more than these, nor again can you find fewer than these (four) Gospels."

All historians agree that the apocryphal Gospels have no historical value, since their authors and dates are unknown. While the Evangelists and St. Paul were official teachers in the Church, the authors of the apocryphal Gospels obviously were not. No doubt, some of them were written by orthodox Christians who,

41. Harnack says: "Paul is the most luminous personality in the history of primitive Christianity, and yet opinions differ widely as to his true significance. Only a few years ago we had a leading Protestant theologian asserting that Paul's rabbinical theology led him to corrupt the Christian religion. Others, conversely, have called him the real founder of that religion. But in the opinion of the great majority of those who have studied him, the true view is that he was the one who understood the Master and continued his work. This opinion is borne out by the facts. . . . As we cannot want to be wiser than history, which knows him only as Christ's missionary, and as his own words clearly attest what his aims were and what he was, we regard him as Christ's disciple, as the apostle who not only worked harder but also accomplished more than all the rest put together." *What Is Christianity?*, New York (Putnam's), 1908, pp. 189–190.

unfortunately, gave free rein to their imagination. Others were written by Jews or heretics to confuse or to mutilate the message of Christ.

B. TALMUD

The "Talmud" is a collection of rabbinical literature published about 500 A.D. No historian takes seriously the vile and scurrilous references to Christ found in its second part. But the work does serve as a source of information about the customs, practices, and beliefs of the Jews.

C. JEWISH WAR

In his "Jewish War" (79), Josephus, a Jewish historian wrote:

Now there appeared about this time Jesus, a man of wisdom, if he is to be called a man, for he was the doer of wonderful works. He drew over to himself many of the Jews and many of the Gentiles. He was the Christ.

Scholars dispute the genuineness of this passage. Without doubt, part of it is an interpolation, for Josephus, as a Jew, would hardly have praised Jesus so highly. Many scholars regard the whole passage as an interpolation for it appears only in a Slavic version, not in the Greek versions of the book. A similar passage in his later book, "Antiquities of the Jews" (94), is generally considered to be an interpolation.

D. ROMAN HISTORIANS

The great Roman historian, Cornelius Tacitus, in his "Annals" (a. 116 A.D.) speaks of Christ when he recalls the great fire of Rome. After the rumor spread that Nero was the guilty party, he attempted to shift the blame upon the Christians. Tacitus relates:

To suppress the rumor that he set fire to the city, Nero fastened the guilt and inflicted the most severe tortures on a group hated for their abominations, called Christians, by the populace. This name comes from Christus who was put to death by the procurator, Pontius Pilate, during the reign of Tiberius. Though checked for a moment, this detestable superstition broke out again not only in Judea, where it originated, but also in Rome, where everything hideous and shameful from every part of the world finds a home and becomes popular.

Historians agree that this passage was written by Tacitus. The precise designation of time and place, the reference to the procurator Pontius Pilate, and to the Emperor Nero rule out any assumption that Tacitus got his information from popular legend. Either he took it directly from the Senatorial records or, as is widely held, he got it from the Consul Cluvius.

Another Roman historian, Suetonius, who wrote about the year 120, also mentions Christ. Unlike Tacitus, he is unreliable. According to him, "in the time of Claudius, there were disturbances among the Jews under the impetus of Chrestus." Evidently, this is a vague and superficial reference.

E. PLINY THE YOUNGER

The letter of Pliny the Younger (112) to the Emperor Trajan is better known. Pliny was the propraetor of the Provincia Pontica or Bithynia. In the letter, he asked the Emperor how he should treat the Christians. "This superstition," he wrote, "has spread widely, not only in the cities and villages, but also in the country. The temples are deserted, and for a long time now no sacrifices have been offered in them." Pliny said that he learned through an investigation that members of this new sect assemble at dawn to chant the praises of a certain Christ whom they adore as God.

No philologist questions the genuineness of this passage. Indeed, its authenticity has always been admitted.

GOSPEL SCEPTICS

Supplementary reading from Arnold Lunn, *The Third Day,* Westminister (Newman) 1945, pp. 23–29. Mr. Lunn is a convert from the Anglican Church.

The positive arguments for Christianity are more than sufficient to support the Christian conclusion, but it is only when we consider rival theories that the full strength of our case emerges, and for this reason the Christian apologist should never be content merely to answer the objections of the sceptic, he should challenge the sceptic to defend his solution. We believe, for instance, that St. John wrote the Fourth Gospel not only because the evidence for his authorship is very strong, but also because no sceptic has ever succeeded in producing a plausible theory to account for the acceptance by the second-century Church of a second-century forgery bearing St. John's name.

The trouble with most sceptics is that they are defective in historical imagination. They approach the problem of the Gospels as if the solution could be found by juggling with texts. They never visualize the conditions under which the Gospels were written and distributed. They never emerge from the valley of dry bones, and the dry bones of their arguments are never clothed with flesh and blood. They fiddle about with texts, rejecting this passage or that as an "interpolation," but never envisage the "interpolator" as a human being, or produce a plausible theory to account for the success of the "interpolator" in imposing his forgery on the faithful. You cannot "coerce" belief. Lunacy, as Chesterton points out, has its own water-tight logic. The fact that a man is in a lunatic asylum does not disprove his thesis that he is the King of England, for if he were the King of England the usurper might be tempted to immure him in a lunatic asylum. His explanation fits "some" facts as well as yours, but it fits far fewer facts.

Similarly, the faddists who object that the "Matthew" and "Mark" mentioned by Papias are not necessarily the same works as the Gospels which we now attribute to those Apostles, is as proof against probabilities as the lunatic. His position is as impregnable to direct assault as would be that of a critic who maintained that the works of Virgil and Horace, referred to by Juvenal —who tells us that these works were in the hands of the schoolboys of his time—were not the works which we now ascribe to those authors. And yet, as Salmon justly says, it would be infinitely easier to alter secular works in private circulation than to effect revolutionary changes in sacred books read Sunday by Sunday in the Churches. We are asked to believe not only that the old Gospels which Papias ascribed to Matthew and Mark disappeared without trace, but also that no Bishop, Presbyter or layman observed that new Gospels have been substituted in their place. It would be easier to believe that Soviet Russia could have substituted the new national anthem for the old "International" without a single Russian being aware of the change.

The theory of new Gospels substituted for old is not only inherently improbable, but is not supported by a shred of evidence. We know from Eusebius that there was controversy in his time, the first half of the fourth century, about the Epistle to the Hebrews and the Epistle to the Corinthians, but Eusebius never discusses the authorship of the four Gospels, for the good reason that he had never heard the traditional authorship challenged. The absence of any tradition as to the manner of the first publication of the Gospels is in itself proof of their antiquity, but more impressive—at least to those who see this problem in terms of human beings rather than of manuscripts—is the fact that the missionary activities of the early Church would have been impossible without some authorised record of the life and teaching of Jesus Christ. We know from Justin Martyr's account of the Sunday meetings of Christians that the reading of the story of Jesus Christ was an established tradition at the weekly meetings of the Christians. So long as a Church was presided over by Apostles, their personal recollections would suffice, but the first requirement of the elders ordained by the Apostles to preside over the churches entrusted to their care was a written and authoritative record of our Lord's life and teaching.

But once we admit the necessity for Gospels in the primitive Church, we have gone a long way to prove that the Gospels which we now possess are the Gospels which were in use in the early years of the Church, for it is impossible to produce a plausible explanation for any substantial alteration of or addition to these Gospels. Nobody has explained how a forger could have obtained credence for a forgery. Theophilus of Antioch, writing about A.D. 180, says: "Writers ought either to have been eye-witnesses themselves of the things they assert, or at least have accurately learned them from those who had seen them." "The feeling here expressed is so natural," writes Salmon, "That I cannot believe that those who were in possession of narratives, supposed to have been written by men of such rank in the Church as Matthew, Mark, and Luke, could allow them to be altered by inferior authority. Little do those who suppose such an alteration possible know of the conservatism of Christian hearers. St. Augustine, in a well-known story, tells us that, when a bishop, reading the chapter about Jonah's gourd, ventured to substitute St. Jerome's 'hedera' for the established 'cucurbita,' such a tumult was raised, that if the bishop had persevered he would have been left without a congregation. The feeling that resents such a change is due to no later growth of Christian opinion. Try the experiment on any child of your acquaintance. Tell him a story that interests him; and when next you meet him tell him the story again, making variations in your recital, and see whether he will not detect the change, and be indignant at it. I do not believe, in short, that any Church would permit a change to be made in the form of evangelical instruction

in which its members had been catechetically trained unless those
who made the change were men of authority equal to their first
instructors. . . . If a bishop of the age of Papias had presumed to
innovate on the Gospel as it had been delivered by those 'which
from the beginning were eye-witnesses and ministers of the Word,'
I venture to say that, like the bishop of whom St. Augustine tells,
he would have been left without a congregation."

The sceptic begins his study of the Gospels by making an act of
faith in the impossibility of the supernatural. His verdict on the
authorship and dates is an unscientific "deduction" from an unproved and false premise. The Christian conclusion is, on the
other hand, a scientific "induction" from the facts. The sceptic
begins with dogma, the dogma that miracles do not occur, and
adjusts the facts to that dogma. The Christian begins with the
facts and ends with the dogmas which are alone consistent with
and imposed by the facts. The sceptic begins with a pre-judgment
that miracles do not occur. The Christian ends with the post-
judgment that miracles have been proved to occur. The conflict
between the Christian and the sceptic is a conflict between post-
judice and prejudice.

If it were not for the unscientific prejudice against miracles,
nobody would waste time attempting to disprove that the Gospels
were written by the Apostles and disciples of the Apostles whose
names they bear. "If we were to apply," writes Salmon, "to the remains of classical literature the same rigour of scrutiny that is used
towards the New Testament, there are but few of them that could
stand the test."

The Jesuit Hardouin tried to prove that the Odes of Horace
and other classical books were written by Benedictine monks in
the dark ages, but it would be easy to refute this theory de-
cisively by producing quotations from the Odes by any writer who
lived within two centuries of the poet's death, and later testimony
would not be thought worth looking at in the case of a New Testament book. "The Roman History of Velleius Paterculus," writes
Salmon, "has come down to us in a single very corrupt manuscript,
and the book is only once quoted by Priscian, a grammarian of
the sixth century, yet no one entertains the smallest doubt of its
genuineness. The first six books of the Annals of Tacitus are also
known to us only through a single manuscript which came to light
in the fifteenth century. Not long ago an elaborate attempt was
made to show that all the books of Annals were forged in that

century by an Italian scholar, Poggio. And it was asserted that 'no clear and definite allusion to the Annals can be found until the first half of the fifteenth century.' The latest editor of the Annals, Mr. Furneaux . . . in answer to the assertion just quoted, can only produce one allusion by no means 'clear and definite' and that of a date 300 years later than the historian . . . where external proof is most abundant in the case of the profane authors, it falls considerably short of what can be produced in support of the chief books of the New Testament."

That the Gospels were "written" in the fourth century is a popular error due to a confusion between date of "authorship" and date of the earliest complete "manuscripts."

In the early centuries of our era manuscripts were still, for the most part, written on papyrus, a frail material compared to vellum which began to take the place of papyrus in the third century. Fragments of papyrus have been recovered from the dry Egyptian soil, many areas of which are virtually rainless, but hardly a contemporary papyrus survives from Greece, Italy, Gaul or Spain. There are many other reasons why the earlier papyrus Gospels should have disappeared. A special effort was made by the persecutors of the Church to search for these manuscripts and to destroy them. The Christians themselves, in so far as they were influenced by the expectation of an immediate second coming, would have made no special efforts to preserve them for the benefit of posterity. And even in more modern times the guardians of priceless manuscripts have often been incredibly careless trustees. Thus we owe the preservation of the famous Codex Sinaiticus of the New Testament to pure chance. A German Professor, Tischendorf by name, discovered forty-three leaves of an ancient manuscript in a basket full of paper intended for the stove to which the monks of Mount Sinai consigned their debris. Tischendorf obtained these for the asking and secured the rest of the Codex some years later.

The case for tradition has been immensely reinforced in recent years by the discovery of the Chester Beatty Biblical Papyri in 1930. The papyri found in a Coptic graveyard, enclosed in one or more jars, near the Nile, include fragments of the Gospels, written in a small hand which palaeographers assign to the first half of the third century. More recently a small fragment of a papyrus containing parts of St. John xviii, 31–33, 37, 38, were discovered by Mr. C. H. Roberts among the papyri in the John Rylands Library at Manchester. Palaeographers assign this fragment to the first half of the second century, a conclusive proof of the early date of the Fourth Gospel, a Gospel which, as we shall see, has been the object of sustained attack. Sir Frederic Kenyon of the British Museum sums up the result of these discoveries in his book 'The Story of the Bible.' "It will now be realised," he writes, "what an epoch-making addition to our knowledge of the history of the Bible has been made by this discovery. Instead of our evidence for the text of the Greek Bible beginning with the fourth century, we now have several witnesses from the third century, and one even from the beginning of the second. . . .

"For all the works of classical antiquity we have to depend on manuscripts written long after their original composition. The author who is in the best case in this respect is Virgil, yet the earliest manuscript of Virgil that we now possess was written some 350 years after his death. For all other classical writers, the interval between the date of the author and the earliest extant manuscript of his works is much greater. For Livy it is about 500 years, for Horace 900, for most of Plato 1,300, for Euripides 1,600. On the other hand the great vellum uncials of the New Testament were written perhaps some 250 years after the date when the Gospels were actually composed, while we now have papyrus manuscripts which reduce the interval by a hundred years. And while the manuscripts of any classical author amount at most to a few score, and in some cases only to a few units, the manuscripts of the Bible are reckoned by thousands."

The case for the traditional authorship and dates of the four Gospels is indeed so overwhelmingly strong that there would be little scope for controversy but for the fact that the Gospels record miracles.

Had the Rylands fragments been discovered a century ago we should have been spared libraries of book, all of which can now be relegated to the limbo of exploded theories . . . shortly before these papyrus fragments were discovered Loisy had decided that the Fourth Gospel was written between 135 and 140 and that Couchod had suggested A.D. 150 as the date when St. Luke's gospel was written. Pere Lagrange writing in 1936 in *La Revue Biblique* remarked drily that critics such as these "ont mal soutenu cette année même le choc d'un petit fragment de papyrus." [1]

1. This phrase may be translated: "This very year (the critics) have been badly shocked by a small fragment of papyrus."

CHAPTER V

Christ's Claims Are Credible

CHRIST claimed to be the incarnate Son of God who came down on earth in fulfilment of God's promise to redeem mankind. The Rationalists and their Christian converts, the Liberal Protestants, reject his claims by denying the historical value of the documents in which they are recorded. We have seen that the historicity of the Gospels cannot be reasonably doubted or denied. Now the problem is this: What proofs did Christ offer to substantiate his truly astounding claims?

For his claim to be the promised redeemer we have the proof from the complete fulfilment in his life and death of all the Old Testament prophecies concerning the Messiah. For his even more astounding claim to divinity we have: 1) the proof from his human perfections considered in the light of this claim; 2) the proof from his miracles; and 3) the proof from his resurrection.

I. THE PROMISED REDEEMER

Jesus himself fulfilled the prophecies about the Messiah found in the books of the Old Testament.[1] In fact, many Jews were converted on this very account. For the religion of the Jews was a religion of expectation centered around a belief in a Messiah or a Deliverer to come. We presuppose that you remember from reading the Gospels how perfectly Jesus fulfilled these messianic prophecies. Here we merely wish to recall a few of them to mind.

1. Read again St. Matthew's Gospel.

ORIGIN

He will be from the seed of Abraham (Gen. 22, 18); from the tribe of Juda (Gen. 49, 10); from the root of David (Ps. 88, 36–38; Is. 11, 1; Jer. 23, 5–6; 30, 9; Exech. 34, 24; 37, 24); his Mother will be a virgin (Is. 7, 14).

Christ was a son of Abraham (Matt. 1, 1; Luke 3, 34); of the tribe of Juda (Matt. 1, 2; Luke 3, 33; Hebr. 7, 14); and the family of David (Matt. 1, 1; Luke 1, 32–33; 2, 4; 3, 31; Rom. 1, 3). He was born of the Virgin Mary (Matt. 1, 18–20; Luke 1, 26–24).

PLACE AND TIME OF BIRTH

He shall come forth from Bethlehem (Mich. 5, 2)—at the time Daniel foretold (9, 24–27).

Jesus was born in Bethlehem (Matt. 2, 1–5; Luke 2, 4; John 7, 42)—at the very moment when expectation, it would appear, was at its highest.

ATTRIBUTES

The Messiah will be begotten of God (Ps. 2, 7). He will be called "God the Mighty, the Father of the world to come, the Prince of Peace" (Is. 9, 6). He will work many miracles (Is. 35, 4–6).

According to historical documents (Gospels) Jesus perfectly fulfilled all these prophesies (Matt. 3, 17; Mark 1, 11; Luke 4, 17–30). We have studied already his miracles (cf. Matt. 11, 2–6).

FUNCTIONS

The Messiah will be a teacher and prophet (Is. 11, 2–9; 61, 1–3)—a spiritual king and a legislator (Zach. 9, 9–10; 13, 21; Ps. 2, 6; Jerem. 23, 5; 1, 31–34; Is. 1, 7; 9, 7; 11, 10–16; 33, 20; 59, 21; 62, 11; Joel 2, 28)—a priest and victim (Ps. 109, 4; Malach. 1, 11; Is. 53, 4–10; 66, 21).

Christ was a teacher and a great prophet as we have proved (Luke 4, 16; Matt. 3, 16; Mark 1, 11). He perfected the old law (Matt. 5). He is a spiritual king (John 18, 33–37). He is a priest who offered himself to God the Father (Luke 22, 15–20; Hebr. 7, 20–28).

PASSION AND DEATH

He will be dishonored, scourged, and spit upon (Is. 50, 6). He will be bruised and wounded for our sins (Is. 53; Ps. 54, 506). The wicked will pierce his hands and feet and cast lots for his vesture (Ps. 21, 17–19). He will die for sinners (Is. 53, 7; 50, 6; Zach. 11, 12; 12, 10; 13, 1; Ps. 21, 7; 68, 22).

From all the gospels it is clear that Jesus suffered and died for sinners (Matt. 26, 47–75; 27, 3; 27, 35; 28, 57; Mark 14, 43–72; Luke 22, 47–71; 23, 1–56; 24, 25–26; John 18, 19).

RESURRECTION

Through his passion and death, he shall enter into his glory (Zach. 11, 12; Is. 50, 6; Ps. 21, 7; 68, 22). He shall rise again (Ps. 5, 10). His church is for all nations (Mich. 4, 2; Ps. 21, 28; 109, 2; Is. 60, 1; 66, 19).

After his resurrection, Christ himself showed the disciples how the prophets had foretold his sufferings (Luke 24, 25–27). All the Evangelists record his resurrection. When the Jews reject the Gospel, the apostles turn to the Gentiles (Acts 14, 46).

These texts were not chosen at random but constitute an integral part of the Messianic tradition. Although the Jews of that time did not think of the sufferings and death of the Messiah, they were clearly foretold by Daniel and Isaias. In all other respects, the texts reflect ideas current among the Jews.

Jesus so perfectly fulfilled all the prophecies that an honest student is forced to admit a providential coincidence between the Messianic prophecies and the life of Christ. Surely the fulfillment of *all* these prophecies in one individual could *not* have been *due* to *chance or human contrivance,* but must have been God's work. Jesus was, therefore, the promised Messiah.

Some object that the Jews, the guardian of the prophecies, did not recognize their fulfillment in Christ. This objection is easy to answer. First of all, it was by Jews—his first followers—that he was recognized as the Messiah. The Gentile Christians only learned of the prophecies and their meaning from the Jewish Christians. Secondly, the Jewish people at that time were, for the most part, morally corrupt. Josephus says that, had not the Romans punished them, some other catastrophe would have struck them. Their evil minds were closed to the message of Christ. Thirdly, their leaders, the Scribes and Pharisees, hated Christ vehemently. After he condemned their pride, arrogance, and hypocrisy, they bitterly opposed him. Finally, the Jews had mis-interpreted some of the prophecies. Blinded by nationalism and materialism they looked for a temporal king rather than a spiritual king. Jesus tried in vain to correct their false notions.

II. THE SON OF GOD

A. The First Proof

This first proof may be summarized in four statements. Christ claimed to be God. Either he was God or, if not, he was either insane or, if sane, a blasphemous liar. But he was not insane or a blasphemous liar. Therefore, he was (and is) God.

We have proved that Christ claimed to be God. Now we are faced with this alternative. Either Jesus Christ is true God as he claimed to be, or the Christian religion is a blasphemous deception and its founder an insane man or a blasphemous liar. He was insane, if he himself was deceived; a blasphemous liar, if he intended to deceive his fellow men.[2]

From reading and listening to the Gospels you should have some appreciation of the incomparable character of Christ. Indeed, anyone who has read the Gospels will never assert that Jesus was insane or a blasphemous liar for, considered from a merely human viewpoint, he was the most perfect man and the finest teacher who ever lived. In fact, such ideas are absolutely contrary to all we know about him; his humility, his love of retirement, his sincerity, his hatred of sham and hypocrisy. Moreover, they are entirely incompatible with his breadth of vision and originality of thought.[3]

2. Koesters remarks: "Our whole human nature protests violently against the assumption that all the blessings and happiness which have come to mankind from faith in Christ have had their source in such a monstrous deception. . . . A serious refutation of those views is surely unnecessary; they are flatly opposed to the unique spiritual majesty and calm of His thinking, to the clarity and consistency of His teaching, as these qualities are revealed to us in the pages of the Gospel. For that reason these views are now rejected by theologians of all faiths, Catholics, conservative and liberal Protestants, Jews, and whoever has any sort of claim to a scientific reputation." *The Believer's Christ,* St. Louis (Herder), 1939, pp. 256–258.

3. A Jewish scholar, Klausner, writes: "In his ethical code there is a sublimity, a distinctiveness and originality in form unparalleled in any other Hebrew ethical code; neither is there any parallel to the remarkable art of his parables. The shrewdness and sharpness of his proverbs and his forceful

Even the Rationalists are quick to note all his good qualities; his ability, his strong personality, his superb courage, and his stainless character. Even they describe him as affable, intelligent, courteous, and humble. Rousseau, for example, said: "Yes, the life and death of Socrates are those of a philosopher, but the life and death of Jesus are those of a God." [4] Renan wrote: "The Christ of the Gospels is the most beautiful incarnation of God in the most beautiful form. His beauty is eternal; his reign will never end."

The Rationalists and the Liberal Protestants profess to admire Christ as a very great man, a model humanitarian. They extol him as the greatest moral teacher of all time, yet they ignore or reject his claim to be God. Such an attitude is unreasonable.

A man who was merely a man and claimed to be God would not be a great moral teacher. He would either be a consummate fool or a demon of hell. Thus a sincere man will either laugh at Christ as a fool; spurn him as a demon; or fall at his feet and worship him as Lord and God. The Rationalists and the Liberal Protestants, however, are too cowardly to face the facts. And so they babble patronizing nonsense about Christ being a great moral teacher. It is like "praising" an ordinary man by describing him as a "magnificent beast."

We are, then, face to face with the great alternative. Either Christ was God as he claimed to be or else he was a madman or something worse. All the evidence indicates that he was not a madman or something worse. Therefore, we should conclude that he was and is God.[5]

B. The Second Proof

Christ performed many miracles while he was on earth. Although we are primarily concerned with his physical miracles, we shall also consider his prophecies (intellectual miracles) as well.

---

epigrams serve, in an exceptional degree, to make ethical ideas a popular possession. If . . . this ethical code be stripped of its wrappings of miracles and mysticism (*sic!*), the Book of the Ethics of Jesus will be one of the choicest treasures in the literature of Israel for all time." Klausner, *Jesus of Nazareth,* New York (Macmillan), 1925, p. 414.

4. Jean J. Rousseau, *Ouevres Completes,* Paris (Hachette), 1905, p. 280.

5. Cf. C. S. Lewis, *The Case for Christianity,* New York (The Macmillan Co.), 1948, pp. 44–45. Knox, *Miracles,* New York (The Paulist Press), 1928, pp. 14–15.

1. His Physical Miracles

Whatever Jesus said was guaranteed by God to be true by his physical miracles. But he said that he was God. Therefore he was (and is) God.

These physical miracles could have been worked only by the power of God. Therefore, even if they do not prove in themselves that Christ is God, they do prove that God was working through him; that God was guaranteeing his message. His own divinity was a part of that message.

Now if Christ was God and wanted to prove it, he would expect some manifestation of Almighty Power. By this we do not mean the inference, "Christ did miracles, therefore Christ is God," is a true one, since the saints also performed them. But we do mean that God would not have vindicated his career by such prodigies of nature, if Christ had been either a deceiver or deceived as to his mission.[6]

a. The Historical Fact

But did Christ really work miracles? This is a question about historical facts. And what does history tell us? First of all, it tells us that for five hundred years before the coming of Christ, pagan and Jewish historians mention very few miracles. The pagan authors connected their stories of the miraculous with antiquity. The Jewish writers record hardly any. In fact, Josephus says there were none. Evidently the people of that age were not gullible; they did not see miracles everywhere.[7] Yet suddenly not merely ignorant peasants but rich men like Zachaeus, educated men like Nicodemus, medical men like Luke, testify that Christ worked countless miracles.[8]

The least you can possibly say is that Christ's lifetime was crowded with amazing events that even his bitter enemies termed "miracles." "So the chief priests and Pharisees summoned a council; What are we about? they said. This man is performing many

6. Cf. Knox, *op. cit.*, p. 122.

7. William F. Albright writes: "The civilization of that day was in many respects comparable to what it is today." *Op. cit.*, p. 311.

8. In this regard, Monsignor Ronald A. Knox says: "When the moderns say that 'ignorant people are always expecting miracles to happen,' what they really mean is that 'ignorant *Christians* are always expecting miracles to happen.' But there were no Christians till Christ came." Knox, *op. cit.*, p. 123.

miracles, and if we leave him to his own devices, he will find credit everywhere" (John 11, 47; cf. John 9, 1–34).

Josephus, the greatest Jewish historian, describes Jesus as "a man of wisdom . . . a doer of wonderful works." Though the authors of the *Talmud* attributed his miracles to the devil, they admit that Jesus worked them. In their sermons, the Apostles referred to them as *facts known to all*. St. Peter declared: "Men of Israel, listen to this. Jesus of Nazareth was a man duly accredited to you from God; such were the miracles and wonders and signs which God did through him in your midst, as you yourselves well know" (Acts 2, 22; cf. Acts 10, 37–39; Rom. 15, 19; I Cor. 15, 13–21).

In the Gospels, we find conclusive evidence of his miracles. Since we have proven that they are genuine, trustworthy, and integral documents, *no part* of them *may be omitted*, according to the principles of historical criticism, *unless* it is proven erroneous. Now it is impossible to omit the miracles from the Gospels [9] without destroying not merely a part but practically the entire historical documents. A few observations will make this clear.

In the Gospels, the Evangelists explicitly enumerate forty-one distinct miracles or groups of miracles.[10] These miracles are distributed throughout the four Gospels. Matthew, Mark, and Luke each mention twenty-two or more. Though John, who presupposed the other Gospels, records only nine, he explicitly states: "There are many other miracles Jesus did in the presence of his disciples, which are not written down in this book; so much has been written down, that you may learn to believe Jesus is the Christ, the son of God . . ." (John 20, 30–31).

9. A person has to prove the existence of an interpolation either by showing that the text in question is not found in an earlier document, or that it differs in linguistic style from the rest of the manuscript, or that it implies knowledge of events later in date than the accepted date of authorship.

10. Cf. Felder, *Christ and the Critics,* London (Burns, Oates, Washbourne), 1924, II, 279–286. A Protestant scholar, Alan Richardson, states: "The evidence that Jesus worked miracles is just as strong, and is of precisely the same quality and texture, as that He taught that God is Father and that His disciples should forgive one another. We cannot on *historical grounds alone* accept the evidence for the one and reject that for the other. The evidence that Jesus healed a dropsical man on the Sabbath day is just as good as the evidence that He told the story of the Good Samaritan or the Prodigal Son." *Christian Apologetics,* London (S.C.M. Press), 1947, p. 170.

These miracles are *interwoven* into the very *context* of the Gospels. On many occasions they stirred up controversies and led to further instructions (Mark 3, 1–6; John 10, 22–39). Often Jesus worked them to illustrate or confirm a point (Mark 2, 5–12). Indeed, there is a natural, logical connection between the miraculous and non-miraculous passages. Since the miracles are so numerous and so evenly distributed, they form an integral part of the Gospel documents. Consequently, if a person rejects the miracles, he logically must reject the Gospels. If he attempts to remove the miracles, he destroys the whole Gospel narrative.

The diversity of these miracles is amazing. Note how Christ cured lepers, paralytics, and the blind by a mere word or touch or even when they were not present (Matt. 8, 2–13; 9, 1–8; 9, 20–22; 9, 27–31; 11, 4–5; 12, 13; 20, 29–34). He raised the daughter of Jairus (Matt. 9, 23–26), the widow's son (Luke 7, 11–17), and Lazarus (John 11) from the dead. He changed water into wine (John 2, 1–11). On two different occasions, he multiplied loaves and fishes (Matt. 14, 15–21; 15, 32–38; Mark 6, 32–34; 8, 1–10; Luke 9, 10–17; John 6, 1–45). One night he walked on the water (Matt. 14, 26–33; Mark 6, 49–56; 6, 19–21). Another day he calmed a tempest (Matt. 8, 23–27; Mark 4, 36–41; Luke 8, 23–25). He himself tells the disciples of John the Baptist: "Go and tell John what your own eyes and ears have witnessed; how the blind see, and the lame walk, and the lepers are made clean, and the deaf hear; how the dead are raised to life, and the poor have the gospel preached to them" (Luke 7, 22).

These miracles were the cornerstone of the faith of the disciples. They were *not* the *results* of faith. They *effected* faith. Nicodemus, for example, believed on account of the signs that he had seen (John 3, 2). Without the miracles you cannot explain the zeal of the people to see and hear Christ (Mark 6, 14–16; John 11, 47–48) nor the hatred of the Scribes and Pharisees. These crafty enemies of Christ were forced to admit that he worked miracles, for they were *facts impossible to deny.* These extraordinary works happened before their very eyes. Jesus performed them openly before large crowds in all the principal cities and towns of Judea.

When they come to the Gospels, a few modern historians abandon their role as historians,—"presenting facts and nothing but facts,"—and try to force their philosophy on us under the guise of history. Happily, their number is small. Even the Liberal Protestant scholar, Harnack, has admitted that the miracles are genuine parts of the Gospel narrative.[11] This is not too surprising, since all the historical evidence at our disposal bids us to acknowledge these historical facts in the life of Jesus. As a historian, a person cannot reject his miracles, for, according to the cardinal principle of historical criticism, his miracles must be considered historically certain since they are integral parts of genuine, complete and trustworthy documents.

b. The Supernatural Fact

No doubt, it is possible to suggest a natural explanation for some of the miracles of Christ. But the prudent Pharisees realized that the vast majority were beyond the realm of natural causes. Thus the investigation into the cure of the man born blind ended in utter confusion.

And Jesus saw, as he passed on his way, a man who had been blind from his birth. Whereupon his disciples asked him, Master, was this man guilty of sin, or was it his parents, that he should have been born blind? Neither he nor his parents were guilty, Jesus answered; it was so that God's action might declare itself in him. While daylight lasts, I must work in the service of him who sent me; the night is coming, when there is no working any more. As long as I am in the world, I am the world's light. With that, he spat on the ground, and made clay with the spittle; then he spread the clay on the man's eyes, and said to him, Away with thee, and wash in the pool of Siloe (a word which means, Sent out). So he went and washed there, and came back with his sight restored. And now the neighbours, and those who had been accustomed to see him begging, began to say, Is not this the man who used to sit here and beg? Some said, This is the man; and others, No, but he looks like him. And he told them, Yes, I am the man. How is it, then, they asked him, that thy eyes have been opened? He answered, A man called Jesus made clay, and anointed my eyes with it, and said to me, Away with thee to the pool of Siloe and wash there. So I went there, and washed, and recovered my sight. Where is he? they asked; and he said, I cannot tell.

11. Harnack says that the miracles of Jesus "cannot be eliminated from the historical reports without fundamentally ruining these reports." Of course, Harnack will have this understood only of the miracles of healing which he thinks can be explained naturally. Harnack, *Dogmengeschichte* (3rd ed.), Freiburg (Mohr), 1898, I, 64.

And they brought him before the Pharisees, this man who had once been blind. It was a sabbath day, you must know, when Jesus made clay and opened his eyes. And so the Pharisees in their turn asked him how he had recovered his sight. Why, he said, he put clay on my eyes; and then I washed, and now I can see. Whereupon some of the Pharisees said, This man can be no messenger from God; he does not observe the sabbath. Others asked, How can a man do miracles like this, and be a sinner? Thus there was a division of opinion among them. And now they questioned the blind man again, What account dost thou give of him, that he should thus have opened thy eyes? Why, he said, he must be a prophet. The Jews must send for the parents of the man who had recovered his sight, before they would believe his story that he had been blind, and that he had had his sight restored to him. And they questioned them, Is this your son, who, you say, was born blind? How comes it, then, that he is now able to see? His parents answered them, We can tell you that this is our son, and that he was blind when he was born; we cannot tell how he is able to see now; we have no means of knowing who opened his eyes for him. Ask the man himself; he is of age; let him tell you his own story. It was fear of the Jews that made his parents talk in this way; the Jews had by now come to an agreement that anyone who acknowledged Jesus as the Christ should be forbidden the synagogue; that was why his parents said, He is of age, ask him yourself.

So once more they summoned the man who had been blind. Give God the praise, they said; this man, to our knowledge, is a sinner. Sinner or not, said the other, I cannot tell; all I know is that once I was blind, and, now I can see. Then they asked him over again, What was it he did to thee? By what means did he open thy eyes? And he answered them, I have told you already, and you would not listen to me. Why must you hear it over again? Would you too become his disciples? Upon this, they covered him with abuse; Keep his discipleship for thyself, we are disciples of Moses. We know for certain that God spoke to Moses; we know nothing of this man, or whence he comes. Why, the man answered, here is a matter for astonishment; here is a man that comes you cannot tell whence, and he has opened my eyes. And yet we know for certain that God does not answer the prayers of sinners, it is only when a man is devout and does his will, that his prayer is answered. That a man should open the eyes of one born blind is something unheard of since the world began. No, if this man did not come from God, he would have no powers at all. What, they answered, are we to have lessons from thee, all steeped in sin from thy birth? And they cast him out from their presence (John 9, 1–34).

If the Pharisees had tried to propose natural explanations for all of Christ's miracles, they would have become the laughing-stocks of Judea. Evidently, there was no proportion between the natural means Jesus used and effects obtained. For example, Lazarus, the daughter of Jairus, and the widow's son were raised from the dead by his words.

Were these people actually dead or, as some Gospel critics suggest, were they merely in some sleep or stupor? If they were not dead, then we have to make three incredible suppositions. First of all, Jesus, who was not present when they died, is the only person who perceives that death is only apparent. Secondly, the dead person in each case recovers just as Christ speaks. Thirdly, Christ deliberately gives the erroneous impression that he has raised them from the dead. Is it reasonable to accept these hypotheses of nineteenth century Rationalists when they contra dict the unanimous testimony of reliable eyewitnesses?

The attitude of the Rationalists and the Liberal Protestants towards the other miracles of Christ is no more reasonable. Even when men permit them to alter the Gospel text, it requires al-most unlimited faith to accept their farfetched suppositions. Since many critics hesitate to reject all the historical facts in the Gospels, they admit the cures were factual. Many of the cures, however, they attribute to fortunate coincidences following mis-taken medical analyses. Usually they ask men to believe in a host of "unknown forces" which suddenly produced in Judea for some unknown reason through this man Christ effects out of all propor-tion to their apparent causes. In their efforts to explain away the Gospel miracles, these Rationalists repeatedly contradict one another. Indeed, their confused, diverse, and contradictory sup-positions merely serve to emphasize the truth.

Some critics, for example, assure us that Jesus did not multiply the loaves and fishes. Since he had always taught a doctrine of re-nunciation, his listeners who wished to fast refused to accept the loaves and fishes which the Apostles offered them.[12] Other critics suggest that the Jews came prepared. When Jesus blessed his loaves and fishes, the people brought out their supplies.[13] Still

12. Cf. Felder, *op. cit.*, II, 357. Felder gives many more examples on pages 321–369.

13. *Ibid.*, pp. 356–357. K. Furrer, for example, says: "How simple is the

others think that the crowd refused to accept any loaves and fishes from the Apostles because they knew Jesus did not have many provisions on hand.[14] St. Mark, however, tells us:

So, when he disembarked, Jesus saw a great multitude there, and took pity on them, since they were like sheep that have no shepherd, and began to give them long instruction. And when it was already late, his disciples came to him and said, This is a lonely place, and it is late already, give them leave to go to the farms and villages round about, and buy themselves food there; they have nothing to eat. But he answered them, It is for you to give them food to eat. Why, then, they said to him, we must go and spend two hundred silver pieces buying bread to feed them. He asked, How many loaves have you? Go and see. When they had found out, they told him, Five, and two fishes. Then he told them all to sit down in companies on the green grass; and they took their places in rows, by hundreds and fifties. And he took the five loaves and the two fishes, and looked up to heaven, and blessed and broke the loaves, and gave these to his disciples to set before them, dividing the fishes, too, among them all. All ate and had enough: and when they took up the broken pieces, and what was left of the fishes, they filled twelve baskets with them. The loaves had fed five thousand men (Mark 6, 34–44; Matt. 14, 14–21; Luke 9, 10–17; John 6, 1–14).

The supernatural fact of the miracles of Christ is clear. Obviously, there is no proportion between the natural means, if any, he employs and the effects achieved. Christ makes the blind see, the lame walk, the lepers clean, the deaf hear, and the dead rise again by a simple command or gesture. Always, the effects follow according to his will. At times he demands faith before a cure. On many occasions, he does not. Sometimes the cured person is not

---

picture! When Jesus had given out the last morsel of bread, then those who had bread did not wish to be backward, but also joyfully distributed from their own provisions, and the others showed themselves modest in taking it, so that all were fed. Some have wanted to poke fun at this interpretation, but that is a very cheap jest."

14. *Ibid.,* p. 357. Albert Schweitzer concluded: "He celebrated, therefore, a sacred cultus-meal the meaning of which was clear to Him alone. He did not count it necessary to explain to them the meaning of the ceremony. The memory, however, of that mysterious supper on the lonely seashore lived on vividly in the tradition and grew to the account of the miraculous feeding." His devoted disciple, E. N. Mozely observes: "Of this there can of course be no proof, but it is a guess of genius." Apparently, Mozely's faith depends upon the guesses of Schweitzer! *Op. cit.,* p. 53.

even present. After several embarrassing experiences, the Pharisees learned that his miracles could not be explained away. In the twentieth century, most Rationalists seem to have reached the same conclusion. They find it simpler to deny the historical fact of the miracles than to "explain" them as natural occurrences.

c. The Apologetical Fact

Once a person is intellectually honest enough to admit the historical and supernatural facts, our major is self-evident. The only reasonable explanation for these miracles is the power (assistance) of God. Surely no one today will dare to attribute them to the Devil. The character of Jesus, his purpose, and his teaching positively exclude that possibility (cf. John 9; Matt. 12, 24; Luke 11, 15).

Evidently, Jesus received his miraculous power from God. God was working through him. "The works which I do, give testimony of me that the Father has sent me" (John 5, 36). God was guaranteeing his message. Obviously, God would never give miraculous power to a liar to confirm his lie. Now, as we have proven, Jesus said that he was God. His divinity was a part of his message. Therefore Jesus Christ was (and is) God.

In speaking to the Jews, Jesus emphasizes this point. "Will you call me a blasphemer, because I have told you I am the Son of God? If you find that I do not act like the Son of my Father, then put no trust in me; but if I do, then let my actions convince you where I cannot; so you will recognize and learn to believe that the Father is in me, and I in him" (John 10, 37–38).

2. THE PROPHECIES OF CHRIST

Besides physical miracles, Jesus performed intellectual miracles, commonly called prophecies. In a strict sense, a prophecy is a certain prediction of future events that are naturally unknowable because they are *contingent* events, that is to say, events which depend upon the free will of God or of one or more men, or they depend upon chance. Although prophecies in themselves are true miracles, they do not have as great an effect upon the modern mind as physical miracles because it is more difficult to ascertain their miraculous character. When the prophecies of Jesus are considered together, however, they appear as clear-cut miracles.

HIS PASSION, DEATH, AND RESURRECTION

Although no mere man could have foreseen his Passion, Death, and Resurrection, Jesus clearly foretells them. "And now Jesus was going up to Jerusalem, and he took his twelve disciples aside on the way, and warned them. Now we are going up to Jerusalem; and there the Son of Man will be given up into the hands of the chief priests and scribes, who will condemn him to death. And these will give him up into the hands of the Gentiles to be mocked and scourged and crucified; but on the third day he will rise again" (Matt. 20, 17–19; cf. Mark 10, 33–34; Luke 18, 31–34; John 2, 18–22; Matt. 16, 21–24; 17, 21–28; Mark 8, 31–33; 9, 30–32; Luke 9, 22–23; 9, 44–45).

"And those who had arrested Jesus led him away into the presence of the high priest, Caiphas, where the scribes and the elders had assembled. . . . And they answered, The penalty is death. . . . And they led him away in bonds, and gave him up to the governor, Pontius Pilate. . . . After this, the governor's soldiers took Jesus into the palace . . . and mocked him . . . and spat upon him . . . and with him they crucified two thieves. . . . He is not here; he has risen, as he told you," (Matt. 26, 57—28, 6; Cf. Mark 14–16; Luke 22–24; John 18–21).

HIS DISCIPLES FLEE

"After this, Jesus said to them, Tonight you will all lose courage over me; for so it has been written, I will smite the shepherd, and the sheep of his flock will be scattered. But I will go on before you into Galilee, when I have risen from the dead" (Matt. 26, 31–32; cf. John 16, 32).

"And now all his disciples abandoned him, and fled. . . . And now the eleven disciples took their journey into Galilee, to the mountain where Jesus had bidden them meet him" (Matt. 26, 56; 28, 16).

PETER'S DENIALS

"Peter answered him, Though all else should lose courage over thee, I will never lose mine. Jesus said to him, Believe me, this night, before the cock crows, thou wilt thrice disown me. Peter said to him, I will never disown thee, though I must lay down my life with thee" (Matt. 26, 33–35).

"And he made denial again with an oath, I know nothing of the man. But those who stood there came up to Peter soon afterwards, and said, It is certain that thou art one of them; even thy speech betrays thee. And with that he fell to calling down curses on himself and swearing, I know nothing of the man; and thereupon the cock crew" (Matt. 26, 72–75).

THE BETRAYAL BY JUDAS

"While they were at table, he said, Believe me, one of you is to betray me. . . . Then Judas, he who was betraying him, said openly, Master, is it I? Jesus answered, Thy own lips have said it" (Matt. 26, 21–25).

"And all at once, while he was speaking, Judas, who was one of the twelve, came near; with him a great multitude carrying swords and clubs, who had been sent by the chief priests and the elders of the people" (Matt. 26, 47).

THE DESCENT OF THE HOLY SPIRIT

He promised to send the Holy Spirit. "Enough for you, that the Holy Spirit will come upon you, and you will receive strength from him; you are to be my witnesses in Jerusalem, and throughout Judaea, in Samaria, yes, and to the ends of the earth" (Acts 1, 8).

"And they were all filled with the Holy Spirit, and began to speak in strange languages, as the Spirit gave utterance to each" (Acts 2, 4). The apostles preached in Judaea, Samaria, Europe, and Asia.

HIS CHURCH

His Church will grow like a mustard plant (Matt. 13, 31–32). It will be a leaven to all mankind (Matt. 13, 33). It will be persecuted. "Do not put your trust in men; they will hand you over to courts of judgment, and scourge you in their synagogues; yes, and you will be brought before governors and kings on my account. . . . (Matt. 10, 17–18). But it shall never fail. "And the gates of hell shall not prevail against it" (Matt. 16, 18). The Gentiles shall be converted. "And this I tell you, that there are many who will come from the east and from the west, and will take their places in the kingdom of God with Abraham and Isaac and Jacob, while that kingdom's own sons are cast into the darkness without. . ." (Matt. 8, 10–11; Cf. Matt. 21, 33–46; 24, 14; Luke 13, 28–29).

The fufillment of these prophecies is evident. Even the apostolic church suffered persecution. "So they sent for the apostles and, after scourging them, let them go with a warning that they were not on any account to preach in the name of Jesus" (Acts 5, 40–41; 4, 1–8). The Gentiles have taken the place of the Jews. "Whereupon Paul and Barnabas told them roundly, We were bound to preach God's words to you first; but now, since you reject it, since you declare yourselves unfit for eternal life, be it so; we will turn our thoughts to the Gentiles" (Acts 14, 46).

JERUSALEM AND THE JEWS

On several occasions, Jesus prophesied the destruction of Jerusalem. "The days will come upon thee when thy enemies will fence thee round about, and encircle thee, and press thee hard on every side, and bring down in ruin both thee and thy children that are in thee, not leaving one stone of thee upon another; and all because thou didst not recognize the time of my visiting thee.

"It will be a time of bitter distress all over the land, and retribution against this people. They will be put to the sword, and led away into captivity all over the world; and Jersualem will be trodden under the feet of the Gentiles, until the time granted to the Gentile nations has run out. Believe me, this generation will not have passed, before all this is accomplished" (Luke 19, 43–44; 21, 20–24, 32; cf. Matt. 23, 36–38; Mark 13, 1–2).

How accurately this prophecy was fulfilled will be understood by all who read the *History of the Jewish War,* by the Jewish historian, Flavius Josephus (37–98). After the death of the Emperor Nero, the Jews rebelled against the Romans. Within a few months a Roman army invaded Galilee. The Christians, mindful of our Lord's words, fled from Jerusalem. Soon afterwards Titus surrounded the city. After a prolonged siege that caused great suffering, the city was entirely destroyed. Since the Romans ordinarily preserved conquered cities, and especially their temples, its complete destruction was totally unexpected. Many of the Jews were killed. Others were led away captives. Josephus who was taken prisoner by the Romans witnessed its fall. He wrote: "When they (the Roman soldiers) went in numbers into the lanes of the city with their swords drawn, they slew those whom they overtook without mercy, and set fire to the houses whither the Jews were fled. . . . (They) made the whole city run with blood, to such a degree indeed that the fire of many houses was quenched with . . . blood." [15]

15. Josephus, *De Bello Judaico,* VI. Cf. Eusebius, *History of the Church,* III, v. In the fourth century, the Emperor, Julian the Apostate (361–363),

Once we study these prophecies and their perfect fulfillment we perceive their miraculous character. The number and nature of the events foretold and their exact fulfillment excludes any possibility of chance or guess work. Thus we cannot give any reasonable explanation for such prophecies without postulating *special divine assistance*. In other words, Jesus must have received miraculous intellectual help from God. God was working through him; guaranteeing his message. His divinity was a part of that message. Therefore he is God. (Note that since prophecies are just another kind of miracle, this addition merely confirms and supplements the preceding proof.)

C. The Third Proof

The miracle of the Resurrection could only be worked by the power of God. Even if it does not prove in itself that Christ is God, it does prove that God was working through him—approving his message. But his divinity was a part of his message. Therefore Christ was (and is) God.

Of all the miracles of Christ, *his physical resurrection* was the *greatest*. Consequently, it was the most certain sign of God's approbation, for he would never work such a miracle to confirm a lie. Indeed, Christ appeals to it as the supreme and final proof of his divine mission.[16]

---

attempted to rebuild the temple in order that he might falsify Christian prophecy. The Jews enthusiastically prepared for the work. Ammianus Marcellinus, a pagan historian, who was an imperial bodyguard, tells of the result which is one of the most remarkable yet one of the best attested events in ancient history: "(Julian) committed the accomplishment of the task to Alypius of Antioch who had before been Lieutenant of Britain. Alypius therefore set himself vigorously to the work, and was seconded by the governor of the province; when fearful balls of fire breaking out near the foundations, continued their attacks until the workmen, after repeated scorchings, could approach no more; and thus, the fierce elements obstinately repelling them, he gave over his attempt." Newman, *Essay on Miracles,* London (Pickering), 1870, Second Edition, p. 337. Newman also mentions the testimony of St. Gregory Nazianzen, St. Ambrose, St. Chrysostom, Rufinus, Socrates, Sozomen, and Theodoret. *Ibid.,* pp. 335–336.

16. Christ speaks of it three times to the Jews: Matt. 12, 39–40; 16, 1–4. John 2, 18–22; six times to his disciples: Matt. 16, 21–27; 17, 9, 21–22; 20, 17–19; 26, 32; Mark 8, 31–38; 9, 9; 9, 30; 10, 32–40; 14, 27; Luke 9, 22–26; 18, 31–34; John 10, 17–18. On three occasions, his enemies indicate their knowledge of it; Matt. 26, 61; (Mark 14, 58), Matt. 27, 39–40 (Mark 15, 29),

Since the Apostles realized its great importance, they preached it first and foremost.[17] St. Peter, for example, declared that by it the Jews were to "know most certainly" that Jesus whom they crucified was "both Lord and Christ." In his First Epistle to the Corinthians (15, 14), St. Paul did not hesitate to say: "And if Christ has not risen, then is our preaching vain, and your faith is vain. Yes, and we are found false witnesses as to God, in that we have borne witness against God that he raised up Christ. . . ."

The Resurrection itself, however, is not a question of faith as opposed to evidence. On the contrary, the *evidence* is *clear* and *convincing*. We have the testimony of the holy women, the twelve apostles, the two disciples on the way to Emmaus, the five hundred mentioned by St. Paul, and St. Paul himself. "We have, too, the negative witness of the Jews and Romans, who saw him dead and, unable to explain away the fact of the empty tomb, invented the clumsy falsehood of theft by the disciples, which even the most hostile critics today do not accept.[18]

This evidence comes to us primarily in the Gospels and Epistles.[19] They are not merely "our" documents but valid historical documents which are almost universally accepted. In fact, they are called into question today only when they record the miraculous. The objection to them, therefore, is *not* based on grounds of history but on a denial of the possibility of a miracle.

Let us follow the natural sequence of events as we consider the evidence.

1. JESUS TRULY DIED

Unbelievers have sought in every possible way to evade the challenge of Christ's resurrection from the dead. Some have proposed what is called the coma theory according to which Christ did not really die but only lapsed into a deep coma because of his

---

Matt. 27, 63–66. Our Lord appeals to it as a conclusive proof of his mission: John 2, 18–22; Matt. 12, 38–40; Luke 11, 29–30.

17. St. Luke writes: "Great was the power with which the apostles testified to the resurrection of our Lord Jesus Christ . . ." (Acts 4, 33). The apostles thought of themselves as "witnesses of the resurrection" (Acts 1, 22; 2, 32; 3, 15; 5, 32).

18. Ward & Sheed, *op. cit.*, p. 218.

19. Matt. 28, 1–20; Mark 16, 1–20; Luke 24, 1–53; John 20, 1–31; 21, 1–25; Acts 1, 3–10; 13, 33–37; Romans 1, 4; 4, 24; 6, 4–9; 8, 11–34; 14, 9; I Cor. 6, 14; 15, 1–48; II Cor. 4, 14; 5, 15; 13, 4; Gal. 1, 1; Eph. 1, 20; Phil. 3, 10; Col. 2, 12; 3, 1; I Thess. 1, 10; 2, 13; II. Tim. 2, 8.

intense sufferings and was entombed alive. Awaking early Easter morning he came forth from the tomb and deceived his followers into believing that he had risen from the dead.

There can be no doubt about the fact that Jesus died. If his prolonged suffering and the manifest signs of death are not sufficient proof, we have the testimony of his friends, his enemies, and the indifferent executioners. All the Evangelists state that he died. His own mother and friends buried him. On Sunday morning the holy women came to anoint his body. When they found the tomb empty, they immediately supposed that someone had stolen the body, since they were sure he was dead.

Similarly, the Jewish leaders who hated Christ were confident that he died (Matt. 27, 63). For years they had waited to kill him. Never would they have permitted his friends to take down the body, if they suspected any spark of life remained. Later, when the Jews tried to explain away the empty tomb, they never even suggested that Jesus did not really die.

Finally, the indifferent executioners (Roman soldiers) would have risked their own lives, if they failed to do their job. Besides, when the Jews asked Pilate to take down the bodies, since the following day was the Sabbath, he made certain that they were dead: "And so the soldiers came and broke the legs both of the one and of the other that were crucified with him; but when they came to Jesus, and found him already dead, they did not break his legs, but one of the soldiers opened his side with a spear; and immediately blood and water flowed out" (John 19, 32–35). (It is interesting to note that scientists today tell us that, after a person's death, blood and water (lymph) will flow out separately from a deep wound.)

After Pilate had made sure that Jesus was dead, he gave Joseph of Arimathea permission to bury the body. "And Joseph taking the body, wrapped it in a clean linen cloth, and laid it in his new tomb, which he had hewn out in the rock. Then he rolled a large stone to the entrance of the tomb and departed" (Matt. 27, 59, 61; cf. Mark 15, 42; Luke 23, 50; John 19, 38; I Cor. 15, 4).

2. CHRIST TRULY ROSE FROM THE DEAD

a. The Tomb Was Found Empty

The chief priests and Pharisees were uneasy, however, and so they came to Pilate saying: "Sir, we have recalled it to memory that this deceiver, while he yet lived, said, I am to rise again after three days. Give orders, then, that his tomb shall be securely guarded until the third day; or perhaps his disciples will come and steal him away. If they should then say to the people, He has risen from the dead, this last deceit will be more dangerous than the old. Pilate said to them, You have guards; away with you, make it secure as you best know how. And they went and made the tomb secure, putting a seal on the stone and setting a guard over it" (Matt. 27, 63–66).

On the third day, the tomb was found empty. There can be no doubt about the fact.

Early in the morning of the first day of the week, while it was still dark, Mary Magdalen went to the tomb, and found the stone moved away from the tomb door. So she came running to Simon Peter, and that other disciple, whom Jesus loved; They have carried the Lord away from the tomb, she said to them, and we cannot tell where they have taken him. Upon this, Peter and the other disciples both set out, and made their way to the tomb; they began running side by side, but the other disciple outran Peter, and reached the tomb first. He looked in and saw the linen cloth lying there, but he did not go in. Simon Peter, coming up after him, went into the tomb and saw the linen cloths lying there, and also the veil which had been put over Jesus' head, not lying with the linen cloths, but still wrapped round and round in a place by itself (John 20, 1–10; cf. Luke 24, 1–8; Mark 16, 1–7; Matt. 28, 1–7).

For the last hundred years Rationalists have been trying to invent some explanation. "They have traced the disappearance of the body to Pilate, as if Pilate might have arranged its removal 'in order to prevent a disturbance'—it is obvious, of course, that this would have been the worst possible way of securing his end; it would be precisely the disappearance of the body which would *create* a disturbance. As Ronald Knox says:

They have traced it to the Jews, who, of all people, were most intimately concerned to see that the Body was not stolen; who, of all people, would most willingly have produced the Body if it had been in their power to do so. They have told us that the holy women must have gone to the wrong tomb by mistake, as if it was likely (apart from what John tells us) that their amazing report was never verified! The palpable futility of all these theories reflects admirably the bankruptcy of the criticism which produced them.

Only one plausible theory of the kind has ever been devised, and it was devised immediately after the event; the Jews maintained that the Body had been secretly carried off by our Lord's own followers. Yet this is an explanation which no scholar has dared to adopt, for obvious reasons. Neither the psychology of the Apostles at the time of the Passion nor their psychology after the Resurrection, lends any color to the idea that their whole story was a gigantic imposition, deliberately foisted on the world by a band of desperate devotees.[20]

All these attempts to explain away the empty tomb have failed miserably. When you think it over, the last one, the so-called "deception theory" is the weakest of all. For after the guards were bribed (Matt. 28, 13) they said that *while they slept* the Apostles stole the body. But if they were asleep, how did they know what had happened? At most, they could say that when they awoke the tomb was empty; the Apostles *probably* stole the body. But can we imagine the dejected Apostles, who were scared to death during the Passion, risking their lives to steal his dead body in order to institute a fraud? And why perpetuate such a fraud? If Christ did not rise, he deceived them and was not God. They had nothing to gain except persecution and death. Moreover, such an "explanation" makes all the Apostles consummate liars. And how account for all the good resulting from this diabolical fraud? The utter absurdity of this "explanation" will become more evident as we proceed. Today, it is rejected by all scholars.

Ultimately, the "critics" were driven to the only possible explanation. Our Lord's body left the tomb alive, for the empty tomb was a fact impossible to deny. But instead of admitting the obvious truth—that our Lord rose from the dead—they asserted that he had not died on the cross. Apart from the fact that it contradicts all the historical evidence (see above), note what the theory implies. It means that Jesus of Nazareth, after he escaped death, had then and there set about deluding posterity into the belief that he had died and risen again.[21] Can anyone "swallow" that? Not if they know anything about Jesus of Nazareth!

20. Knox, *op. cit.*, pp. 126–127.
21. Even Strauss says: "A person who had crawled from the tomb half-dead, a gravely ill person just managing to drag himself along, a person in need of medical care, of bandaging, of nursing, a person who even after such treatment might in the end still die of his wounds, could not have made upon the disciples the impression that he was the victor over death and the

b. The Resurrection Appearances

The empty tomb, however, is not their only difficulty. Indeed, the *resurrection appearances* pose a *greater problem* for them. These appearances have not been recounted by any Evangelist in full chronological order for the *Evangelists* were *primarily concerned* with the *fact of the Resurrection* and *not* with the facts of his *various appearances*. Although each Evangelist enumerates a number of them, no one gives an exhaustive list. In fact, it seems from a study of the Gospels that they mention only those appearances when Jesus convinced them of the physical reality of his body, or when he taught them some new truth. We have no idea how often he appeared to his mother or the Apostles simply to converse with them.

Evidently, the records are incomplete. From two sources, for example, we hear of a meeting between our Lord and St. Peter that is not recorded elsewhere (Luke 24, 34; I Cor. 15, 5). St. Paul alone recounts his appearance to five hundred people at one time (I Cor. 15, 6). But as Ronald A. Knox says: "The fact that the reminiscences preserved to us are preserved to us in so fragmentary a form is all the better proof of their authenticity. Plainly, the Apostles never met and said, 'We must have a story; what shall it be?' Plainly, no later editor with historical instincts has been through the evidence and tried to work up a brief. We are left with the naked testimony, such as it is, of first-hand witnesses." [22]

This is confirmed by the extreme sobriety of the gospel accounts. The Evangelists relate merely the bare, historical facts. They never go beyond their own experience. Humbly, they acknowledge their own incredulity and hesitancy. Though the various narratives are incomplete, they are not incompatible.

The historical evidence for the real and bodily resurrection of Christ is most convincing for two reasons. First of all, the Apostles *never expected the resurrection*. Secondly, when Christ did appear, they *feared it was a vision* or spirit *until he proved that* he had a *physical body*. Let us consider these two points.

---

grave, that he was the prince of life; yet, it was precisely this impression that lay at the bottom of their later life." Strauss, *Das Leben Jesu*, 1864, p. 298.

22. Knox, *op. cit.*, p. 128.

After Jesus was seized by the Jews, the Apostles fled in terror. As St. John admits (John 20, 19) "for fear of the Jews, they had locked the doors of the room in which they had assembled." There, "they mourned and wept" (Mark 16, 11). Although Jesus had clearly foretold his resurrection, the Apostles never expected it. Frankly, they *admit their fault.* They offer no excuses. St. John says: "They had not yet mastered what was written of him, that he was to rise from the dead" (John 20, 9). Since they had refused to think of his death (Matt. 16, 22), they apparently never thought of his resurrection. Even if they had, the dreadful spectacle of the crucifixion would have blotted out all their hopes. Like us, they seemed too earthly minded—measuring success by material prosperity and power.

By their *actions,* they clearly *manifested* their *lack of hope.* On the third day, Mary Magdalen and the other holy women set out to anoint his body (Mark 16, 1). Evidently, they were not thinking about his resurrection—much less expecting it. When they found the tomb empty, their first thought was that someone had stolen the body. "So she came running to Simon Peter, and that other disciple, whom Jesus loved; They have carried the Lord away from the tomb, she said to them, and we cannot tell where they have taken him" (John 20, 2).

According to St. Luke, "this story seemed to them (Peter and John) *nonsense* and they did *not believe* the women. But Peter arose and ran to the tomb; and stooping down, he saw the linen cloths laid there; and he went away *wondering* to himself at what had come to pass" (Luke 24, 11–12).

Surely the discovery of the empty tomb does not have the effect we would naturally expect, if the Apostles were anxiously awaiting the resurrection. Notice how its discovery precedes any belief in the resurrection. It merely causes Peter to "wonder." The attitude of the Apostles is reflected well by the two disciples leaving Jerusalem. St. Luke writes:

It was on the same day that two of them were walking to a village called Emmaus, sixty furlongs away from Jerusalem, discussing all that had happened. They were still conversing and debating together, when Jesus himself drew near, and began to walk beside them; but their eyes were held fast, so that they could not recognize him. And he said to them, What talk is this you exchange between you as you go alone, sad-faced? And one of them, who was called Cleophas, answered him.

What, art thou the only pilgrim in Jerusalem who has not heard of
what happened there in the last few days? What happenings? he asked;
and they said, About Jesus of Nazareth, a prophet whose words and acts
had power with God, and with all the people; how the chief priests,
and our rulers, handed him over to be sentenced to death, and so crucified him. For ourselves, we *had hoped* that it was he who was to deliver
Israel; but now, to crown it all, today is the third day since it befell.
Some women, indeed, who belonged to our company, alarmed us; they
had been at the tomb early in the morning and could not find his body;
whereupon they came back and told us that they had seen a vision of
angels, who said that he was alive. Some of those who were with us went
to the tomb, and found that all was as the women had said, but of him
they saw nothing (Luke 24, 13–24).

From the evidence, it is clear that the Apostles did not expect
to see the risen Christ. Even the discovery of the empty tomb
merely caused Peter to "wonder." Since the Apostles were so slow
to believe, they are most reliable witnesses.

Secondly, when Christ did appear, the Apostles at first feared
it was some sort of a vision. Our Lord had to demonstrate the
reality of his physical body.

The experience of the holy women should have prepared the
Apostles. According to St. Matthew (28, 9), the holy women "embraced his feet and worshipped him." Since they embraced his
feet, he must have been physically present. In like manner, the
two disciples should have perceived the nature of his body when
"he took bread, and blessed, and broke it, and offered it to them"
(Luke 24, 30). We do not know whether they did or not because
St. Luke is anxious to give a better proof. After the two disciples
hurried back to Jerusalem, they were told:

The Lord has indeed risen, and has appeared to Simon. And they too
told the story of their encounter in the road and how they recognized
him when he broke bread. Now while they were talking of these things,
Jesus stood in their midst, and said to them, "Peace to you! It is I, do not
be afraid." But they were startled and panic-stricken, and thought that
they saw a spirit. And he said to them, 'Why are you disturbed, and
why do doubts arise in your hearts? See my hands and feet, that it is I
myself. Feel and see; for a spirit does not have flesh and bones, as you
see I have.' And having said this, he showed them his hands and his
feet. But as they still disbelieved and marvelled for joy, he said, 'Have
you anything here to eat?' And they offered him a piece of broiled fish
and a honeycomb. And when he had eaten in their presence, he took

what remained and gave it to them (Luke 24, 35–48; cf. John 20, 20; Mark 16, 14).

Because the Apostles never expected the resurrection, they are "startled and panic-stricken" when he appears. They fear it is an apparition until Christ proves the reality of his physical body. If any further doubts remained, the proof given to Thomas dispelled them.

There was one of the Twelve, Thomas, who is also called Didymus, who was not with them when Jesus came. And when the other disciples told him, We have seen the Lord, he said to them, Until I have seen the marks of the nails on his hands, until I have put my finger into the mark of the nails, and put my hand into his side, you will never make me believe. So, eight days afterwards, once more the disciples were within, and Thomas was with them; and the doors were locked. Jesus came and stood there in their midst; Peace be upon you, he said. Then he said to Thomas, Let me have thy finger; see, here are my hands. Let me have thy hand; put it into my side. Cease thy doubting, and believe. Thomas answered, Thou art my Lord and my God. And Jesus said to him, Thou hast learned to believe, Thomas, because thou hast seen me. Blessed are those who have not seen, and yet have learned to believe (John 20, 24–29).

After reading carefully these Gospel accounts, no honest man can find a good reason for doubting the *physical* resurrection of Christ. By physical resurrection, we mean that his human body, which was dead, was restored to life. It is clearly the conviction of all the witnesses that our Lord, after his resurrection, had a physical body. The holy women "embraced his feet." Because the Apostles fear that he is merely a spirit, our Lord commands them: "Feel and see; for a spirit does not have *flesh and bones,* as you *see* I have." Later, he offers the same tangible proof to the sceptical Thomas. For forty days the Apostles often saw, heard, touched, walked, ate, drank, and carried on conversations with him. Although they do not intend to give a complete list of his appearances, the Evangelists do mention eleven or more. At first, he appears to them to make known his physical resurrection. Afterwards, he comes to give them final instructions. After he physically ascends into heaven, they see him no more for his physical body is in heaven.

In the light of these historical facts, the "hallucination" theory of the Rationalists and the Liberal Protestants appears in its true colors. According to them, the Apostles had hallucinations. By a hallucination, they mean a perception of an object to which no reality corresponds. In other words, the Apostles were "seeing things." Though Jesus was not really present, they "thought" he was. This was due to their "overwhelming desire to see him, to a state of tense, nervous excitement as they awaited the resurrection." Since normal men do not have hallucinations, the Rationalists and the Liberal Protestants must suppose these or similar dispositions [23] in the Apostles to account for their hallucinations. Obviously, they are groundless suppositions fabricated by men with an "overwhelming desire" to reject the resurrection. The plain historical facts are that the Apostles never expected the resurrection; that they feared they were having a vision until Christ demonstrated the reality of his physical body. Moreover, the "hallucinationists" conveniently forget about the empty tomb and other historical facts.

In every age, sceptics have asked why Christ did not show himself publicly after his resurrection to his enemies and to all the people. Though it is one of their best objections, it is easy to answer. For God does not ordinarily use superabundant means to convert the evil-minded. As a rule, he is content with giving men clear and amply sufficient proofs. In fact, Christ taught us this in one of his parables. A rich man in hell begged Abraham to send a messenger from the dead to warn his five brothers. Abraham refused, saying: "They have Moses and the prophets; let them listen to these. They will not do that, father Abraham, said he, but if a messenger comes to them from the dead, they will repent. But he answered him, If they do not listen to Moses and the prophets, they will be unbelieving still, though one should rise from the dead (Luke 16, 19–31). . . . Even if Christ had appeared publicly, after his resurrection, depraved men would have found "reasons" to deny him. And today unbelievers would ask: "If Christ appeared to all men after his resurrection, why doesn't he appear to all men now?" Christ himself refused the Pharisees a special sign from heaven (Mark 8, 11–13) and did not come down from the cross (Matt. 27, 40). Although he does give extraordinary graces to some like Paul, they are exceptions to the rule. Remember his words to Thomas: "Thou hast learned to believe, Thomas,

---

23. A man dying of thirst in the desert, for example, may see a mirage of water.

because thou hast seen me. Blessed are those who have not seen, and yet have learned to believe" (John 20, 29).

D. Confirmations

Everywhere we turn we find new confirmations of the truth of this great historical event. The conversion of St. Paul is a good example. By the words of the risen Christ, Paul was converted from a violent persecutor of the Church into its greatest missionary [24] (Acts 9, 1–26). And no "critic" today doubts Paul's account of his miraculous vision. In fact, no "critics" challenge the authenticity of his epistles, yet Paul constantly presupposes that the resurrection is a known fact. (In his Epistle to the Romans, for example, he refers to it in 1, 4; 2, 16; 4, 24; 6, 4; 8, 11; 8, 34; 10, 9; 14, 9). Now it is inconceivable that a man of his strict honesty, high intelligence and learning, would have joined a gang of liars. It is inconceivable that he would have been completely deceived by them. The only reasonable explanation for the conversion of St. Paul is his encounter with the risen Christ.

The conversion of St. Paul was hardly a more remarkable miracle than the *change wrought in the Apostles themselves*. From dejected, discouraged, fearful men,[25] they are transformed into courageous, inspired, fearless Apostles. On the day of Pentecost, they come forth boldly in the very city where Christ was crucified to preach the gospel. By his first sermon, St. Peter converted three thousand to belief in Christ "whom God has raised up, and we are all witnesses of it," and five thousand more were added a few days later, when he spoke again of "the author of life whom God raised up from the dead" (Acts 10, 34–43).

For after the resurrection, the Apostles and disciples had realized fully for the first time that the man Jesus was also "their Lord and their God." "The Lord has indeed risen and has appeared to Simon," was the cry of the Eleven as they greeted the two disciples returning from Emmaus (Luke 24, 34). "Thou art my Lord and my God," answered Thomas after he felt the wounds of Jesus (John 20, 28). "It is the Lord," St. John shouted when

24. St. Paul's conversion occurred at the latest from three to five years after the death of Christ. Harnack thought Paul was converted either in the year of Christ's death or in the year following it.

25. Subconsciously we seem to think that the Apostles and martyrs feared suffering and death less than we do. This mistaken impression is corrected, however, by considering their conduct during our Lord's passion.

he recognized Christ on the lake shore (John 21, 7). Jesus himself answers Saul's "Who art thou, Lord?" "I am Jesus whom Saul persecutes" (Acts 9, 5).

By the resurrection the Apostles were convinced that God had put his divine seal on the life of Jesus. Thus Peter tells the Jews: ". . . God had made him Lord and Christ, this Jesus whom you crucified" (Acts 2, 36). Again and again, they assert "God raised Jesus from the dead" (Acts 2, 32; 3, 15; 4, 10; 10, 40; 13, 30, 37). Though many futile efforts were made to silence them, not even one denial of the facts they narrated is recorded during the first hundred years of Christianity. In their judgment, God had manifested by this tremendous miracle his unmistakable approbation of the claims of Jesus (Acts 10, 33–43).

For them his resurrection was a cosmic event since it guaranteed the resurrection of all men (I Cor. 15, 21). In his new life, they found the positive assurance of their own eternal life (Phil. 3, 10). By living and conversing with the risen Christ, their hearts and desires were raised above this world of time and space. The things of this earth no longer seemed important. After the descent of the Holy Spirit, they feared no man. Thus when they were forbidden to speak, they replied: "It is impossible for us to refrain from speaking of what we have seen and heard" (Acts 4, 20). Scourging did not deter them. "And they left the presence of the Council, rejoicing that they had been found worthy to suffer indignity for the sake of Jesus' name" (Acts 5, 41). And the dauntless courage of the Apostles was found, too, in disciples like Stephen (Acts 7, 51–59). Indeed, the history of the early Church, recorded in the *Acts of the Apostles,* is a story of courageous men, men of strong faith and burning love (II Cor. 11, 23–33). The resurrection of Christ alone explains the great change that took place in the Apostles.

In Palestine and beyond its borders *converts of every rank and race multiplied rapidly.* Within a few centuries they constituted a majority in the Roman Empire. As St. Augustine said, if the resurrection had not been a fact, then the conversion of the world to belief in it by a few Galilean fishermen would have been as great a miracle as the resurrection itself.

Among the first converts, there were "many (Jewish) priests" (Acts 6, 7). Prior to their conversion, they belonged to the very class that hated Christ and had condemned him to death. Now they broke away from their leaders who were still refusing to consider the evidence (Acts 6, 33–42). Voluntarily, they gave up the privileges of their priesthood for a life of unmitigated persecution. Before they made such a great sacrifice, they must have been completely convinced of the truth of the resurrection.

Apparently, the evidence was so clear that they preferred to be branded as traitors to their race and nation rather than deny Christ any longer. And they had the opportunity to study first-hand evidence.[26] They could question and cross-examine the witnesses of the resurrection.[27] They could study anew the Messianic prophecies and how Jesus fulfilled them. They could investigate the miracles worked by the Apostles in the name of the risen Christ. In fact, the Apostles worked so many miracles that "fear came upon every soul" (Acts 2, 7–8; 2, 43; 3, 1–10; 4, 13–22; 5, 18–23; 6, 8; 8, 13; 12, 6–10). (Note that we might prove even from these miracles alone that God approved of the message of the Apostles.)

The entire primitive Church shared the Apostles' conviction about the real and bodily resurrection of Christ.[28] In the first century, St. Clement of Rome [29] is just as certain of it as St. Ignatius of Antioch [30] is in the second century, or as Tertullian [31] and St. Irenaeus [32] are in the third century, or as St. Augustine [33] and St. John Chrysostom [34] are in the fourth century. All the creeds, all the confessions of faith [35] and many doctrinal defini-

26. The Gospels mention the time and place of many miracles. At Capharnaum, for example, Christ healed the paralytic man, the servant of the centurion, and raised the daughter of Jairus, the head of the synagogue, from the dead. Many of the sick whom Christ healed and the dead who had been restored to life by him were living witnesses confirming the words of the Apostles.

27. St. Paul states that the majority of the five hundred people who had seen Christ after his resurrection were still alive when he wrote his First Epistle to the Corinthians. (I Cor. 15, 6)

28. Cf. Koesters, *op. cit.*, pp. 25–41.

29. Cf. *Letter to the Corinthians*, I, XXXVI, 1 (PG., I, 280).

30. Cf. *Letters to the Ephesians*, XVIII, 2 (PG., V, 660); *Magnesians*, XX, 2 (PG., V, 661); *Smyrnaeans*, I. 1 (PG., V, 708).

31. Cf. *De Praescr.*, XIII (PL., II, 26); *Adv. Marcionem*, III, 8 (PL., II, 331); *Adv. Prax.*, II (PL., II, 156).

32. Cf. *Against Heresies*, I, x, 1 (PG., II, 549).

33. Cf. *Enarrationes in Ps.* 63:15 (PL., XXXVI, 767).

34. Cf. *In Princip. Act. Hom.*, IV, 8.

35. Cf. Denzinger, *op. cit.*, nos. 2–13, 16, 20, 40–42, 54, 86, 994.

tions of the early Church reflect this firm faith of all Christians in the resurrection of Christ. As St. Athanasius (325) said: "We prove, therefore, that this doctrine (of the divinity of Christ) has been handed down from fathers to fathers; you, however, who are Jews of later birth and disciples of Caiphas, what fathers can you produce to support your view? You can quote no one of any note; all manifest horror of you." [36]

At the present time, approximately 485,000,000 Catholics, 129,000,000 Eastern Christians, and the majority of 207,000,000 Protestants believe that Christ is the true Son of God. This is a religious profession unequaled in the world. If we add to these numbers all those who have believed in Christ in past centuries, we have a vast multitude, united by their faith in Christ and inspired by his life and teachings. This faith in Christ has been passed on from generation to generation, from century to century. It is not the opinion of a day or the tendency of an age; it is the invaluable inheritance of the great family of Christians.[37]

These confirmations of the resurrection are undeniable facts of history. If their apparent cause, the resurrection, is denied, they are totally inexplicable. Although it is possible to develop each one of these points and to add new confirmations, it seems unnecessary. If anyone is interested in further discussion, he can consult any one of the many books written about the resurrection.[38] The more we study it, the more firmly we are convinced of its truth. *All* the evidence bids us acknowledge that Christ truly rose from the dead. And the positive arguments are reinforced by the absurdity of the theories proposed to explain them away. We must, of course, keep in mind that historical evidence cannot produce mathematical certitude; it can only exclude *reasonable* doubt! In the present case, no reasonable doubt should remain.

E. Resurrections in Other Religions

In recent years many scholars have labored to develop the science of Comparative Religion.[39] Without doubt, this is a valuable

36. *De Decr. Nicaen. Syn.*, XXIV (PG., XXV, 465).
37. Cf. Koesters, *op. cit.*, pp. 21–54.
38. *The Third Day* by Arnold Lunn is a splendid popular work on the subject.
39. Often it is referred to as a History of Religions.

science. Unfortunately, some Rationalists have endeavored to use it to discredit Christianity. Their works usually follow the same pattern.[40] In the first volumes, the author considers the pagan religions of antiquity. Since the evidence is sparse, he interprets it. Ordinarily, he notes every similarity in morals, doctrines, or ritual between the pagan religions and Christianity. Although he never states definitely that Christianity receives any certain doctrine or practice from another religion, he insinuates that it did. In other words, he implies that Christianity is a fortunate syncretism of the best in all the pagan religions. Christ consciously or unconsciously selected the best features of all religions prior to his. Thus Christianity is reduced to a natural religion.[41]

Naturally intelligent Christians object strongly to such a suave presentation of untruths. Without doubt, the pagan religions and Christianity have some things in common. As we have seen, men can figure out some truths about God by reason alone. We are not surprised, then, if a pagan religion teaches that God is one, spiritual, infinite, or all-good. Obviously, Christianity teaches those same truths.

By reason, man can know a number of moral principles. Because Christ includes those principles in his teaching, it does not mean he got them from the pagans. If in some detail a pagan sacrifice corresponds to the Christian sacrifice, it does not mean they are related.[42] In fact, it is obviously wrong to imply, that because they are similar, the one is derived from the other.

40. A good example is J. Frazer's *The Golden Bough* (12 vols., 3rd ed.), London (Macmillian), 1911–15. He merely re-echoes men like Pfleiderer, Gunkel, Cheyne, and Fiebig. Even extreme liberals like B. Carl Clemen and Johannes Weiss were indignant at the great wrong those men did in the name of science. Cf. Felder, *op. cit.,* p. 399.

41. As G. K. Chesterton remarked, popular scientists keep repeating that Christianity and Buddhism are very much alike. Usually, they base their arguments on resemblances that mean nothing at all. Mr. Blatchford, for example, used this method. Thus he observed that both Christ and Buddha were called by a divine voice from the sky, as if one would expect the divine voice to come from a hole in the ground. Or, again, he pointed out that these two Eastern teachers washed the feet of others. A person wonders why he did not regard it as a significant coincidence that their disciples had feet to wash. Cf. Chesterton, *op. cit.,* pp. 240–242.

42. As Ronald A. Knox says: "He (Mencken) is on more familiar ground elsewhere, when he details more significant resemblances between Christian and non-Christian rites; always careful, like Professor Huxley, to emphasize

As you may suspect, these Rationalists conveniently forget about the vast differences. They may find a pagan religion that worships three gods or god under three aspects, but they have never found one that worships three persons in the one God. They may discover that in some mystery religion, a man became god or a god became a man, but they have never discovered one where God becomes man and yet retains his divine nature. And although they discover similarities in external and secondary matters,[43] they have never found a parallel to the sublime, well-balanced figure of Christ depicted by the Evangelists.

Above all, the Rationalists note carefully any similarities between the resurrection of Christ and those of pagan gods. Again and again, they indicate where the notion of Christ's resurrection *might* have originated. After they write chapters on legends, folklore, and nature-myths about resurrections, they speak of the

---

the similarities and keep a severe silence about the differences. Christians use beads to count the prayers they are saying; so do the Buddhists; therefore . . . The symbol of the Cross is used in Christian art; it is also found among the relics of several early religions: therefore. . . . The ancient Aztecs celebrated a ceremonial and probably sacrificial meal, which reminded the Spaniards of their own Mass and Communion: therefore. . . . Therefore what?

"Mr. Mencken draws no conclusions. Or, rather, he does so occasionally, but not with more than his usual success. . . . By dwelling on resemblances and neglecting differences, by presenting the Incarnation as one among a series of theophanies, the Resurrection as one among a series of fertility-legends, you can hypnotize the reader into a state of fumbling agnosticism; 'it would take me too long,' he feels, 'to go into all this mass of detail'; he cannot see the wood for the trees. I do not know whether Mr. Mencken talks on the wireless, but he has caught the method to perfection; he dazzles by excess of light, nauseates the intellectual digestion with a surfeit of facts, and leaves the reader, from sheer weariness, disinclined to hear the word 'religion' ever mentioned again." *Broadcast Minds,* New York (Sheed & Ward), 1933, pp. 138–142.

43. Often they refer to Krishna, Buddha, and Gilgamesh. Krishna was the eighth incarnation of the Hindu god Vishnu. The earliest *legends* about him (second to seventh century) mention some similarities between his childhood and Christ's. Krishna, however, is represented as the natural son of his parents and his morality is far inferior to that of Christ. In regard to Gotama Buddha, the emphasis was first put on his doctrines and only later on his person. The fundamental teachings of Christ and Buddha are diametrically opposed, namely, theism vs. atheism and monism. Moreover, Buddha never claimed to be divine. All we know about Gilgamesh is found in an epic on the cuneiform tablets in the brick library of Ashurbanipal (668-626 B.C.).

resurrection of Christ as if it were just another myth. In some old mythologies, for example, the gods of the sun die at night and rise in the morning. The Hellenic gods of vegetation [44] die in the Fall and rise in the Spring. "Is not Jesus supposed to have risen at sunrise, and in the Spring? This can hardly be pure coincidence."

Although the Rationalists cannot point out any direct influence of these mythologies on Christianity, they "know" that they must have influenced the authors of the Old Testament and through them the early Christians. Their method is sufficiently vague, sufficiently discreet about making direct statements that would have to be proved and sufficiently erudite on the surface to lead many astray. Because they write volumes on the subject, people conclude that they "must have something." Unfortunately, some who read their books fail to grasp the all-important difference between all these mythical resurrections and the resurrection of Jesus. They are merely poetic fancies—timeless myths or symbols—*without any historical basis*. The resurrection of Jesus is a *well-authenticated historical event* concerning a historical personage. There is a world of difference between the two.

III. CONCLUSION

In this chapter we have indicated three reasons why every man should believe in the divinity of Christ. These reasons or proofs are based upon a great deal of evidence found in proven historical documents. When we examine the objections Rationalists have proposed against these proofs we realize that it is not the believer but the unbeliever who is unreasonable and who is blinded by his philosophy. The difficulty is not to find sufficient evidence to establish, for example, the resurrection of Christ for all the historical evidence at our disposal leads us to believe in the resurrection. The difficulty is to select and present the best evidence in a few pages.

44. Babylonian Tammuz, Egyptian Osiris and Isis, Phoenician Adonis and Astarte, Phrygian Attis, Syrian Atargatis, Thracian Dionysos and Zagreus. Cf. Felder, *op. cit.*, 398–401.

THE HALLUCINATION THEORY

Supplementary reading from Arnold Lunn, *The Third Day*, London (Burns, Oates), 1945, pp. 74–80.

We must not confuse hallucination with mal-observation. A clever conjurer can deceive his audience and they may fail to observe things which only a keen-sighted and quick-witted person would detect, and the resultant hallucination is due to mal-observation. Abnormal people who are mentally unbalanced suffer from isolated illusions. Normal people under abnormal circumstances may suffer hallucinations. Many years ago Mr. Claud Elliott, now headmaster of Eton, and I, searched a Pyrenean peak on which a friend of ours had been killed. We had travelled all through the night from London and started on our search-party within an hour or two of arriving at the little inn from which he started his last climb. We were out of training and tired, and the strain of the search gradually began to tell. Every time we turned a corner we expected to see our friend; again and again we thought we saw his body stretched out on the rocks, and heard the other members of the party shouting that they had found him. A vulture hovering near the cliff, as vultures will often hover for days before attacking a dead body, provided a macabre touch. These hallucinations were vivid while they lasted, but they never lasted for more than a second or two.

Monsignor Knox, in one of his sermons, quotes my experiences on the Pyrenean search-party and adds, "Isn't it possible, ask the critics of our religion, that the people who thought they saw our Lord after his Resurrection were in the same position as that?" To which we answer, No. Whatever position they were in, they were not in the same position as that. Rather, they were exactly in the opposite position. A hallucination means seeing something else, and mistaking it for what you are looking for, as Arnold Lunn did in the Pyrenean peak; these people saw what they were looking for and, one and all, mistook it for something else. St. Mary Magdalene did want to find the Crucified, and it would have been natural enough if she had seen the gardener and mistaken him for our Lord. The curious thing is that she saw our Lord and mistook him for the gardener. The two disciples on the Emmaus road, who were thinking about our Lord and talking about him as they went, might have been pardoned if they had recognised his figure, wrongly, in that of some casual passer-by. But the fact is that they thought he was a casual passer-by when they really met him. The apostles in the Upper Room might easily have seen a ghost and taken it for their Master; but they didn't, they saw their Master and took him for a ghost. And again by the lake-side, they might have been deceived by the accents of a strange voice, and thought it was his. It is more significant that they should have been deceived by the accents of his voice, and thought it was a strange one. They didn't run away with their first impressions, and tell unauthenticated stories of a miracle. They examined their first impressions and only by examination learned the miraculous truth."

And as Monsignor Knox remarked on another occasion, "Nobody is sure that he has found a half crown in his pocket as a man who puts his hand into a pocket expecting that it will contain a solitary copper."

Exhaustion, strain and fear, all played their part in creating those fleeting hallucinations on the Pyrenean peak, but no such background can be invoked to explain the appearances of our Lord to the disciples.

Nothing could be more natural than the setting in which Christ appeared to the disciples on their way to Emmaus. The story is told by St. Luke. Jesus joins them on their walk, just as any other pilgrim might. It was broad daylight, and the appearance of Jesus provokes none of the astonishment and perturbation which we associate with the appearance of phantoms. And the stranger who joins them asks them why they were so depressed. "You must be a stranger in Jerusalem," is the reply, "or you could not have failed to hear the things that have happened these days." "What things," asks the stranger; and the two disciples re-tell the sad story of their vanished hopes. "For, of course, we had hoped that it was he who was to deliver Israel."

Or again read the story of doubting Thomas as told by St. John. No prejudice could be stronger than St. Thomas'. He insists on experimental proof before he believes, and yields only to the irresistible pressure of stubborn fact. It is impossible to fit this story into the familiar pattern of hallucination. . . .

Our problem is to account for the origin of a belief so contrary, not only to human experience, but also to their own expectations, for the disciples hoped for an earthly triumph, and refused to believe that Jesus would be rejected by his own people. And because they did not wish to believe in the Cross, they found no room in their minds for the Resurrection which, like the Cross, had been foretold. Very significant in this context is the conversation of two disciples with the risen Christ whom they had failed to recognise on the walk to Emmaus. They told him how the chief priests and our rulers, handed Christ over to be sentenced to death. "For ourselves, we had hoped that it was he who was to deliver Israel, but now to crown all, today is the third day since it befell." And they describe with no apparent conviction, the finding of the empty tomb by the women and also by some of the apostles "but of him they saw nothing," and it is clear that these disciples at least were unpersuaded by the fact that the women reported "that they had seen a vision of angels who said that he was still alive." It was not until they returned to Jerusalem that the disciples who walked to Emmaus learned that "the Lord had appeared to Simon." The reluctance to accept the evidence of women is a convincing touch, for if the story had been invented we may be very sure that the discovery of the empty tomb would not have been attributed to women. . . .

It was not until St. John entered the tomb and found it empty "and the napkin that had been about his head not lying with the linen clothes" that "he saw and believed. For as yet they knew not the scriptures that he must rise again from the dead."

It was difficult for the disciples to believe in the Resurrection because this belief conflicted with all human experience. It was difficult to believe in Christ because loyalty to Christ involved a breach with the church of their Fathers. We are tempted to forget that the disciples were Jews, for the influence of Christian art is so strong that we tend to think of them as Nordic or Latin Christians and not as Asiatic Jews. Religion is never more powerful than when it is closely associated with the national loyalties of an oppressed race, as for instance in Palestine under the Romans, or in Serbia during the Turkish occupation, or in Ireland during the long Anglo-Protestant ascendancy. It was as difficult for the disciples to break away from the Synagogue as it would have been for Irish peasants during the penal times to apostatise from the Catholic Church.

It is inconceivable that a mere hallucination could have provoked and maintained this spiritual dislocation of their lives, a dislocation which involved a complete breach with their past. Sooner or later the remonstrances of those who loved them, and the bitter reproaches of those who despised them as apostates must have eroded their faith in the objective reality of what they believed that they had seen. As the opposition increased and as the possibility of martyrdom became more and more apparent, their confidence in the hallucination must inevitably have weakened. Moreover, no hallucinations are identical, and inevitably as the memory of the phantoms faded the disciples must have begun to compare their own memories of what they believed that they had seen, and the inevitable discrepancies must have reinforced their growing doubts. Finally, these men had to stand the supreme test of martyrdom, and they were not of the stuff of which martyrs are made, for they abandoned Jesus and fled at the moment of his arrest and Peter subsequently denied him.

It is very hard for a man to eradicate even small failings, for character is stubborn in its resistance to change. The disciples were average men, neither heroes nor cowards, but subject—as ordinary men are subject—to collapse under great strain, and it is difficult to believe that a mere hallucination could have transformed these men, who panicked in Gethsemane, into the dynamic Apostles who were not only ready to break with their Church, their relations and their friends, but also proved themselves undaunted by flogging, imprisonment and the ever present prospect of martyrdom. Nothing but a certitude, rock-like in quality, could have produced this amazing transformation.

CHAPTER VI

The Testimony of History

IF Christ's claims are credible, I should be a Christian, a follower of Christ. But what *kind* of a Christian? This question brings us to the heart-breaking problem of a divided Christianity. There are approximately 821,000,000 Christians in the world today. Of these, some 485,000,000 are Roman Catholics; 129,000,000 belong to the Separated Eastern Churches; [1] and 207,000,000 are Protestants.[2] There are nineteen Separated Eastern Churches and many more Protestant Churches.[3] The problem then is this: Should I be a Roman Catholic, a member of the Roman Catholic Church, and, if so, why?

The Roman Catholic Church offers three reasons for its claim to be the one and only true Church of Christ. The most basic of these reasons is known as the *historical* proof for the Church's

1. These are also called the Dissident Oriental Churches or the Orthodox Churches. After centuries of intermittent schism they separated themselves definitively from Rome in the fifteenth century. Some of these churches, or parts of them, have since returned to communion with the Holy See. Consult the chart at the end of this chapter.

2. This includes the members of the Protestant Episcopal Church, the American offshoot of the Church of England. The "high-church" group within the Protestant Episcopal Church resents the term Protestant and has tried unsuccessfully to have it eliminated from the official title of their Church.

3. Here in the United States there are around four hundred Protestant sects. Most of them are small; more than 90% of American Protestants belong to two dozen denominations.

claim. It runs like this. Christ himself established his Church as a visible society, giving to it a determinate constitution as a visible society. He commanded all men to become members of this one Church. Now the only Church that can trace its lineage back to the apostolic Church founded by Christ is the Roman Catholic Church. Therefore, the Roman Catholic Church is the true Church of Christ. Therefore, if a Christian, I should be a Roman Catholic Christian.

The critical point in this proof is the statement: Christ established his Church as a visible society, giving to it a determinate constitution as a visible society. The proof for this statement is as follows. He who 1) gathers around himself a group of disciples, 2) places before them a goal to be achieved, 3) supplies them with the means to its achievement, and 4) establishes an authority in their midst to direct them to this goal by the use of these means, is the founder of a visible society. But Christ himself did all these four things in the case of the apostolic church: 1) *he* gathered together a group of disciples; 2) *he* placed before them a goal to be achieved; 3) *he* supplied them with the means to its achievement; 4) *he* established an authority in their midst to direct them to this goal by the use of these means. Therefore Christ himself founded the apostolic Church as a visible society.

The first statement is indisputable; the man who does all these four things is unquestionably the founder of a visible society. It is around the second statement that the Roman Catholic-Protestant controversy revolves, although not around all four parts of this statement nor with equal importance around those in dispute. As to the first part—Christ himself gathered together a group of disciples—there can be no question. As to the second part—Christ placed before them an end to be achieved—there is, at least along general lines, no dispute; that end is eternal salvation in the kingdom of God. As to the third part of the statement—Christ supplied them with the means to the achievement of this end—there is much dispute but this disagreement has its roots in the fourth part of the statement. It is around this fourth and last part that the controversy really revolves—which is not surprising, since without authority a visible society cannot exist [4] and since the nature of the authority determines the nature of the visible society.

4. Authority is the formal element in a visible society and the distribution of authority determines the nature of the visible society.

Thus our primary question—Did Christ himself establish his church as a visible society?—is reduced to the question—Did Christ himself establish an authority in the apostolic church and, if so, what was the nature of that authority? Some Protestants deny that Christ established an authority in the apostolic church. Others admit that he did so but disagree with us as to the nature of that authority. A review of their opinions will throw much light on our own position as Roman Catholics and will at the same time indicate what must be proved in order to validate the historical proof for the Roman Catholic position.

I. CATHOLIC AND PROTESTANT VIEWS

A. The Catholic View

The Roman Catholic position is that Jesus Christ established his Church as, at one and the same time, an invisible and a visible society. Here we are interested in that Church as a visible society. What kind of an authority did he set up in his Church?

First of all, we maintain that Christ bestowed authority to govern, teach, and sanctify his followers upon the Apostles and their successors, the bishops of the Church. Secondly, we hold that Christ bestowed supreme authority over the whole Church upon St. Peter and his successors, the bishops of Rome. Thus, we believe that the Church of Christ according to the will of its founder is ruled by bishops who are the successors of the Apostles. We believe that among the bishops, as among the Apostles, one of their number is chief. Although each Catholic bishop receives his jurisdiction from God, he must use it in obedience to the Bishop of Rome who succeeds St. Peter as supreme ruler. In other words, just as every diocesan bishop is a visible vicar with authority delegated from Christ over his own diocese, so the Pope is a still higher vicar with authority delegated from Christ over the whole Church. As Fortescue says: "We know that Christ governs, teaches, sanctifies his Church through men, his vicars. Christ baptizes, Christ consecrates, Christ forgives sins, rules the diocese. Christ rules the whole body too, at Headquarters: here, too he does so through his minister." [5]

What is the scope of their authority, the authority of a bishop

5. Cf. Fortescue, *The Early Papacy*, London (Burns, Oates and Washbourne), 1920, p. 21.

in his diocese, of a Pope over the whole Church? Neither a bishop nor a Pope is an irresponsible tyrant who can do anything he pleases in the territory under his jurisdiction. They have authority over matters of religion and in those adjacent matters that closely affect it. But they have no authority from Christ in purely temporal matters, in political questions, or in the experimental sciences. Moreover, even in religious matters, their powers are *not* unlimited; they are limited by the constitution of the Church as established by Christ. Not even the Pope can modify or change any article of divine revelation; his task is to guard it against attack and false interpretation. He can neither omit a text from the Bible nor add one to it. He must believe the revelation of Christ as all Catholics believe it and he must preach it to the world. He can neither make nor abolish a sacrament. Nor could a Pope decide to abolish the college of bishops and directly rule the entire Church.

B. Protestant Views

It is very difficult to present accurately the manifold Protestant views on this matter.[6] The best one can do is to indicate trends of thought. They can be reduced to two.

First of all, we have those Protestants who agree with us that Christ did establish his Church as a visible society but disagree with us as to the kind of society he established. Here we have two divergent views. The "high-church" Episcopalians and the "Orthodox" Churches maintain that Christ bestowed spiritual authority upon the Apostles and their successors, the bishops of the Church. They deny that he gave supreme authority to St. Peter and his successors, the bishops of Rome. At best, they will admit that the occupants of the see of Rome possess a primacy of honor; that they are the first among equals.[7] We have another view favored by some Lutherans. This not only denies that supreme authority was granted to St. Peter and his successors but also that spiritual authority was conferred upon the Apostles and their successors, the bishops. It holds that spiritual authority was given to

6. Cf. Weigel, Gustave, S.J., *A Survey of Protestant Theology in Our Day,* Westminster (The Newman Press), 1954, pp. 3–12.

7. They do not agree as to the source of this primacy of honor. Some hold that it is of ecclesiastical origin while others will admit that it was bestowed upon St. Peter and his successors by Christ himself.

all of Christ's followers, insisting upon the priesthood of all believers. *They* are the immediate subject of spiritual authority. It is they who not only designate those who shall exercise authority in the Church but likewise communicate this authority to them.

Secondly, we have those Protestants who deny that Christ established his Church as a visible society. In their opinion, the Church as founded by Christ has no earthly organization.[8] It is something greater and wider than any defined body of Christians. In other words, the Church of Christ embraces all believers.[9] Of course, members of this one invisible Church may form individual churches, if they find it spiritually helpful to do so. Although these churches are useful, they are not essential.[10] They have been compared to clubs within a city. Some citizens of a city, for example, may find it useful to join a club (K. of C., Elks, Odd Fellows, etc.) but all remain citizens whether they join a club or not. Thus,

8. A well-known Protestant editor, Charles C. Morrison, writes: "No denomination claims that Christ is the head of its denomination! It may claim that it has 'the truth,' that it is 'the true New Testament church,' that its creed is the true statement of the Christian faith, and that its practices and mode of organization conform strictly to the 'pattern' of the primitive church; but no denomination, or only a negligible few, has ever pretended that Christ is the head of its denomination. Such a claim would sound either ridiculous or blasphemous in the ear of any Protestant. Only Rome makes such a claim, and it was against this very pretension that Protestantism revolted." *Can Protestantism Win America,* New York (Harper), 1948, p. 180. Cf. Harnack, *What is Christianity?,* New York (Putnam's), 1908, pp. 281, 293, 295–296.

9. Ronald A. Knox, who is a convert to the Church, said: "Ninety per cent of the people who reject the Catholic Church reject it, not because they believe in some other visible Church, but because they do not believe in a visible Church at all." *The Mystery of the Kingdom,* London (Sheed & Ward), 1928, p. 41.

In this regard, Protestants are following the lead of Luther and Calvin. They maintained that Christ did not found his Church as a visible institution. In their opinion, the true church is composed of those whom God has predestined to Heaven. In recent years, Harnack and Sabatier proposed a different opinion. According to them, Christ merely revealed his *spirit* of love for God and men. His "Kingdom" or "Church" is made up of those who try to feel in their *hearts* what he felt.

10. Morrison says: "Protestantism thus knows at least this much of the mind of Christ with respect to the differences which divide his church into 'churches': He totally disregards them as having no relevancy at all in the constitution of his church. Protestants confess that Christ and his church transcend their sectarian contentions and the sectarian 'churches' that are maintained upon them. The sheep of other sectarian folds belong to him no less than those of their own sectarian fold." *Ibid.,* p. 180.

all Christians belong to the one true Church of Christ whether they attend the services of any particular denomination or not. Consequently, many Protestants feel that one church is as good as another.[11] And they do not think that any Church has an exclusive authority from God to teach and guide men.[12]

The historical proof for the Church's claim is directed mainly against those Protestants who admit that Christ founded a visible Church but who disagree with us as to its nature. Our immediate task, then, is to show that Christ himself conferred spiritual authority upon the Apostles and their successors, the bishops of his Church—this against the view of some Protestants that he established his Church on democratic lines; and that he bestowed supreme authority upon St. Peter and his successors, the bishops of Rome—this against those Protestants who maintain that he established his Church on oligarchic lines. The identification of the Catholic Church with the one established by Christ follows without any difficulty.

II. EPISCOPAL AUTHORITY

In this section we seek to prove that Christ himself conferred spiritual authority upon the Apostles and their successors, the bishops of his Church. To do so we will appeal to the evidence from Scripture and Tradition.

A. Evidence from Scripture

At the beginning of his public ministry, Jesus declared his intention of inaugurating "the kingdom of God" or "the kingdom of heaven" or "my Church." [13] In fact, the greater part of his teaching centers around it. It was the "kingdom" vaguely described by the prophets in which a remnant of the Jews would take part.[14]

---

11. Cf. *ibid.*, pp. 180–181.

12. There are exceptions. The Seventh Day Adventists, for example, hold that their church is the one true Church because they alone have preserved the faith of the Apostles and the reformers, which faith is lost in all the other Christian denominations.

13. Of course, the earthly kingdom instituted by Christ is a preparation for the heavenly; the relation is one of means to end. Cf. Y. de la Briere, "Eglise," in *Dictionnaire Apologétique*, I, 1246–1247.

14. Like the other institutions of Christianity, the Church was foreshadowed under the Old Jewish dispensation so that the world would be prepared for it. Under the old dispensation, the Ecclesia (Church) of God was coter-

Obviously, it was not a political kingdom, for Jesus resisted any effort to make him a temporal monarch. And yet "his kingdom" is inaugurated on earth for he compares it to a field that contains both wheat and cockle; to a net that takes in both good and bad fishes; to a bridal party including both wise and foolish virgins. It is a sheepfold of which he makes Peter the shepherd.[15] The resurrection is to take place at the end, not at the beginning of it.[16]

Indeed, Christ speaks of himself as a king who departs for a far country. During his absence, his deputies will administer his kingdom. And it will grow rapidly, like a mustard tree, serving as a leaven to all mankind.[17] When he, the King, returns (at the end of the world), he will reap the harvest. He will separate the

---

minous with the Jewish nation. God has "called" the Jews from among all the nations to his unique Assembly. As a member of this Assembly, the Jew claimed what he claimed, and hoped what he hoped. In God's Providence, this Church-nation served as the rough model for the Christian Assembly that followed and superseded it.

The Christian Church was to differ in many respects from the old "Church of God." "It was to differ from it in being international; it was to differ from it in being guided and indwelt by the Holy Spirit; it was to differ from it in being indefectible, irreplaceable. But plainly the new Church was to be, like the old "Church," a visible Society; for in all his teaching our Lord uttered no hint of a difference which must have proved so momentous." Knox, *The Church on Earth*, New York (Macmillan), 1929, pp. 6–7.

15. John 10, 16; 21, 15–18.

16. Surely, there is no foundation for the old Calvinist notion that the Church is the sum of those predestined to eternal life.

17. "This kingdom of his is not to appear suddenly. Recent scholars have sometimes imagined that our Lord expected his own death to be followed by some sudden world catastrophe, which would usher in a new order of things, and that this new order was the 'kingdom' referred to. But he has been careful to explain that his kingdom is a slow growth which you might compare to the action of a man who plants a mustard seed, or that of a woman who hides leaven in three measures of meal. So far from encouraging his followers to think that a world-catastrophe is to be expected shortly, he goes out of his way to assure them that a long period of waiting must precede it; and that period of waiting will be his kingdom. The householder must sleep and rise night and day while the seed grows; it is a far country that the king is visiting, and his return from it is delayed. Thus the kingdom may be identified with a period of time, namely—our Lord will not specify its length—which is to intervene between its institution and his coming again." Knox, *The Belief of Catholics*, New York (Sheed & Ward), 1940, pp. 146–147.

cockle from the wheat, the bad fish from the good, the goats from the sheep. Then the good will be invited to his heavenly kingdom, the consummation of his kingdom on earth.

As the nucleus of this kingdom or Church, Christ chose a small number of disciples whom he carefully trained. "Then he went up onto the mountain side, and called to him those whom it pleased him to call; so these came to him, and he appointed twelve to be his companions, and to go out preaching at his command . . ." (Mark 3, 13–15).

His principal concern seemed to be *their* ministry which was to be a posthumous continuation of his own. In fact, he spent most of his time instructing them. While he preached only to the lost sheep of Israel, they were to represent him before the whole world. Thus his heart is filled with joy and gratitude when they recount the successes of their first mission. Repeatedly, he stresses their role. They are to be "fishers of men," the "salt of the earth," and the reapers of an abundant harvest. To them alone he entrusts the secrets of the kingdom.

For three long years he instructed and trained them. Then, just before his Ascension, he sent them forth as his representatives to
1) teach,
2) govern, and
3) sanctify all nations.

He sent them to *teach* all nations. "All power in heaven and on earth has been given to me. Go, therefore, and make disciples of all nations . . ." (Matt. 28, 19; Mark 16, 16). "You shall receive power when the Holy Spirit comes upon you and you are to be my witnesses in Jerusalem and throughout Judaea, in Samaria, yes, and to the ends of the earth" (Acts 1, 8).

Obviously, their mission is a continuation of his own. They are his *official* teachers. To them he promises the Holy Spirit who will aid them to recall and understand all his teachings. "So much converse I have held with you, still at your side. He who is to befriend you, the Holy Spirit, whom the Father will send on my account, will in his turn make everything plain, and recall to your minds everything I have said to you" (John 14, 25–26).

He sent them to *govern* men. "Go, therefore, and make disciples of all nations . . . teaching them to *observe* all that I have commanded you" (Matt. 28, 19–20). Notice that our Lord not only commands them to teach, but to teach them to *observe* (obey) his commandments. In other words, they teach with *his authority.* Peter is given charge [18] of all his lambs and sheep (John 21, 15–17).

And the Christians are bound to obey them. "I promise you, all that you bind on earth shall be bound in heaven, and all that you loose on earth shall be loosed in heaven" (Matt. 18, 18). "He who listens to you, listens to me; he who despises you, despises me; and he who despises me, despises him that sent me" (Luke 10, 16).

He sent them to *sanctify* men by sacred rites. "And he said to them, Go out all over the world . . . he who believes and is baptized will be saved; he who refuses belief will be condemned" (Mark 16, 16; Matt. 28, 18–20).

"When he had said this, he breathed upon them, and said to them, 'Receive the Holy Spirit; whose sins you shall forgive, they are forgiven them; and whose sins you shall retain, they are retained" (John 20, 22–23).

And the Apostles carried out his command. Following St. Peter's first sermon, the Apostles baptized three thousand (Acts 2, 41). After Philip baptized the Samaritans, Peter and John laid their hands upon them and they received the Holy Spirit (Acts 8, 12–17). Peter baptized the first Gentile converts even though they had already received the Holy Spirit (Acts 11, 15–18). In fact, until the time of the Protestant revolt, the public rite of baptism clearly distinguished members of the Church from non-members. Through it, they were initiated into the society of Christ.

Everywhere the Apostles taught his doctrines, governed according to his precepts, and sanctified men with his sacraments. It was to the Apostles as teachers, rulers and sanctifiers of his society that Christ promised his constant divine assistance. "Go, therefore, make disciples of all nations . . . and behold, I am with you all days, even to the consummation of the world" (Matt. 28, 19–20).

Soon after Christ's Ascension the apostolic Church appeared as an organized, visible society. There is no indication of any period of organization. The Apostles seemed to know their roles. Immediately they *acted together, under the leadership of Peter, as the official teachers and rulers* of the infant Church.

Indeed, they presupposed that everyone recognized their position in the Church. Thus, they appointed and ordained the first deacons.

18. The nature of St. Peter's authority will be discussed in the next section.

So the twelve called together the general body of the disciples, and said, It is too much that we should have to forego preaching God's word, and bestow our care upon tables. Come then, brethren, you must find among you seven men to put in charge of this business, and to the ministry of preaching. . . . These they presented to the apostles, who laid their hands on them with prayer (Act 6, 2–6).

Note how *the twelve* called together the general body of disciples. They told them to select seven men whom *the twelve ordained* and *put in charge* of the less important business of the Church.

On their own responsibility, they chose another Apostle (Acts 1, 15–26). They took for granted that their successors would also *rule* the Church. St. Paul states that a bishop "must be one who is a good head to his own family, and keeps his children in order by winning their full respect; if a man has not learned to manage his own household, will he know how to *govern God's Church?*" (I Timothy 3, 4–5).

The Council of Jerusalem (49–50 A.D.) serves as another good example of how the Apostles governed the apostolic Church. In the *Acts of Apostles,* we read:

But now some visitors came down from Judea, who began to tell the brethren, You cannot be saved without being circumcised according to the tradition of Moses. Paul and Barnabas were drawn into a great controversy with them; and it was decided that Paul and Barnabas and certain of the rest should go up to see the apostles and presbyters in Jerusalem about this question. . . . When they reached Jerusalem, they were welcomed by the church, and by the apostles and presbyters; and they told them of all that God has done to aid them. But some believers came forward and declared, They must be circumcised; we must call upon them to keep the law of Moses. When the apostles and presbyters assembled to decide about this matter there was much disputing over it, *until Peter rose and* said to them . . .Thereupon it was *resolved by the apostles and presbyters,* with the agreement of the *whole church,* to choose out some of their number and despatch them to Antioch with Paul and Barnabas. . . . It is the Holy Spirit's pleasure and ours that no burden should be laid upon you beyond these . . . (Acts 15, 1–35).

Note how the Christians at Antioch referred their question to the *Apostles and presbyters* of the central Church. When their representatives arrived at Jerusalem, they were *welcomed by the*

Church and by the Apostles and presbyters. Evidently, the members of the Church as well as its leaders were well known and united.

The dispute continued *until Peter rose.* Following Peter's directions, the Apostles made a law for Gentile converts. Thus, as the recognized leaders of the Church, the Apostles governed it.

Obviously, Peter was the leader of the Apostles. In this chapter, we do not intend to discuss how it was possible for him to be the undisputed leader despite his threefold denial and his poor education. But we merely note the fact that Peter directed the election of a successor to Judas; that he preached the first sermons before the Jews; that he judged Ananias and Saphira; that his word was final at Jerusalem.[19] In other words, the Apostles governed the Church under the leadership of Peter.[20]

Indeed, the apostolic Church appeared as exclusive and authoritative as the Catholic Church seems today. Thus, St. Paul declared:

Friends, though it were an angel from heaven that should preach to you a gospel other than the gospel we preached to you, a curse upon him! I repeat now the warning we gave you before it happened, if anyone preaches to you what is contrary to the tradition you received, a curse upon him (Gal. 1, 8–10)!

Again, St. Paul told Titus: "Give a heretic one warning, then a second, and after that avoid his company; his is a perverse nature, thou mayest be sure . . ." (Titus 3, 11).

In his first epistle to the Corinthians, St. Paul instructed them to expel habitual sinners from their company.

Why, there are reports of incontinence among you, and such incontinence as is not practiced even among the heathen; a man taking to himself his father's wife. And you, it seems, have been contumacious over it, instead of deploring it and expelling the man who has been guilty of such a deed from your company. . . . Call an assembly, at which I will be present in spirit, with all the power of our Lord Jesus Christ, and so, in the name of our Lord Jesus Christ, hand over the person named to Satan. . . . The other questions I will settle when I come (I Cor. 5, 1–5; 11, 34).

19. Acts 1, 15–16; 2, 14–42; 3, 12–26; 4, 16–20; 5, 1–12; 5, 26–32; 15, 1–35.
20. The nature of this leadership, as already noted, will be discussed in the following section.

Like St. Ignatius and St. Irenaeus, St. Paul insisted on obedience.

Obey those who have charge of you, and yield to their will; they are keeping unwearied watch over your souls, because they know they will have an account to give. See to it that theirs is a grateful task, not a laborious effort; you would gain nothing from that. . . . Greet all those who are in authority and all the saints (Hebrews 13, 17 and 24).

Note how St. Paul instructed the bishops to be real shepherds.

Keep watch, then, over yourselves, and over God's Church, in which the Holy Spirit has made you bishops; you are to be the shepherds of that flock which he won for himself at the price of his own blood (Acts 20, 27–28).

It is possible to quote other passages of Sacred Scripture but it seems unnecessary. From the texts we have quoted, it is clear that the apostolic Church was an organized society. It was composed of rulers and subjects, teachers and taught, working towards the same objective. The members were known, for they were admitted to the Church through the *public rite* of baptism (Acts 2, 41; 11, 48). As a group, they joined in public worship. All of them believed in the same truths of faith. If anyone differed from the *official teachers* of the Church, they were expelled. It is likewise clear that the authority which the Apostles exercised was not one that they usurped nor was it one that had been bestowed upon them by the disciples of Christ. It was an authority that had been granted to them by Christ himself.

B. Evidence from Tradition

1. THE GENERAL COUNCILS

The organization of the early Church is clear from the General Councils. They were composed of bishops from all over the world. These bishops who were the local rulers of the Church were called together to decide questions of faith and morals. When their decisions were approved by the Pope, they were binding on all members of the Church. Thus all the followers of Arius were cut off from the Church by the Council of Nicaea.

In the first five centuries there were four General Councils, held at Nicaea (325), Constantinople (381), Ephesus (431), and Chalcedon (451). Even the canons of these Councils indicate that the early Church was a visible society composed of rulers and subjects, teachers and taught, working together towards the same objective with the same means. The Council of Chalcedon, for example, declared:

Clerics of poor-houses, monasteries and oratories shall remain under the jurisdiction of their respective bishop in each city . . . and shall not indulge in selfwill or rebel against their bishop. Those who dare in any manner transgress this ordinance and refuse submission to their bishop, are if clerics, to incur canonical censure (deposition), if monks or laymen, to be excommunicated.[21]

Evidently, the bishops had *supreme* authority in their respective cities. If a person wished to remain in the Church, he had to obey his bishop. Disobedience led to *expulsion from* the society. But the bishops themselves had to conform to the canons of the Church. Thus the Council of Ephesus decreed:

Similarly in regard to all those who shall aim to undo in any way any decision of this holy council of Ephesus, the holy council decides that if they be bishops or clerics, they are to be expelled from their ranks (deposed); if laics, excommunicated.[22]

Apparently, the whole Church was a strongly knit society under the same authority. The decrees of the Councils of Constantinople and Nicaea confirm this truth. Thus the Council of Nicaea declared:

In regard to those who call themselves Cathari (heretics), should they desire to enter the Catholic and Apostolic Church, this holy and great council decrees that they receive the imposition of hands . . . they must certify in writing that they will accept and follow the teachings of the Catholic and Apostolic Church. . . .[23]

Even these few decrees reveal how well organized the early Church was. Obviously, the Fathers of the Councils did not think the Church was invisible. And the more you study the Councils the more you realize that primitive Christianity was Catholic in every respect. Consider, for example, the attitude of the Council of Chalcedon towards the Pope.

21. The Council of Chalcedon, Canon VIII. Translation by H. J. Schroeder, *The Disciplinary Decrees of the General Councils*, St. Louis (Herder), 1937, p. 97.
22. Council of Ephesus, Canon VI. *Ibid.*, pp. 76–77.
23. Council of Nicaea, Canon VIII. *Ibid.*, p. 34.

Six hundred and thirty bishops were present at the Council. Although the vast majority of them were from the Eastern Empire, they recognized Pope Leo as their head. In a letter to him they declared: "In your representatives you didst take the presidency over the members of the Synod, as the head over the members." [24]

And Pope Leo *acknowledged this fact* when he remarked that "my legates have presided in my place over the Oriental Synod." [25]

Indeed, the papal legate, Paschasinus, declared at the first session of the Council:

We have a commission from the most holy and most apostolic Bishop of Rome, who is head of all Churches, to see that Dioscorus (Archbishop of Alexandria) shall have no seat in the Council, and if he shall venture upon this, that he be expelled.[26]

No bishop questioned the fact that the Bishop of Rome was the *head of all the Churches.* Evidently, it was a truism. Indeed, the Pope objected to Dioscorus because he attempted to hold an Ecumenical Synod "without the consent of the Apostolic See, which had never been done before, and ought never to be done." [27]

As a result, the Archbishop of Alexandria was denied a vote in the Council. This is factual proof of the power of the Pope in the early Church. It reminds one of the attitude of Pope Coelestine towards the Council of Ephesus. In his first letter to it (May 3, 431), Pope Coelestine *assumes* that *all* the bishops will *agree* with *his* decisions.

The (papal) legates are to be present at the transactions of the Synod, and will give effect to that which the Pope has long ago decided with respect to Nestorius, for he does not doubt that the assembled bishops will agree with this.[28]

In other words, the bishops are merely to *confirm* the decision of the Pope. Apparently no bishop questioned his *right to direct the Council.* Indeed, Archbishop Firmus of Caesarea, one of the leading bishops, declared:

24. Quoted in *History of the Councils,* Charles J. Hefele, Edinburgh (Clark), 1883, III, p. 297.
25. *Ibid.,* p. 297.
26. *Ibid.,* p. 298.
27. *Ibid.,* p. 297.
28. *Ibid.,* p. 42.

The former letter of the Apostolic See to Cyril had already contained the sentence and direction respecting the Nestorian question, and they (the assembled bishops) had . . . *only fulfilled this direction,* and pronounced the canonical and apostolical condemnation against Nestorius.[29]

At the second session of the Council of Chalcedon, when the Nicene Creed was read, the bishops exclaimed:

That is the orthodox faith, that we all believe, into that we were baptized, into that we also baptize; thus Cyril taught, thus believes Pope Leo.[30]

In like manner, when another letter from Pope Leo in regard to faith was read, the bishops cried out:

That is the faith of the fathers, that is the faith of the apostles! We all believe thus, the orthodox believe thus! Anathema to him who believes otherwise! Peter has spoken by Leo.[31]

Later, the papal legate, Paschasinus, speaks of Leo as the *Archbishop of all the Churches.*

In the third place, the letter of the most holy man Leo, the Archbishop of all the Churches, who condemned the heresy of Nestorius and Eutyches, shows quite clearly what is the true faith, and this faith the Synod also holds, and allows nothing to be added to it or taken from it.[32]

From these historical facts it should be evident that the early Church was organized as the Catholic Church is today. (At present, we are interested only in organization of the early Church— not in the actual supremacy of the Pope in every age.) Indeed, the Catholic Church alone teaches and rules its members through priests and bishops who are subject to the Pope. It alone speaks and acts like the early Church.

2. The Fathers of the Church

In the works of the Fathers of the Church we also find innumerable passages indicating the organization of the Church in the first few centuries. Since these works are available in both Catholic and non-Catholic translations, we need not go into detail. But let us consider a few passages.

29. *Ibid.,* p. 63.
30. *Ibid.,* p. 316.
31. *Ibid.,* p. 317.
32. *Ibid.,* p. 330.

When St. Ignatius of Antioch was on his way to martyrdom at Rome (107 A.D.), he wrote seven letters to the Christian communities he passed. In his letter to the Trallians, he says:

You must continue, then, to do nothing apart from the bishop. Be obedient, too, to the priests as to the apostles of Jesus Christ. . . . In the same way all should respect the deacons as they would Jesus Christ, just as they respect the bishop as representing the Father and the priests as the council of God and the college of the Apostles. Apart from these there is nothing that can be called a Church.[33]

Evidently bishops and priests are essential to the Church. And the members should respect and obey them just as they would respect and obey our Lord and the Apostles. In his letter to the Ephesians, St. Ignatius repeats the same lesson.

For if the prayer of one or two men has so much force, how much greater is that of the bishop and that of the whole Church. Anyone, therefore, who fails to assemble with the others has already shown his pride and set himself apart. . . . Let us be careful, therefore, not to oppose the bishop, so that we may be obedient to God.[34]

In his letter to the Smyrnaeans, he again emphasizes the dignity and power of the bishop, priests and deacons.

Shun schisms, as the source of troubles. Let all follow the bishop as Jesus Christ, did the Father, and the priests, as you would the Apostles. Reverence the deacons as you would the command of God. Apart from the bishop, let no one perform any of the functions that pertain to the Church. Let that Eucharist be held valid which is offered by the bishop or by one to whom the bishop has committed this charge. Wherever the bishop appears, there let the people be; as wherever Jesus Christ is, there is the Catholic Church.[35]

Note how St. Ignatius in the year 107 *presupposes* that the Church exists as an organized institution in every town he passes. The bishop and priests rule it as representatives of our Lord. The faithful are obliged to obey them in order to remain in the Church. Apparently, St. Ignatius has never heard of an invisible Church.

33. *Letter to the Trallians*, III, 2–3 (PG., 5,677). Translated by G. Walsh, New York (Fathers of the Church Inc.), 1947, pp. 102–103.
34. *Ibid.*, I, 5, p. 89 (PG., 5, 643).
35. *Ibid.*, VI, 8, p. 121 (PG., 5, 714).

The same is true of all the Fathers. Listen to the words of St. Irenaeus:

In every church, all who wish to see the truth may study the tradition of the apostles that is known throughout the world. Indeed, we can name those who were instituted bishops in the (various) churches by the apostles and trace their successors to our own times. . . . And they (the Apostles) wanted these men, who were to be their successors, to be perfect and blameless in every way, for they were committing the government of the Church into their hands.[36]

St. Irenaeus who was taught by St. Polycarp, the disciple of St. John the Apostle, declares that the Apostles instituted bishops to *take their place in the government of the Church*. They *committed the Churches to their care*. In fact, Irenaeus can name the bishops instituted by the Apostles and their successors. He uses "the greatest, the most ancient and the universally known Church founded and organized at Rome by the two most glorious Apostles, Peter and Paul," as an example.[37] Like Ignatius, Irenaeus stresses obedience to the bishops.

Therefore one should obey the presbyters who are the successors of the Apostles. . . . But, as I have already said, we should follow those who retain the doctrine of the Apostles, and who are qualified, with the order of the priesthood, to instruct and correct others privately and publicly.[38]

It is possible to quote many more passages from the Fathers, but it seems unnecessary. All their works testify to the *hierarchical constitution of the Church*.[39] They continually speak of bishops, priests, and deacons as men whom the laity are bound to obey. St. Ignatius, for example, assumes that the Church is an external,

36. St. Irenaeus, *Adversus Haereses*, III, 3, 1–4 (PG., 7, 848–855). Transl. mine. Cf. *ibid.*, IV, 26, 2 (PG., 7, 1053); IV, 33, 8) PG., 7, 1077).
37. *Ibid.*, III, 3, 2 (PG., 7, 848).
38. *Ibid.*, IV, 26, 2–3 (PG., 7, 1053–1054).
39. The great Protestant scholar, Harnack, speaks of the *episcopal organization* of the Church in the second century when the Gnostic heresy sprang up. He writes: "There can be no doubt that the Gnostic propaganda was seriously hindered by that inability to organize and govern Churches which is characteristic of all philosophic systems of religion. The Gnostic organization of schools and mysteries was not able to contend with the episcopal organization of the Churches." Harnack, *History of Dogma*, London (Williams & Norgate), 1894, I (transl. from 3rd German ed.,), 252 n. 1.

organized society. This assumption is the strongest proof, for it means that no one even questions the fact. And St. Ignatius was an immediate successor of the Apostles whom he knew. Evidently, the constitution of the Church did not change over night. The Church of St. Ignatius was a well-organized society because the Apostolic Church was constituted that way, and it was constituted that way by Christ himself, through his bestowal of the power to teach, govern and sanctify upon his apostles. That their successors, the bishops of the Church, exercised this same Christ-given authority is the clear testimony of Tradition.

III. PAPAL AUTHORITY

In this section we seek to prove that Christ bestowed supreme authority upon St. Peter and his successors in the see of Rome. To do so we will again appeal to the evidence from Scripture and Tradition.

A. Evidence from Scripture

In regard to papal supremacy, the most important scriptural passage is found in the sixteenth chapter of St. Matthew's Gospel. Of course, Catholics do not rest their case on it alone. As usual, we study it together with other passages from Scripture and consider how they were understood in the early Church. But we do regard this text as strong evidence in favor of St. Peter's supremacy. On account of its importance, it has been subjected to the most searching criticism.

1. PROMISE OF THE PRIMACY

Then Jesus came into the neighborhood of Caesarea Philippi; and there he asked his disciples, What do men say of the Son of Man? Who do they think he is? Some say John the Baptist, they told him, others Elias, others again, Jeremy or one of the prophets. Jesus said to them, And what of you? Who do you say that I am? Then Simon Peter answered, Thou art the Christ, the Son of the living God. And Jesus answered him, Blessed art thou, Simon son of Jona; it is not flesh and blood, it is my Father in heaven that has revealed this to thee. And I tell thee this in my turn, that thou art Peter, and it is upon this rock that I will build my church; and the gates of hell shall not prevail against it; and I will give to thee the keys of the kingdom of heaven; and whatever thou shalt bind on earth shall be bound in heaven, and whatever thou shalt loose on earth shall be loosed in heaven (Matthew 16, 13–19).

There are three metaphors in this passage, namely,

a) the metaphor of the rock,
b) the metaphor of the keys, and
c) the metaphor of the ropes (binding and loosing).

In order to understand our Lord's meaning we should consider each one carefully.

a. Metaphor of the Rock

"Thou art Peter, and it is upon this rock that I will build my Church."

Here Christ speaks to Peter alone and speaks of Peter alone in a figurative way.

Without a doubt, the English translation weakens the force of the passage. The new name, Peter, which Christ gives to Simon, son of Jona, is the Greek word for rock ($\pi\acute{\epsilon}\tau\rho\sigma$). In Aramaic, the word for Peter is *Kepha* which means rock. Thus the sense of the passage is: "Your name is Rock, and it is upon this Rock I will build my Church." In other words, Christ plays on the two words, rock and church.

We may put the argument in syllogistic form like this:

What a rock foundation is to a church in the material order, so Peter is to the whole group of the faithful or the church in the social order.

But the natural foundation is the ultimate and basic principle in the material order for the coherence and stability of the church.[40]

Therefore, Peter in the social order is the ultimate and basic principle of union and stability for the universal Church of Christ.[41]

40. In the Sermon on the Mount, our Lord contrasts the wisdom of one man who built his house upon rock with the foolishness of another who built his house upon sand (Matt. 7, 24–27; Luke 6, 18). Evidently, Christ is building his church upon a rock so that it will perdure.

41. In every society, the real principle of union and stability is authority. Peter, as the foundation upon which the unity and stability of the church depends, must have authority. Obviously, this does not lessen the authority of Christ, for he merely delegates power to Peter who in Christ's name and by his authority presides over the church on earth. Christ, therefore, remains the ultimate and divine principle of its stability, the font of all authority. The authority of Peter, as visible head of the church, is participated and exercised in union with Christ (Ephesians 2, 20–22).

b. Metaphor of the Keys

"I will give thee the keys of the kingdom of heaven." Evidently, the keys are a symbol of authority.[42] They are natural signs for designating power or authority for whoever has charge of the keys, has charge (i.e. *authority*) over the place that is locked, that the keys open.

When Christ designated Peter as the rock upon which he would build his Church, he indicated that Peter would be the central authority in his Church. By this second metaphor, Christ reemphasizes the authority of Peter. He gives him the keys to the very kingdom of heaven. And he places no limitation on his power as the next metaphor reveals. It does not make any difference whether Christ meant the Church on earth or the heavenly kingdom by the phrase, "kingdom of heaven." In either case, he gives Peter supreme authority.

c. Metaphor of the "Ropes"

"Whatever thou shalt bind on earth shall be bound in heaven, and whatever thou shalt loose on earth shall be loosed in heaven."

In Rabbinical law, the Jews often used the words, "bind" and "loose." They are literal translations of the Hebrew words, "asar" meaning to bind in the sense of prohibiting, and "hittir" which means to loose in the sense of permitting. "Asar" and "hittir" represented legislative powers to the rabbis. Hence Peter is given the power of obliging to or dismissing from a moral obligation.

This metaphor completes the text by showing the practical effects of Peter's supreme power. His power is practically unlimited, for *whatever* Peter binds or looses on earth, Christ will ratify in heaven. In other words, our Lord will approve what Peter does.

"And the gates of hell shall not prevail against it." This parenthetical phrase signifies that "it" will be *perpetual*. But to what does "it" refer? According to grammatical rules "it" refers to "church" for church comes after the noun, rock. Moreover, the object of siege would be the edifice, not merely the foundation. "Gates" is a symbolic word meaning "powers." At the time of Christ, "hell" meant either the place of the dead where the spirits of men dwell after this life or the place of the damned. It does

42. In Sacred Scripture, "keys" are often used as symbols of power. Cf. Isaias 22, 22; Apoc. 1, 18; 3, 7.

not matter how "hell" is understood here since in either case the Church is shown to be perpetual. If "hell" connotes the place of the dead, then the phrase means that death will not prevail against the Church. If "hell" signifies "the place of the reprobate," then the phrase means that diabolical powers will not prevail against it. Hence the Church will be perpetual.

Now, that the Church is perennial is due to its foundation (cf. Matt. 7, 24–27). Christ explicitly says: "It is upon this rock that I will build my Church; and (i.e., therefore) the gates of hell shall not prevail. . . ." Otherwise the parenthetical phrase is not logically connected with what goes before. Peter, therefore, must exist as long as the Church, that is, perpetually. But Christ himself foretold Peter's death (John 21, 18–19). Thus we must conclude that our Lord speaks, not of Peter personally, but of the office he holds. Peter will ever live and rule in his successors.

If the sense of this passage is so clear, you may wonder why non-Catholic scholars do not agree with its exegesis.[43] As a matter of fact, many of them do. In the last hundred years, many non-Catholic scholars have rejected the interpretations of Calvin and Luther.

According to Calvin, Christ said: "You are Peter (and then pointed to himself, and said) and upon this rock (i.e., myself) I will build my church." [44]

In Luther's opinion, the faith of Peter was the rock to which Christ referred. Our Lord really meant that the Church is built upon the faith of Christians. Other Protestants suggested that the confession of Peter was the rock upon which Christ intended to build his Church.

In recent years, leading Protestant scholars have rejected these interpretations. Dr. Henrich Holtzmann, for example, who was a

43. Most Protestants never consider the passage. A Methodist minister admitted that he never thought of it in relation to the Pope.

44. To justify this interpretation Calvinists point out that Christ is often spoken of as a rock in Scripture. We agree that during his life on earth, Christ had the titles of Rock, Keybearer, Teacher, and Shepherd. Then the Christian body consisted of a visible head (Christ), subsidiary teachers (the apostles) and the rank and file. But before his death Christ conferred those titles on Peter who was to take his place as visible head on earth. (Matt. 16, 18; Luke 22, 31; John 21) Thus the outline of his Church is preserved: the visible head (Peter, representing Christ), the subsidiary teachers, and the rank and file. Cf. Ward & Sheed, *op. cit.,* p. 101.

Lutheran professor of Scripture at Strasbourg, commenting on this text said:

In the Aramaic original in both places the word employed was *kepha;* but in the Greek when the metaphor is applied to the person of Peter (and on this point the interpretation of Catholic exegetes must be accepted without qualification, in reference to the traditional Protestant exegesis which explains the Rock as Peter's faith or confession) on the first occasion the masculine form is necessarily used, though for this reason it is employed also as an appellation. The same man (Peter) who just now was brought before us as the foundation of the building appears in verse 19 as the steward (see Zacharias 12, 42) and keybearer in the house when it has been built, like Jesus Himself in the house of His father (Apoc. 3, 7). When Christ is no longer present in person, Peter will exercise the supreme authority as steward and master of the house, symbolized by the keys which open and shut (Is. 22, 22).

The ecclesiastical spirit expressed throughout this entire *pericope* is specifically Catholic, as is shown by the identification of the concepts Church (verse 18) and *Kingdom of Heaven* (verse 19).[45]

Note how Dr. Holtzmann accepted the Catholic exegesis of this passage. Another commentator on the New Testament who was admired by many Protestants was August Meyer. He was a prominent Lutheran professor and minister for over forty years. His works have been re-edited by Dr. Bernard Weiss who is also a Lutheran minister. In regard to this passage, Meyer and Weiss say:

The expedient to which anti-Roman controversialists so frequently have recourse, to explain the Rock as meaning not Peter himself but his firm faith and its confession (so Luther, Melancthon, Calov, Ewald, Zauge, Wiesehr, Keil) is inadmissible, since the allusion to "this Rock" following as it does the words "thou art a Rock" can refer only to the Apostle himself, as also the succeeding words, "I will give thee. . . ." [46]

When they discuss the second metaphor, Meyer and Weiss say:

In reference to Peter, however, the metaphor shifts, inasmuch as it changes from that of a foundation-rock, not indeed to the inferior metaphor of a porter but (Luke 12, 42; I Cor. 4, 1 and 9, 17; Titus 1, 7)

45. Heinrich Holtzmann as quoted by Friedrich von Hugel in his book, *Some Notes on the Petrine Claims*, London (Sheed & Ward), 1930, pp. 25–26.

46. *Ibid.*, pp. 21–22.

to that of the steward, expressing no longer the constant relation of the Apostle to the Church but the future authority which was its consequence. It is the authority of the steward who is entrusted with the supreme charge and supervision of the economy of the household, and possesses full powers of administration in it, symbolized by the keys of the house (Isaiah 22, 22; Apoc. 3, 7). To this authority belongs beyond all doubt the right mentioned in these passages to open and shut.[47]

It is possible to quote many more Protestant scholars to the same effect.[48] Since they reject the old interpretations of Calvin and Luther, it is hardly necessary for us to refute them. Calvin's interpretation demands that we read a good deal into the text. If it were true, St. Matthew did not mean what he said. The same objection is made against Luther's interpretation. If Christ intended to establish his Church on the faith of all Christians, why did he not say so? Apparently, Luther and Calvin did not want to admit the truth because of the consequences.

Although their modern disciples admit the Catholic interpretation of this text is correct, most of them deny that the passage itself is a genuine part of St. Matthew's Gospel. They regard it as an interpolation. Of course, the Liberal Protestants are noted for "discovering" interpolations. It is one of their weaknesses. But there are signs of improvement. Fifty years ago they rejected all four gospels as non-historical. Now they merely reject those passages which displease them.

But according to the principles of historical criticism, no part of an historical document may be rejected unless it is proven erroneous. Consequently the *burden of proof lies with the Liberal Protestants.* Most of them, however, deny the genuineness of this passage merely because the other Evangelists, although they record the scene, do not mention the words of Christ conferring the primacy on Peter. Without a doubt that is an important omission but is it a sufficient reason to doubt the genuineness of the text in St. Matthew? We do not think so for a number of reasons.

First of all, all existing codices of St. Matthew's Gospel and all translations, with one exception, contain the passage in question. The one exception is the *Syrus Synaiticus.* This exception causes

47. *Ibid.,* pp. 22–23.
48. Cf. *ibid.,* p. 30 and Lebreton, *Life and Teaching of Jesus Christ,* I, London (Burns, Oates and Washbourne), 1935, 355–356.

no difficulty because the whole page on which this passage occurs is missing from the manuscript.

Secondly, there is no speck of evidence indicating that the passage was an interpolation.[49] In the sixth chapter, we proved that any substantial change in the Gospels was impossible. Since the people knew the Scriptures by heart and reverenced them as God's words, they were opposed to any change. St. Augustine tells us how the people of Oea objected vehemently when St. Jerome's new translation was read in their church because he changed one word in the Book of Jonas. If they detected even an incidental change in the Old Testament, how would it have been possible to add a whole new passage with great significance to the New Testament.[50] Above all, how could this have been done without arousing any controversy? But there is no record of any controversy.

Finally, do you think the other bishops would permit the bishop of Rome to assume supremacy contrary to the intentions of Christ without even protesting? Being human the bishops are jealous of their prerogatives. History recounts many quarrels between bishops over matters of far less importance. At the Council of Nicaea (325), for example, the archbishops of Jerusalem and Caesarea fought over the right of precedence. Yet there is no indication that anyone in the early Church questioned the supremacy of the bishop of Rome. On the contrary, all the evidence indicates that other bishops acknowledged his supremacy from the beginning.[51]

There is, then, no reason for doubting the genuineness of this passage. The difficulty is not to explain its presence in Matthew, but to account for its absence in Mark and Luke. This is a problem for scriptural scholars.[52] It has no bearing on the proof. Cer-

---

49. "There is not a passage in the whole of the four gospels which is more clearly Aramaic in terms, metaphors, and construction." Lagrange, *op. cit.*, I, 262.

50. If the text was added in the second century, it would have certainly alluded to St. Peter's successors.

51. Although St. Irenaeus, for example, urged Pope Victor (190 A.D.) not to excommunicate some Greek bishops, he never questioned his power to do so.

52. Perhaps a study of the text itself furnishes, at least, a partial explanation. Evidently, its full significance cannot be grasped unless a person knows the meaning of several key Aramaic words. Since Matthew wrote to Jews, he could quote these words of our Lord and feel sure of being understood.

tainly, the silence of Mark and Luke does not weaken the testimony of Matthew unless it is proven that they should have cited these words. But this cannot be shown.

Indeed, St. Luke relates how Christ foretold the important role Peter would play despite his coming fall.

And the Lord said, Simon, Simon, behold Satan has claimed power over you all, so that he can sift you like wheat; but I have prayed for thee, that thy faith may not fail; when, after a while, thou hast come back to me, it is for thee to be the support of thy brethren (Luke 22, 31–32).

This is the only record we have of Christ offering prayer for an individual. After his fall and conversion, Peter will become the support of his brethren.[53] His faith will never fail for the Son of God has prayed for him. The Protestant scholars, Meyer and Weiss, comment:

'That thy faith fail not': i.e., that thy faith in me may not cease, that thou mayest not become unbelieving and fall away from me. Jesus knew this prayer had been heard despite the temporary lapse of the denial, whose occurrence He equally foreknew. That is why He continues: 'and thou (thou, the counterpart of I), once converted, confirm thy brethren (thy fellow-disciples) be their support and strengthen them when their faith wavers.' [54]

2. The Bestowal of the Primacy

And when they had eaten, Jesus said to Simon Peter, Simon, son of John, dost thou care for me more than these others? Yes, Lord, he told him, thou knowest well that I love thee. And he said to him, Feed my lambs. And again, a second time, he asked him, Simon, son of John, dost thou care for me? Yes, Lord, he told him, thou knowest well that I love thee. He said to him, Feed my lambs. Then he asked him a third

---

But Mark and Luke who wrote to Greeks apparently judged it better to omit the words lest they confuse their readers. As we shall see, Luke puts over the same idea in a different way (Luke 22; 31–32). Professor Cuthbert H. Turner, a Protestant, in an article in *Theology* (Aug., 1926) attributes St. Mark's silence to Peter's humility. Speaking of the four gospels as a whole, he says: "What impresses me more than anything else is the convergence of the testimony of these four documents in the prerogative position allotted to St. Peter."

53. Note how our Lord once again warns the Apostles of the power of Satan (gates of hell) and promises them security through Peter (upon this rock).

54. Hugel, *op. cit.*, p. 27.

question, Simon, son of John, dost thou love me? Peter took it ill that he should ask him a third time, Dost thou love me? and said to him, Lord, thou knowest all things; thou canst tell that I love thee. Jesus said to him, Feed my sheep (John 21, 15–17).

This episode took place in Galilee after the resurrection of our Lord. Without a doubt, it was a magnificent reparation on Peter's part for his threefold denial of Christ. But it was far more, for our Lord not only forgives Peter but makes him universal shepherd in his stead.[55]

Previously, Christ had referred to himself as the Good Shepherd; to his followers as his sheep (John 10, 1–11). Now he hands over to Peter the care of his whole flock. Peter must take his place as pastor of all the lambs and sheep.[56]

At Caesarea Philippi Christ designated Peter as the rock upon which he would build his Church; the steward who would have charge of the house of God. Now he bestows that supreme authority upon Peter. Since Christ will shortly ascend into heaven, he names Peter to take his place on earth.

The obvious literal sense of the three passages of Scripture which we have been discussing is that Christ gave Peter supreme authority over his Church. Any other interpretation demands that we read something into the words of our Lord; that he does not mean exactly what he says. Moreover, any other interpretation is faced with the problem of explaining how (and why) St. Peter or, at least, one of his immediate successors *assumed* supremacy *contrary* to the intentions of our Lord.

55. Most Liberal Protestant scholars agree with the Catholic interpretation of this passage. But they deny its historicity. Their "reasons" for rejecting it are no better than their "reasons" for rejecting the passage from Matthew. Until they offer proofs, we shall reject their doubts as unreasonable since the passage is an integral part of a proven historical document.

56. In the Old Testament, the leaders of the people are often called shepherds (I Par. 17, 6; II Kings 5, 2; Jer. 2, 8). Of course, the supreme shepherd of the Jewish people is God (Ps. 22, 1; 79, 1; Is. 40, 11; Jer. 31, 10). The Messiah, whom God promises to send the Jews, will be the prince of shepherds (Jer. 23, 1–8; Ezechiel 34, 1–31). Christ pictures himself as the Good Shepherd (John 10, 1–18). Before his ascension, Christ puts his flock under the care of Peter (John 21, 15–17). Of course, Christ continues to be the owner of the flock and the supreme shepherd ("Feed *my* sheep." John 10, 27–29). Thus Peter calls our Lord the Prince of shepherds in his first epistle (I Peter 5, 4; 2, 25).

3. EXERCISE OF THE PRIMACY

The Gospels indicate Peter's position in relation to the other Apostles. When the Evangelists list the Apostles, for example, they name Peter first though he was not the Beloved Disciple nor the best educated. Often they refer to "Peter and the other apostles" or "Peter and the twelve" (Mark 16, 7). Peter's name occurs in some sixty passages scattered over the four Gospels. No other Apostle is mentioned more than twenty-five times. St. Luke notes that after the resurrection Christ appears to Peter before he appears to the other Apostles (Luke 24, 35).

In the *Acts of the Apostles,* we read how St. Peter on five important occasions acted as head of the apostolic Church. 1) In the presence of all the Apostles, Peter directs the election of a successor to Judas (Acts 1, 15–26). 2) After the descent of the Holy Spirit, Peter preaches the first sermons (Acts 2, 14; 3, 12; 3, 8; 5, 29). 3) He alone judges and punishes Ananias and Saphira (Acts 5). 4) As a result of divine revelation, he leads the way in the admission of Gentiles into the Church (Acts 10 and 11). 5) At the Council of Jerusalem there was much disputing over the admission of Gentiles to the Church until Peter spoke in favor of it (Acts 15).

So long as the Apostles remained together in Jerusalem, Peter's supremacy was manifested on every important occasion.[57] His right to act as supreme ruler was never questioned by the other Apostles.[58] Evidently, they understood the words of our Lord in their literal sense.

57. "There are in Westcott and Hort's edition of the New Testatment, 1027 lines in the first twelve chapters of Acts: of these 622 relate what was done and said by Peter, including 197 devoted to the single episode of the conversion of Cornelius." Dr. Foakes Jackson as quoted by Selden P. Delany, *Why Rome,* New York (The Dial Press), 1930, p. 130.

58. Sometimes non-Catholics mention St. Paul as an exception. Paul wrote: "But when Cephas (Peter) came to Antioch, I withstood him to his face, because he was deserving of blame. He had been eating with the Gentiles, until we were visited by certain persons from James; but when they came, he began to withdraw and to separate himself, fearing the circumcised. And the rest of the Jews dissembled with him . . ." (Gal. 2, 11–13). Certainly, Peter taught that the Mosaic laws no longer bound Christians (Acts 15, 7–10, 28–29). Yet in this case, Peter obviously did not practice what he preached. Perhaps he hoped to avoid an unpleasant scene. Paul himself had circumcised Timothy to avoid needless trouble (Acts 16, 3). When Paul, however, saw the other

Today many non-Catholics are disposed to admit that Peter was the supreme ruler and teacher of the apostolic Church.[59] But they ask,—did it pass on from him to the Bishops of Rome? "To which our most natural answer is," as Ronald Knox says, "If not to them, to whom?" [60] Surely the promises Christ made to Peter are out of all proportion to the role Peter *personally* played.

When we commented on the passage in St. Matthew's Gospel, we noted that since Peter is the foundation of the Church, he must exist as long as the Church, that is perpetually. Since Christ foretold Peter's death, he evidently meant that Peter would live and rule in his successors. His office would be perennial.

Moreover, does it seem reasonable that Christ would establish a Church, that would last to the end of the world, with a form of government that would change within fifty years? Certainly, there is no evidence to support that opinion. Indeed, if a visible authority was necessary when the Church was small, it would be still more so with the growth of the Church and the passage of time.

Jewish Christians and even Barnabas following Peter's example, he feared the consequences. And so Paul reprimanded Peter for his actions. Though Paul censured Peter's conduct, he never questioned his authority.

Indeed, Paul seems conscious of the gravity of his action. Do you think Paul would have mentioned it if he had merely corrected another apostle? It seems not for if one brother rebukes another, it causes no comment. But if a bishop rebukes the Pope, it is extraordinary. Thus when Paul mentions that he criticized Peter's conduct, he leaves us with the inference that Peter was his superior. We also get that impression when Paul mentions how, after his conversion, he had gone to Jerusalem to visit Peter alone (Gal. 1, 18).

59. The old Protestant contention that Peter never went to Rome has been abandoned. The critical Protestant scholar, Bishop Lightfoot, considered it a proven fact that Peter went to Rome and was martyred there. Harnack wrote: "No community in the Empire could regard with indifference its relationship to the great Roman Church; almost everyone had connections with her; she contained believers from all the rest. As early as 180 this Church could point to a series of bishops reaching in uninterrupted succession from the glorious apostles Paul and Peter down to the present time . . . she decided all questions of faith with admirable certainty. . . . It is highly probable that Peter was really in Rome like Paul (see Clem. V., Ign. ad Rom. IV.); both really performed important services to the Church there, and died as martyrs in that city." *History of Dogma,* London (Williams & Norgate), 1896, II (2nd transl. ed. from 3rd German ed.), 159, and n. 1.

60. Knox, *op. cit.,* p. 160. As we shall see, the early churches jealously kept the record of their spiritual pedigrees. The Roman bishops traced their pedigree back to Peter. Certainly, the Antiochene bishops never contested this.

Finally, all the evidence at our disposal indicates that the successors of St. Peter exercised supreme authority and their authority was acknowledged by the vast majority of bishops and Christians.

B. Evidence from Tradition

At the present time, non-Catholic scholars have practically given up their attempts to prove that the immediate successors of St. Peter did not exercise supreme authority over the Church. The evidence is too clear and abundant. Certainly, no non-Catholic scholar will question the fact that papal supremacy was universally acknowledged after the fifth century. But in the past, some have denied that the Christians of the first centuries admitted the supremacy of the Pope. Because this old error still perdures, we should devote some attention to it.

In this matter, we must be on guard against judging according to our feelings or prejudices. In the past some Catholic authors have been too intent on proving their point—arguing from one or two quotations rather than from the whole tradition. We hope to avoid this error. Since the value of evidence increases as it is multiplied, we will consider many texts. Then we will draw our conclusion, *not from one text,* but from all of them put together.

On the other hand, some non-Catholic scholars seem more intent on explaining away passages favorable to papal supremacy than explaining them. When one of the Fathers, for example, addresses the Pope in words that state or imply his supremacy, they conclude it was only a polite compliment. Obviously, this is an easy means of discounting texts. Maybe in a few years they will tell us that the Vatican Council merely intended to compliment Pius IX when they defined the infallibility of the Pope. Surely we must hold that an intelligent man means what he says—especially when he uses expressions with definite implications—unless the contrary can be proven. To dismiss a statement with which you disagree by declaring the author did not mean what he said is puerile.

Naturally we do not expect to find numerous proofs of papal supremacy in the first few centuries. First of all, the early churches founded by the Apostles offered few occasions for the exercise of papal supremacy. Secondly, since the Church was subjected to recurrent persecutions, communication with the Pope was difficult. Thirdly, there are relatively few documents of that period still extant.

Before we examine the documents, we should note an important distinction. If a non-Catholic could *prove* that the early Christians believed some article of faith, the contrary of what we believe now, or at least, logically incompatible with our belief, that would destroy our faith since we maintain that faith does not change. But if we cannot prove that the first Christians believed what we believe now, it is not at all logical to conclude that our beliefs differ from theirs.

Suppose, for the sake of argument, that we could find no statement of any kind about some dogma. This would not affect our faith. It would simply mean that there is no proof, either for or against the dogma, in the given period. We should still accept it for we believe the Church has always been guided by the Holy Spirit.[61]

All the fundamental institutions and doctrines of the Church existed in the practice and teaching of the Church from the beginning, but not as explicitly and completely, as in the course of time. The apostolic Fathers did not intend to give a comprehensive coverage of dogma. The doctrine of the Trinity, for example, was not treated explicitly by any Father until the fourth century.

We have labored this point because people so often confuse not saying a thing is true with saying it is not true. Happily we have a good deal of historical evidence indicating that the Catholic Church in the first five centuries did believe what we believe about the papacy. And no non-Catholic scholar questions the fact that after the fifth century it was the common belief of Christendom.

In regard to the supremacy of the Bishop of Rome in the first five centuries, we have two sources of evidence: the works of the Fathers of the Church, and the decisions of the Councils. Often the Fathers and Councils state or imply his supremacy. Indeed, they mention cases where his jurisdiction was used, where a Pope decides a question and his decision is accepted, in such a way that they can be understood only on the supposition that his universal jurisdiction was admitted by all Christians. Let us consider some of the better examples of each.

61. Cf. Fortescue, *op. cit.,* p. 9.

1. Works of the Fathers

In the works of the Fathers who lived prior to the sixth century [62] we find many indications of the power of the Bishop of Rome.[63]

a. The Letter to the Corinthians

The first case is astounding unless we see in it the Providence of God, who intends that we should have a clear example of the Pope's universal jurisdiction before the year 100. It is, of course, the famous letter of St. Clement to the Corinthians. Near the end of the first century, the Christians of Corinth rebelled against their hierarchy.[64] Thereupon "the Church of God dwelling at Rome" wrote to the "Church of God dwelling at Corinth." Most authorities agree that "the Church of God dwelling at Rome" means the authority of that Church, that is, its bishop. In fact, authors of the second and third centuries attribute the letter to Clement, Bishop of Rome.[65]

In the letter Clement does not merely counsel the Corinthians to be obedient to their hierarchy; he *commands* them. He writes: "But, if some shall disobey the words which have been spoken by him (God) through us, let them know that they will involve themselves in no small transgression and danger." [66]

Again, he states: "For you will afford us joy and gladness if you obey what we have written through the Holy Spirit. . . . We have done this in order that you may know our entire preoccupa-

62. Most Christians admit the orthodoxy of the Fathers of the Church in the first five centuries. Seldom have any Christians doubted the faith of such saints as Clement, Ignatius, Cyprian, Jerome, and Augustine.

63. Belloc says: "All Church history is full of Roman Primacy from the moment when church history becomes open to detailed examination. . . . If you would call it corruption, you must put the origin of that corruption very early; indeed, you will be compelled to put it within the lifetime of those who had talked familiarly with the Apostles and knew their mind and all the tradition of the very beginnings of the Church." *The Catholic Church and History*, London (Burns, Oates, & Washbourne), 1930, p. 44.

64. Harnack, Funk, Bardenhewer, Lightfoot, Hilgenfeld, and many other scholars date the letter about the year 96.

65. Irenaeus, *Adversus Haereses*, III, 3, 3; Hegesippus (Eusebius, *Historia Ecclesiae*, IV, 22, 1); Dionysius Corinth. (*ibid.*, IV, 23, 9); Hieronymus, *De Viris Illustribus*, 15.

66. Clement, *The Letter to the Corinthians*, 59, 1.

tion has been and remains that you may quickly achieve peace." [67]

What are the implications of this letter? The Bishop of Rome sends categorical orders to Christians in Greece. In those days of sailing boats, Corinth seemed to be on the other side of the world. Yet the Bishop of Rome reminds them that disobedience of his commands would be sinful. Does Pius XII claim any more authority over any diocese? Now the "Pope" who wrote this letter "saw the Apostles themselves and lived with them." [68] When Clement wrote this letter, it is probable that one of the Apostles, St. John, was still alive at Ephesus. Yet it was not St. John but the Bishop of Rome who feels obliged to correct the abuses.[69] Does this not mean that the Bishop of Rome had the care of all the churches.[70]

There is no evidence that the Corinthians questioned Clement's jurisdiction. On the contrary, the letter was praised and quoted as an admirable document.[71] Imagine how Protestants would react to such a letter. Apparently, the Corinthians were Catholics. Order was restored in the Church.[72]

b. The Letters of St. Ignatius

Another indication of the position of the Bishop of Rome comes from the pen of the great martyr-bishop, St. Ignatius of Antioch. When he was on his way to martyrdom at Rome (107 A.D.) he wrote seven letters. In his letter to the Romans he speaks

67. *Ibid.*, 63, 2–4.

68. Irenaeus, *op. cit.*, III, 3, 3.

69. Clement, *op. cit.*, I. 1.

70. Harnack wrote: "That letter to the Corinthians proves that, by the end of the first century, the Roman Church had already drawn up fixed rules for her own guidance, that she watched with motherly care over outlying communities, and that she then knew how to use language that was at once an expression of duty, love, and authority." *Op. cit.*, II, 155.

71. St. Irenaeus describes it as "a most powerful letter to the Corinthians exhorting them to peace, renewing their faith, and declaring the tradition which the Church in Rome had received from the apostles. . . ." (*Op. cit.*, III, 3, 3). Bishop Dionysius of Corinth mentions (a. 170 A.D.) that it was still read during divine worship. Harnack said: "Bishop Dionysius of Corinth in his letter to Bishop Soter (166–174), affords us a glimpse of the vast activity manifested by the Christian Church of the world's metropolis on behalf of all Christendom and of all brethren far and near; and reveals the feelings of filial affection and veneration with which she was regarded in all Greece as well as in Antioch." *Op. cit.*, II, 156–57.

72. Hegesippus as quoted in *History of the Church* by Eusebius, 22, 2.

of their church with the utmost respect as "the president of the bond of love." A noted Protestant scholar, Harnack, concluded:

Soften as we may all the extravagant expressions in his Epistle to the Romans, it is at least clear that Ignatius conceded to them a precedence in the circle of sister Churches; and that he was well acquainted with the energy and activity displayed by them in aiding and instructing other communities. . . . Lastly, Ignatius is convinced that the Church will interfere quite as energetically on behalf of a foreign brother as on behalf of one of her own number.[73]

The non-Catholic historians, Shotwell and Loomis, think that to this Eastern bishop the Roman church appears "to stand on a level somewhat above that of the others to which he writes." [74]

c. The Easter Question

Towards the end of the second century, we have another good example of the power of the bishops of Rome. When the bishops of Asia Minor refused to conform to the universal custom of celebrating Easter on Sunday every year, Victor I (189–199) threatened to excommunicate them. St. Irenaeus, the bishop of Lyons and others, however, protested because they thought the penalty was too severe for the fault. As a result, Victor never published the excommunication or he withdrew it at once. But no one even suggested that Victor could not do what he threatened.

Obviously, Victor was claiming real jurisdiction over the Christians in Asia Minor. Though some bishops thought he was too severe, they never questioned his claim. In regard to Victor's action, Harnack wrote:

Victor ventured to issue an edict, which we may already style a peremptory one, proclaiming the Roman practice with regard to the regulation of ecclesiastical festivals to be the universal rule in the Church, and declaring that every congregation, that failed to adopt the Roman arrangement, was excluded from the union of the one Church on the grounds of heresy. How would Victor have ventured on such an edict . . . unless the special prerogative of Rome to determine the conditions of the "common unity" in the vital questions of the faith had been an acknowledged and well-established fact? How could Victor have addressed such a demand to the independent Churches, if he had not been

73. Harnack, *op. cit.,* II, 156 and n. 3.
74. Shotwell and Loomis, *The See of Peter,* New York (Columbia Univ. Press), 1927, p. 239.

recognised, in his capacity of bishop of Rome, as the special guardian of the "common unity."[75]

d. The Testimony of St. Irenaeus

The testimony of St. Irenaeus (125–202), who was Bishop of Lyons in France, is well-known. Irenaeus was a Greek who had been taught by St. Polycarp, the pupil of St. John the Apostle. In his book, *Against Heretics,* Irenaeus speaks of the Roman Church as "the very great, the very ancient, and universally known Church founded and organized at Rome by the two most glorious Apostles, Peter and Paul." Then he states: "For because of its pre-eminent authority, every church . . . must agree with this church. . . ."[76]

It has been extremely difficult for Protestant scholars to explain the meaning of these statements of St. Irenaeus.[77] Apparently, St. Irenaeus was a Roman Catholic.

e. Tertullian

In bitter irony, Tertullian, who was a Montanist heretic, speaks of Pope Calixtus (213–222) as "the Supreme Pontiff, that is, the Bishop of bishops."[78] The implication is clear. Tertullian means

75. Harnack, *op. cit.,* II, 160. As Harnack pointed out, Victor in this case "set the authority of Rome against that of Greek apostolic Churches." *Ibid.,* 163, n. 3. In reference to the *Philosoph.* (a. 200 A.D.) of Hippolytus, another Protestant scholar Sohm, remarked: "One cannot help concluding that the Roman bishop has the power of appointing and deposing not merely presbyters and deacons, but also bishops. Moreover, the impression is conveyed that this appointment and deposition of bishops takes place in Rome, for the passage contains a description of existent conditions in the Roman Church. Other communities may be deprived of their bishops by an order from Rome, and a bishop (chosen in Rome) may be sent them." Quoted by Harnack, *ibid.,* I, 162 n. 1.

76. Irenaeus, *Against Heretics,* III, 3, 2. Cf. Batiffol, *Cathedra Petri,* Paris (Cerf), 1938, pp. 36–37.

77. Harnack granted: "The truth rather is that the Roman community *must* have been named, (by way of example), because its decision was already the most authoritative and impressive in Christendom." *Op. cit.,* II, 157.

78. Tertullian, *On Modesty,* I. Harnack said: "The sarcastic titles 'pontifex maximus,' 'episcopus episcoporum' . . . are so many references to the fact that Calixtus already claimed for himself a position of primacy. . . ." *Ibid.,* II, 163. Indeed, Harnack conceded: "Beyond doubt the Roman Church possessed an acknowledged primacy in the year 250; it was the primacy of active participation and fulfilled duty." *Ibid.,* II, 162 note 2.

that the Catholics regard the Bishop of Rome as the Supreme
Pontiff, the Bishop of bishops.

f. St. Cyprian

In the past, some Protestants have spoken of St. Cyprian (210–
258) as if he had been an adversary of papal supremacy.[79] It is
true that Cyprian argued with the Bishop of Rome and even resisted some of his orders. But he also affirmed the supremacy of
Rome in clear and emphatic terms.

As his letters reveal, Cyprian disagreed with papal decisions
on several occasions. When Pope Cornelius, for example, admitted
several of Cyprian's rebellious priests to communion, Cyprian
protested.[80] This, however, was a question of discipline, not of
faith. Cyprian never questions the power of the Pope. Indeed,
he urges Pope Stephen I (254–257) to excommunicate the Bishop
of Arles who was a Novation heretic.[81] This shows that Cyprian
acknowledged the Pope's jurisdiction over even bishops of France.

In regard to the rebaptism of heretics, Cyprian again differed
from the Pope. He maintained that only Catholics could baptize validly. Today all Christians agree that Cyprian was wrong
and Stephen was right.[82] As usual, Rome took the tolerant, reasonable position and opposed strongly just what many Protestants
would suppose to be popish intolerance. Fortunately, the dispute
was settled before Cyprian's glorious death as a martyr. In his

79. Unfortunately, Protestants do not pay much attention to Cyprian's main
point, the necessity of one Church. Harnack admitted: "According to Cyprian,
the Catholic Church, to which all the lofty predictions and predicates in the
Bible apply, is the one institution of salvation outside of which there is no
redemption (ep. 73, 21). She is this, moreover, not only as the community
possessing the true apostolic faith, for this definition does not exhaust her
conception, but as a harmoniously organized federation. This Church therefore rests entirely on the episcopate, which sustains her, because it is the con-
tinuance of the apostolic office and is equipped with all the power of the
Apostles. Accordingly, the union of individuals with the Church, and therefore with Christ, is effected only by obedient dependence on the bishop, i.e.,
such a connection alone makes one a member of the Church." *Ibid.*, II, 85–86.

80. *Ep.* LIX.

81. *Ep.* LXVIII.

82. St. Augustine and St. Jerome regarded Cyprian's views as heretical and
his conduct reprehensible. Of course, they agreed his martyrdom atoned for
his faults. Harnack said: "In his conflict with Stephen, Cyprian unmistakably
took up a position inconsistent with his former views as to the significance of
the Roman see for the Church. . . ." *Op. cit.*, II, 88 note 2.

favor, we must remember that Cyprian never denied papal supremacy. In fact, he affirms it repeatedly. In a letter he writes: "Cornelius was made bishop . . . when the place of Fabian, that is, when the place of Peter and the high degree of the priestly throne was vacant." [83]

For Cyprian the Roman see is the "mother and root of the Catholic Church." [84] In another letter he says that the African schismatics "dare to set sail and bring letters to the throne of Peter and the chief Church, whence priestly unity came forth." [85]

Cyprian knew there is "one Church and one see, founded by the Lord's voice on Peter. No other altar can be set up, no new priesthood made, except the one altar and one priesthood. Whoever gathers elsewhere scatters." [86] There is "one Church founded by Christ our Lord on Peter, by the source and reason of unity." [87]

g. The Patriarchs of Alexandria

In this same century, Pope Denis (259–269) judged the case of Denis, Patriarch of Alexandria. After some members of his diocese denounced him to Rome, the Pope asked his namesake to present his side of the case. Denis of Alexandria did so and was exonerated.[88] Note the implications. If the Bishop of Rome had the right to judge the Patriarch of Alexandria, then all bishops and Christians were subject to him.

Even the great St. Athanasius acknowledged the supreme authority of the Pope. When he and four other bishops were denounced to Pope Julius I (337–352), they went to Rome. "When they had explained their cause to Julius, Bishop of the city of Rome, he sent them back to the East and restored to each his see, as is the prerogative of the Roman Church. . . ." [89]

83. *Ep.* LV, 8.
84. *Ep.* XLIII, 3. Commenting on this phrase, Harnack said that it was an "acknowledged fact that the Roman community was the most distinguished among the sister groups and as such had had and still possessed the right and duty of watching over the unity of the whole." *Ibid.*, II, 165.
85. *Ep.* LIX, 14. Harnack admitted that Cyprian acknowledged the Roman primacy. Cf. *op. cit.*, II, 165.
86. *Ep.* LXVIII, 5.
87. *Ep.* LXX, 3.
88. St. Athanasius, *Ep. de Sent. Dionysi*, 13 (PG., 25, 499).
89. Socrates, *Hist. Eccl.*, II, 15 (PG., 67, 211).

In the fourth century, references to the supreme authority of the Bishop of Rome are more numerous. We will mention only a few of them. If you are interested, books on this subject will give many more.

h. St. Jerome

In a letter to Pope Damasus (366–384) St. Jerome wrote:

I speak with the successor of the fisherman and the disciple of the cross. I, following no one as my chief but Christ, am joined in communion with thy Holiness, that is, with the See of Peter. On this rock I know that the Church is built. Whoever eats the lamb outside this house is profane. Whoever is not in the ark of Noah will perish when the deluge comes.[90]

2. THE COUNCILS OF THE CHURCH

In like manner, the acts and decrees of the local and general Councils of the Church prior to the sixth century can be understood only on the supposition that the bishop of Rome was universally recognized as the supreme ruler of the Church.

a. Council of Milan

The Council of Milan under St. Ambrose applauds Pope Siricus (384–389) for condemning the heretic, Jovinian.

We see in the letter of your Holiness the vigilance of a good shepherd keeping faithfully the gate entrusted to you, watching over the fold of Christ with holy care, worthy that the sheep of the Lord should hear and follow you.[91]

b. Council of Sardica

The Council of Sardica (344) acknowledges the jurisdiction of the Pope over all bishops. It declares that any bishop may appeal to the Pope. If the Pope deems it necessary, he may appoint judges for the trial. The Council declared: "It seemed best and most proper that the bishops from every province should refer to the head, that is to the see of the Apostle Peter." [92]

No one questions the fact that the Council of Sardica recognized the Bishop of Rome as supreme ruler of the Church. And

90. *Ep.* XV, *Ad Damasum,* 2 (PL., 22, 355–356).
91. Ambrose, *Ep.* 42.
92. *Ep. syn. Sard. ad Iul.* (Harduin I, 653).

its decrees became the common law of the Church both in the East and West.

c. General Councils

In chapter nine, we indicated the attitude of the General Councils toward the Bishops of Rome.[93] As we have seen, they recognize him as the unerring teacher and supreme ruler of all the churches. Pope Coelestine, for example, rightfully assumes that all the bishops at the council of Ephesus will agree with his decisions. Nor does anyone object when Philip, the Papal Legate at Ephesus, declares:

There is no doubt, indeed it is known to every age, that the holy and most blessed Peter, prince and head of the apostles, column of faith and foundation of the Catholic Church, received the keys of the kingdom from our Lord Jesus Christ, Saviour and Redeemer of the human race, that to him was given power of forgiving and retaining sins, who to this time lives and judges in his successors.[94]

At the first session of the Council of Chalcedon, the papal legate declared:

We have a commission from the most holy and most apostolic Bishop of Rome, who is the head of all the churches, to see that Dioscorus (Archbishop of Alexandria) shall have no seat in the council, and if he shall venture upon this, that he be expelled.[95]

The Pope objected to Dioscorus because he attempted to hold an Ecumenical Synod "without the consent of the Apostolic see, which has never been done before and ought never to be done." [96]

Although the vast majority of the bishops at the Council were from the East, no one questioned the right of the Roman bishop to judge the archbishop of an apostolic see. Now if the Pope had jurisdiction over the archbishop of Alexandria, he evidently had episcopal jurisdiction over all the members of the Church.

The General Councils were primarily concerned with the con-

93. The seven ecumenical councils were all held in the East and dealt mostly with Eastern heresies. In fact, they were almost like provincial synods of the East for few Western bishops attended them. Non-Catholic scholars find it difficult to explain why legates of the Bishop of Rome presided over all of them.

94. Mansi, IV, 1295.

95. Hefele. *op. cit.*, III, p. 298.

96. *Ibid.*, p. 297.

demnation of heresies that disrupted the Church. They were not concerned with doctrines accepted by all Christians. Consequently, they never discussed the supremacy of the Pope. But repeatedly they acknowledged his supremacy by their words and actions.

V. CONCLUSION

Let us now draw together the elements of the historical proof for the Church's claim to be the one true Church of Christ. Christ, we maintain, established his Church as a visible society, giving it a determinate constitution. He commanded all men to become members of this one Church. Now the only Church that can trace its lineage back to the apostolic Church founded by Jesus Christ is the Roman Catholic Church. Therefore the Roman Catholic Church is the true Church of Christ. Therefore I should be a Roman Catholic.

The attack upon this proof has centered around the statement: Jesus Christ established his Church as a visible society, giving it a determinate constitution. Since authority is the formal element in any visible society, the attack has been focussed above all else upon the question: did or did not Christ himself set up an authority to rule his Church and, if so, what was its nature? We, as Roman Catholics, hold that Jesus Christ did establish an authority to rule his Church; that he gave spiritual authority to the Apostles and their successors; that he conferred supreme authority over the whole Church upon St. Peter and his successors, the bishops of Rome. We have presented sound historical evidence for that position.

CHART OF CATHOLIC EASTERN CHURCHES [1]

CHURCH	WHERE FOUND	NUMBER OF FAITHFUL (Round Numbers)	LITURGICAL LANGUAGE	VERNACULAR LANGUAGE	DATE OF DEFINITIVE SEPARATION OF ORIGINAL CHURCH	DATE OF REUNION OF PRESENT CATHOLIC BODY
ALEXANDRIAN RITE						
1. Copts	Egypt	63,000	Coptic and Arabic	Arabic	451	1741
2. Ethiopians	Ethiopia, Eritrea	30,500	Ge'ez	Amharic, etc.	550	1839
ANTIOCHENE RITE						
1. Syrians	Syria, Irak, U.S.A.	74,500	Syriac and Arabic	Arabic, Syriac	543	1656
2. Maronites	Syria, U.S.A.	391,000	Syriac and Arabic	Arabic	c. 650	1182
3. Malankarese	India	50,000	Syriac and Malayalam	Malayalam	1653	1930
ARMENIAN RITE						
1. Armenians under the patriarch	Syria, Near East	45,000	Classical Armenian	Armenian	c. 525	1198: 1742
2. Other Armenians	Europe, Russia, U.S.A.	100,000 (?)				
BYZANTINE RITE						
1. Bulgars	Bulgaria	5,500	Church Slavonic	Bulgarian	c. 1472	1860
2. Greeks	Greece, Turkey, etc.	3,300	Greek	Greek	c. 1472	1860
3. Hungarian-Ruthenians	Hungary	140,000	Magyar	Magyar	c. 1472	1652
4. Italo-Greek-Albanians	Italy, Sicily, U.S.A.	60,000	Greek	Italian, etc.	Never separated	1724
5. Melkites	Syria, Egypt, U.S.A.	173,000	Arabic	Arabic	c. 1517	1724
6. Rumanians	Rumania, U.S.A.	1,434,000	Rumanian	Rumanian	c. 1472	1701
7. Russians (a) in U.S.S.R.		18,000	Church Slavonic	Russian	c. 1472	1595: 1920
(b) elsewhere	Europe, America, Far East	4,500	Church Slavonic	Russian	c. 1472	1905
8. Ruthenians (a) in U.S.S.R.	Galicia	3,500,000	Church Slavonic	Ukrainian	c. 1472	1595
(b) Podcarpathian	U.S.S.R.	500,000	Church Slavonic	Ukrainian	c. 1472	1652
(c) elsewhere in Europe	Bukovina, "displaced," etc.	250,000	Church Slavonic	Ukrainian		
(d) in the Americas		927,000	Church Slavonic	Ukrainian		
9. Yugoslavs	Yugoslavia	55,000	Church Slavonic	Croat, etc.	c. 1472	1611
CHALDEAN RITE						
1. Chaldeans	Irak, Syria, U.S.A.	96,000	Syriac	Arabic, Syriac	500	1551
2. Malabarese	India	632,000	Syriac	Malayalam	?	Before 1599

1. Reprinted by permission of the Bruce Publishing Company from "The Christian Churches of the East," by Donald Attwater, Copyright, 1935–1937 (Rev. ed.) by the Bruce Publishing Company. The original also gives the chief bishop of each of these churches and his residence.

CHAPTER VII

The Stamp of God's Approval

THE Roman Catholic Church presents a second argument in favor of its claim to be God's official Church here on earth. It is the so-called "empirical" proof. The Vatican Council expressed it in these words: "The Church itself, by reason of its marvelous growth, its eminent holiness and inexhaustible fruitfulness in all good things, by reason of its catholic unity and its unconquered stability, is itself a great and perpetual motive of credibility and an irrefutable witness of its own divine mission." [1]

The empirical proof, therefore, can be presented in argumentative form in this way. That Church is the true Church of God to which he has been giving extraordinary assistance and, doing so, has been guaranteeing its claim to be God's official Church here on earth. But there are five aspects of the life of the Catholic Church which clearly manifest that it has been receiving extraordinary divine assistance, namely, its marvellous growth, its eminent holiness, its inexhaustible fruitfulness in all good things, its catholic unity, and its unconquered stability. Therefore the Catholic Church is God's Church and God himself is guaranteeing its claim. (Note that Christ's name does not enter directly into this proof; the conclusion is that the Roman Catholic Church is *God's* Church.)

The first statement in this proof—That Church is God's Church to which he has been giving extraordinary help and, doing so, has been guaranteeing its claim to be his official Church on

1. Session III, cap. 3—Denz, 1794.

earth—needs no proof. If a particular Church lays claim to be exclusively the true Church of God and if God gives it extraordinary assistance, then certainly he is backing up this claim. But the second statement—But the Roman Catholic Church has been receiving extraordinary divine assistance and, therefore, God himself is guaranteeing its claim—does require proof. Let us examine each of the five aspects of the life of the Roman Catholic Church to which the Vatican Council appealed to justify the claim that it has been receiving extraordinary divine assistance.

I. ITS MARVELLOUS GROWTH

The founding of the Roman Catholic Church was historically a miraculous event. That this is so can be shown from the fact that there was no proportion between the natural causes and the effect produced. An examination of the circumstances under which the Church came into existence and spread rapidly throughout the length and breadth of the then-known world will make this amply clear.

From the Acts of the Apostles and the Epistles we know that after Peter's preaching, following upon Pentecost, first about 3,000 souls,[2] then 5,000 were converted to Christ; and daily "the multitude of men and women who believed in the Lord increased still more."[3] When St. Stephen was stoned to death a persecution of the Christians broke out in Jerusalem and "all except the apostles were scattered abroad throughout the land of Judea and Samaria. . . . Now those who were scattered abroad went about preaching the word."[4] "Now those who had been dispersed by the persecution that had broken out over Stephen, went all the way to Phoenicia and Cyprus and Antioch . . . . and a great number believed and turned to the Lord."[5] Barnabas and Saul were sent to Antioch and taught "a great multitude. And it was in Antioch that the disciples were first called 'Christians.'"[6]

Later the Apostles founded churches throughout the Roman Empire and even beyond its boundaries. Thus, about twenty years after Christ's ascension, Peter was able to write an epistle

2. Acts 2, 41; 4, 4.
3. Acts 5, 14.
4. Acts 8, 1–4.
5. Acts 11, 18–21.
6. Acts 11, 26.

"to the sojourners of the dispersion in Pontus, Galatia, Cappadocia, Asia and Bithynia." [7] About the same time Paul wrote to the Romans: "Your faith has become known to the whole world." [8] About the end of the first century, John wrote his Apocalypse "to the seven churches, to Ephesus, and to Smyrna, and to Pergamum, and to Thyratira, and to Sardis, and to Philadelphia, and to Laodicea." [9] Thus, even during the life of the Apostles, Christianity had spread over a vast area.

After the death of the Apostles, the number of Christians increased so rapidly that by the middle of the second century St. Justin could say that there is no race of men, whether barbarians or Greeks among whom prayers are not offered through the name of the crucified Christ.[10] About the same time, St. Irenaeus testifies to the fact that there were churches in Germany, in Spain, in Gaul, in the East, in Egypt, in Lybia, in Jerusalem, and in Judea.[11] By the beginning of the fourth century, Christianity prevailed in Asia Minor, Thrace, Cyprus, Edessa and was diffused throughout Syria, Egypt, Greece, southern and central Italy, proconsular Africa and Numidia, Spain and Gaul. Many of the early Christians were indeed of the common people,[12] but many also were from among the rich and the illustrious,[13] as also from among the learned.[14]

This marvelous growth took place despite great impediments and despite the weakness of the natural means employed. That the impediments were great is all too clear. This little band of Jews taught that all men must bow down in worship to Jesus of Nazareth, a Jew who had died the death of a criminal on the cross, a teaching which was, as St. Paul says,[15] a scandal to the Jews and folly to the Gentiles. They condemned and refused to recognize the civic deities—and this at a time when the worship

7. 1 Peter 1, 1.

8. Romans 1, 8.

9. Apoc. 1, 11.

10. Dial. cum Tryphon, n. 117, P.G., t. VI, 749–750.

11. Adv. haereses, I, 1, c. 10, n. 2. P.G., 553, sq 1, 111, c. 3, n. 2, P.G., 848, sq.

12. I. Cor. 1–26.

13. Cf. Acts 13, 12; 17, 34; Phil. 4, 3, 22; Acts 17, 4–12; 18, 2–26; I Cor. 7, 12; 11, 5.

14. Cf. Arnobius, Adv. Gentes, 1, II, 5. P. L. V, 816.

15. I Cor. 1, 23.

of the national gods was considered to be a part of the recognition due to the State itself. They insisted on a lofty and difficult code of moral conduct in startling contrast with the corrupt practices of the pagan world. Finally, from the very beginning they were faced with bitter opposition. First of all came persecution by their Jewish compatriots. Peter and John were arrested by them.[16] The Apostles were imprisoned and scourged.[17] Stephen, the deacon, was stoned to death.[18] Paul was repeatedly manhandled.[19] James was put to death by Herod when he realized that the persecution of the Christians was pleasing to the people at large.[20] At first the Romans thought the trouble was between two factions within the Jewish people and remained on the outside. But during the reign of Nero the Christians were blamed for setting fire to Rome. From then on until the Edict of Milan in 313 the Christians lived under the official ban of the Roman Empire and, time after time, were subjected to some of the most savage persecutions ever recorded in human history.

The weakness of the means employed is also clear. The Apostles were a group of men lacking in any special education. Nor did they possess any political power. "And I, brethren," says St. Paul,[21] "when I came to you, did not come with pretentious speech or wisdom, announcing unto you the witness to Christ. For I determined not to know anything among you, except Jesus Christ and him crucified. And I was with you in weakness and in fear and in much trembling. And my speech and my preaching were not in the persuasive words of wisdom, but in the demonstration of the Spirit and of power, that your faith might rest, not on the wisdom of men, but on the power of God." "What is really hard to believe," says St. Augustine,[22] "for anyone who stops to think, is the way the world came to believe. The fishermen whom Christ sent with the nets of faith into the sea of the world were men unschooled in the liberal arts and utterly untrained as far as education goes, men with no skill in the use of language, armed

16. Acts 4, 1–22.
17. Acts 5, 17–42.
18. Acts 7, 54–60.
19. II Cor. 11, 23–33.
20. Acts 12, 1–3.
21. I Cor. 2, 1–5.
22. City of God, Bk. XXII, chap. 5.

with no weapons of debate, plumed with no rhetorical power. Yet, the catch this handful of fishermen took was enormous and marvelous. They hauled in fish of every sort, not excluding those rare specimens, the philosophers themselves. . . . The world has believed this insignificant group of lowly, unimportant, and uneducated men precisely because the divine character of what happened is more marvelously apparent in the insignificance of such witnesses."

Weighing the natural causes involved in the birth of the Church against all the impediments to her existence, it is clear that the growth of the Church was a miracle of the social order. This is confirmed by the manifold miracles that accompanied her growth. Many of them are explicitly mentioned. At Pentecost, each man in the crowd heard the message in his own language, although the members of the crowd were from every section of the diaspora.[23] Peter's miraculous curing of the lame man at the gate of the temple brought many converts into the Church.[24] When Ananias and his wife Saphira lied to Peter, they were immediately struck dead by God.[25] That many other miracles were performed by the Apostles is clear from the Acts; their miraculous powers became so well and widely known that a multitude of non-Christians from the cities near Jerusalem brought their sick to them to be healed, which they were.[26] The Apostles were freed from prison through the intervention of an angel,[27] as was Peter later on.[28] Stephen, the deacon, performed miracles which aroused the fear and hatred of his countrymen.[29] Philip, one of his companions, did likewise.[30] The conversion of the great St. Paul to Christ was clearly a miracle.[31] St. Paul himself worked many miracles. He cast out an evil spirit from a girl in Philippi.[32] In fact, so great was his reputation as a miracle worker that some of the Jewish exorcists at Ephesus tried to cast

23. Acts 2, 4–11.
24. Acts 3, 1–10.
25. Acts 5, 1–10.
26. Acts 5, 11–26.
27. Acts 5, 18–20.
28. Acts 12, 5–11.
29. Acts 6, 8.
30. Acts 8, 6–8.
31. Acts 9, 1–19.
32. Acts 16, 16–18.

out devils by using his name.³³ Two incidents are explicitly mentioned in which the Apostles restored the dead to life: St. Peter raised up Dorcas at Joppe; ³⁴ St. Paul revived Troas.³⁵

II. ITS LOFTY HOLINESS

At first glance, a claim to holiness may seem to spring from inordinate pride. But let us examine this claim. In speaking of the holiness of the church, we do not pretend to show that, man for man, Catholics are holier than non-Catholics. Nor do we intend to expose our own consciences or the consciences of other Catholics to settle the argument. No! That is impossible! We are not concerned with the holiness of *individual* Catholics but with the holiness of *the Church*.

Now the holiness of the Church is manifest, first of all, in its *doctrines*. For two thousand years amid the greatest variety of circumstances the Catholic Church has ever taught the complete doctrine of Christ as it is found in Sacred Scripture and tradition. The Church has always urged its children not only to avoid sin but to seek the highest perfection by practicing the evangelical counsels. As a result, it has become the mother of innumerable religious orders whose members consecrate themselves to the practice of poverty, chastity and obedience.³⁶

The Church has never been content to teach merely "the golden rule" or general moral principles. It has applied the precepts of God to every detail of life. Even the Church's enemies are forced to admit that its doctrine has never varied from the highest moral standards.³⁷ Perhaps they may point to a few bad

33. Acts 18, 11–17.
34. Acts 9, 36–42.
35. Acts 20, 9–12.
36. In his book, *Design for Giving*, Harold J. Seymour, an Episcopalian, who was general manager of the National War Fund, makes an interesting observation. "They (Catholics) have also given 186,000 of their sons and daughters to lives of complete and final consecration; 39,000 priests, 7,000 lay brothers, and 140,000 sisters. With all these, and with those who gave freely of their time to the Ladies of Charity, and to the Society of St. Vincent de Paul, this Church can indeed call itself 'Mother of Charities,' both here at home and around the world." Seymour, *Design for Giving*, New York (Harper), 1947, p. 125.
37. In his book, *The Catholic Church and Conversion*, G. K. Chesterton comments on the accusation: "Roman Catholics are taught that anything is

popes. But they have never discovered any evil doctrines. And the very fact that the Church's teaching has ever remained pure and sublime, despite some bad popes and bishops, is even a greater miracle than if all its rulers were saints.

As history shows, the Church has preferred to lose anything rather than compromise God's teaching. In the fourth century, for example, when it looked as if the whole world would succumb to the Arian heresy, which was supported by all the power of the Roman empire, the Church preferred to suffer extinction rather than compromise. Or rather it was confident, even in the midst of terrible persecutions, that the gates of hell would not prevail against it.

In the sixteenth century the Church refused to bargain with Luther even though she might have "kept" Germany. It rejected any such compromise rather than betray its Founder. In like manner, it refused to make any exception to the law of God for King Henry VIII. Surely, if it believed that the end justifies the means, these were ideal places to apply the principle. No doubt, the Catholic Church could make peace with Russia today if it would agree to Russia's terms. And it would gain more members if it would permit divorce. But the whole world knows that the Church will never compromise. This conviction is based upon the more or less conscious realization that it will ever preach the unadulterated law of God—no matter how strong the opposition.

In the past, its enemies used to accuse it of teaching immoral doctrines. Although they could never put their finger on one, they were sure they existed. Even today many people "swallow" ridiculous stories about us. Unfortunately, they are too ignorant to investigate the charges.

Recently, more intelligent enemies of the Church have tried a new tack. They declare that the teaching of the Catholic Church is *too* holy. In their opinion, it teaches far more than Christ did. In fact, they are convinced that no one can live out its doctrines. They are beyond the powers of human nature.

And strange to say, the Church agrees with them, that is if a

---

lawful if done for the good of the Church." Since it is supposed to be a definite statement of an institution whose statements are very definite, it can be proved to be totally false. Chesterton compares it to the statement that the Pope has three legs or that Rome is situated at the North Pole. Cf. *ibid.*, pp. 35–36.

man relies upon his own powers alone. The Church, however, does not leave its members on their own. It offers them inestimable help. Of course, the real secret of its powerful assistance lies in the Mass and the Sacraments. For Catholics believe that they receive the Body and Blood of our Lord as their spiritual food; that God strengthens them by powerful graces through the other sacraments. At Mass, they participate in the very sacrifice of Calvary. But since these are hidden sources of grace appreciated only by Catholics, we will not stress them here. Yet non-Catholics should keep them in mind, when they investigate the possibility of living the Catholic religion.

But the very fact that hundreds of millions of Catholics are living according to its teaching is sufficient proof. In fact, this close union of so many Catholics gives confidence and encouragement to the individual. He feels himself to be a part of a victorious army struggling to follow Christ. And all are strengthened by the absolute confidence of the Church in their ability to live as real Catholics.

In the second place, the holiness of the Church is manifest in its results. "By their fruits you will know them. Do men gather grapes from briers, or figs from thistles? Even so, every good tree bears good fruit, but the bad tree bears bad fruit" (Matt. 7, 16–17).

The *real fruits* of the Catholic Church are *the saints*. They are its undeniable results for they endeavored to practice what it teaches and to use the means of sanctification which it offers. Surely a sincere man would not be so unfair as to judge the Church by those "Catholics" who disregard its teaching and its sacraments.[38] They are not its products. A doctor does not judge

---

38. James Cardinal Gibbons wrote: "It is easy to explain why so many disedifying members are always found clinging to the robes of the Church, their spirtual Mother, and why she never . . . disowns them as her children. The Church is animated by the spirit of her Founder, Jesus Christ. He 'came into this world to save sinners.' He was the Friend of Publicans and sinners that He might make them the friends of God. . . . The Church, walking in the footsteps of her divine Spouse, never repudiates sinners . . . no matter how grievous or notorious may be their moral delinquencies; not because she connives at their sin, but because she wishes to reclaim them. She bids them never to despair, and tries, at least, to weaken their passions, if she cannot reform their lives." *The Faith of Our Fathers,* Baltimore (Murphy), 1892, pp. 45–46.

the value of a diet by the patient who ignores it; or the effects of a medicine by a patient who never takes it. In like manner, a man should not judge the Church by men who do not make use of it. Remember that man's will remains as free within as without the Church.[39]

Yet, as Monsignor Ronald A. Knox, who was an Episcopalian before his conversion, points out:

There is no single excuse so freely used by people who want to justify themselves in remaining outside the Church as the behavior of some of us who are inside it. . . . There is nothing more jealously watched or more bitterly criticized today by people who criticize religion than the behavior of professed Christians. Fifty years ago, people did not pay very much attention to what we did; today, when the Catholic Church is the only considerable religious body that dares to claim an increasing and not a diminishing membership, we have a heavier responsibility. . . . We do not want that scrutiny, so often Pharisaical, to make hypocrites of us. But do let us take care, not only about our motives, as God sees them, but about the external appearances of our actions, lest they should be keeping back souls from God. . . . A scandal carries further than a tale of sanctity; our Blessed Lady lived and died unknown, but all Jerusalem knew when Judas hanged himself.[40]

39. A noted convert points out: "The Church has always insisted that bad belief breeds bad conduct, and that right belief is a help to right conduct, but none the less the Church has never lost sight of the distinction which Protestantism tends to blur. *Credo* means 'I believe'; it does not mean 'I behave.' Catholicism is often a test not only of character but of intelligence, and there is no reason why a man should cease to be intelligent because he has ceased to be good. There is no reason why he should stop believing because, for the moment, he has stopped behaving. . . .

"In the course of nineteen centuries the Church has discovered that sinners sometimes sin, and is therefore not so scandalized as her critics by the frailties of her children. Like her Master, she comes to call not the righteous but sinners to repentance, and like her Master she continues to give scandal by her uncompromising hostility to fashionable sins and by her infinite charity to unfashionable sinners." Arnold Lunn, *Within That City*, New York (Sheed & Ward), 1936, pp. 38, 40.

40. Ronald A. Knox, *The Mystery of the Kingdom*, London (Sheed & Ward), 1928, pp. 44–45. In 1950, the vice-chancellor of the diocese of Kansas City summarized the Catholic attitude towards crime at the funeral of an accused gangster. He stated: "The doubt (whether he should have been given ecclesiastical burial denied to public sinners) in favor of the deceased stems from the fact that recently he was seen receiving the sacraments and attending Sunday Mass. . . . As Catholics we abominate and we condemn syndicated

The Church, however, *should be judged by its saints* for they alone used it fully. Now their holiness has never been attacked or questioned by anyone. In fact, most non-Catholics have a real admiration for a saint like Francis of Assisi. The well-known Protestant scholar, Harnack, concedes that the Catholic Church produces saints today. He says:

In all ages it (Roman Catholicism) has produced saints, so far as men can be so called, and it still produces them today. Trust in God, un- affected humility, the assurance of redemption, the devotion of one's life to the service of one's brethren, are to be found in it; many brethren take up the cross of Christ and exercise at one and the same time that self-judgment and that joy in God which Paul and Augustine achieved.[41]

The saints come from every walk of life. Men and women, clergy and laity, the married and the unmarried, the rich and the poor—all are represented on the calendar of the saints. Thou- sands of saints are mentioned in the *Roman Martyrology* alone. They are found in every century. At the time of the Protestant revolt, for example, when the Church was supposed to be in a bad state, there were great saints like Francis de Sales, Philip Neri, Charles Borromeo, Vincent de Paul, Peter Claver and Alphonsus Ligouri. In the nineteenth century, three hundred and ten were declared Blessed (the second great step towards canonization) and seventy-eight were canonized. As *Time* maga- zine pointed out in an article about Mother Cabrini, the process of canonization is long and difficult.

But good works and great sanctity are not all it takes to make a saint. One of the things it takes is a lawsuit—long-drawn, intricate and com- plex. In the first step toward canonization a diocesan tribunal is ap- pointed in each diocese where the candidate has lived. Before the tri- bunal a local Vice Postulator pleads the candidate's "Cause" while a Promoter of the Faith (the "devil's advocate") makes all possible objec- tions at every turn.

------

crime and vice. It is as despicable as it is evil. We condemn the underworld and all its barbarous and cowardly ways. But we condemn also the overworld —liquor executives, public officials . . . and the like who, though able to retain the aura of respectability, sacrifice every decent principle for their own contemptible and selfish ends" (April 18, 1950).

41. Harnack, *What Is Christianity?* New York (Putnam's), 1908, p. 285.

When all local examinations are completed, the documents of the case proceed to the Congregation of Rites in Rome, where they are meticulously reviewed, approved by the Pope (in his Christian name, so as not to compromise papal authority) and returned to the diocesan tribunals for a second pleading. . . . If they and the Congregation of Rites find that the Servant of God was not just an extremely virtuous person but practiced in "heroic degree" the . . . Virtues of Faith, Hope, Charity, Prudence, Justice, Fortitude and Temperance, the primary degree of Venerable is awarded.

For a Venerable to become Blessed and finally a Saint, two miracles are required at each stage. Miracles must be "of the first order"; *i.e.*, instantaneous healing of a grevous disease of a nonpsychological or nervous nature, attested to by doctors of known reputation, preferably non-Catholics.

Saint Frances Xavier Cabrini's best known miracle occurred in March 1921. A nurse at the Cabrini-founded Columbus Hospital in Manhattan accidentally washed out the eyes of an infant named Peter Smith with a 50 per cent solution of silver nitrate instead of the routine one per cent. Three doctors who examined the child's scarred eyes said that there was no hope for his sight. But the hospital's Superior pinned a relic of Mother Cabrini to the baby's nightdress and called the sisters to the chapel to pray all night. Next morning the doctors admitted that a miracle had occurred—the scars were miraculously gone.

But day-old Peter now had pneumonia, was running the normally fatal temperature of 108. Once again the doctors gave him up. Once again the Sisters of the Sacred Heart prayed all night for Mother Cabrini's intercession. Once again morning found the child completely cured. Last week, while the bells of Rome rang out and the Holy Father said High Mass in honor of the first U. S. saint, 25-year-old Peter Smith, now a veteran of the Pacific war and a candidate for the priesthood, retired with his mother to the Catskills to meditate on St. Francis Xavier Cabrini.[42]

In regard to the holiness of the Church, then, the evidence is clear and convincing. Never have the enemies of the Church proved that it has ever departed even in the least degree from the highest moral teaching. Never do they question the heroic sanctity of its numberless saints. No doubt, some of the members of the Church commit private and public sins. But do not its critics realize that its children are still human and free? If they are bad despite the holy doctrines and sacraments of the Church,

42. Time, XLVIII, 3 (July 15, 1946), 76.

what would they be without them? If critics of the Church are sincere, they will investigate its doctrines, its means of sanctification and its innumerable saints. Then they will know most assuredly that the Catholic Church is holy.

How do you explain this amazing fact that the Catholic Church has given undeniable manifestation of its holiness for two thousand years? Apparently, no natural explanation suffices.

III. ITS INEXHAUSTIBLE FRUITFULNESS

The extraordinary fruitfulness of the Church is manifest in the influence it has had upon 1) the individual, 2) the family, and 3) upon civil society.

1) The Church has always provided for the poor, the orphans, the aged, the sick, for all those in distress, by founding charitable institutions to minister to their needs.[43] It has been moved to do so because the love of one's neighbor is nothing more than an extension of the love of God. "Blessed are the merciful," said Christ, "for they shall receive mercy." [44] Again he said: "But when the Son of Man shall come in his majesty, and all the angels with him, then he will sit on the throne of his glory; and before him will be gathered all the nations, and he will separate them one from another, as the shepherd separates the sheep from the goats; and he will set the sheep on his right hand, but the goats on the left. Then the king will say to those on his right hand, 'Come, blessed of my Father, take possession of the kingdom prepared for you from the foundation of the world; for I was hungry and you gave me to eat; I was thirsty and you gave me to drink; I was a stranger and you took me in; naked and you covered me; sick and you visited me; I was in prison and you came to me.' Then the just will answer him saying, 'Lord, when did we see thee hungry, and feed thee; or thirsty, and give thee drink? And when did we see thee a stranger, and take thee in; or naked, and clothe thee? Or when did we see thee sick, or in prison, and come to thee?' And, answering, the king will say to them, 'Amen I say to you, as long as you did it for one of these, the least of my brethren, you did it for me.' Then he will say to those on his left hand, 'Depart from me, accursed ones, into the everlasting fire which was prepared for the devil and his angels. For I was

43. Many Roman Catholics are unaware of the scope of these works.
44. Matt. 5, 7.

hungry, and you did not give me to eat; I was thirsty and you gave me no drink; I was a stranger and you did not take me in; naked, and you did not clothe me; sick, and in prison, and you did not visit me.' Then they also will answer and say, 'Lord, when did we see thee hungry, or thirsty, or a stranger, or naked, or sick, or in prison, and did not minister to thee?' Then he will answer them, saying, 'Amen I say to you, as long as you did not do it for one of these least ones, you did not do it for me.' And these will go into everlasting punishment, but the just into everlasting life." [45]

2) The Church has always promoted the welfare of the family by protecting the rights of wives, children and servants.

It has unceasingly defended the dignity of womanhood, rejecting and condemning the cruel and licentious notions of the pagan world. It has insisted upon the Christian law of the unity and indissolubility of matrimony and this, indeed, even under the most difficult circumstances.[46]

It has defended the rights of children by prohibiting and punishing with severe spiritual penalties such pagan practices as abortion, the exposure of unwanted infants, the buying and selling of children. It constantly urges parents to give their children a religious education. In order that they may fulfil this obligation, it has founded schools, colleges and universities at great effort and expense.

3) Finally, the Church has exercised a profound influence for good upon civil society, both national and international.

In the early centuries its enemies sought to arouse popular indignation against the Church by acusing it of every crime and, in particular, of treason against the State. During the persecutions they stepped up their attack. As a countermeasure, the early apologists insisted upon the contribution Christians were making to law and order in civil society. The Church has always been mindful of St. Paul's words: "Let everyone be subject to higher authority; for there exists no authority except from God, and those who exist have been appointed by God. Therefore he who resists the authority resists the ordinance of God; and they that resist bring on themselves condemnation." [47] Yet,

45. Matt. 25, 31–46.
46. Two notable cases: Philip of Hesse and Henry VIII of England.
47. Rom. 13, 1–2.

while preaching respect and obedience to lawful authority in the State, the Church has always condemned and opposed its unlawful use. For that reason every tyrant from Nero to Stalin has sought to destroy the Church.

An outstanding example of the Church's influence for good came during the break-up and disappearance of the Roman Empire. It is difficult to exaggerate the enormity of the task that faced the Church in the so-called "Dark Ages." It was the task of converting, taming, and civilizing the barbarian hordes that had invaded the crumbling Roman Empire. True to its divine mission, the Church accepted the burden. It sent out missionaries; it founded monasteries; it opened schools. In time these labors bore their fruit; by the eighth century the barbarians had achieved some semblance of civilization and spiritual culture. As soon as life had become sufficiently settled again, centers of higher learning were founded. It was to the monastic schools of England and Ireland, where the lamp of learning had continued to glow during these trying times, that Charlemagne, the king of the Franks, turned to begin his schools in France and Germany. Slow at first, the progress of learning gained momentum so that by the end of the eleventh century a revival had already begun. Sublime art and architecture and enduring literature, all the fine arts found their noblest inspiration in the life of the Church. The renaissance of the fifteenth century, which produced some of the greatest masterpieces of human history, flourished under the patronage of the Church.

The Church has likewise exercised a tremendous influence for good in the sphere of international relations. It has done so in many ways: by condemning wars of conquest, by determining what is licit and illicit even in a just war, by affirming the necessity and excellence of the Christian law of charity and fraternity over and above the special laws of different nations, by arbitrating conflicts between nations. Always has it insisted upon the fact that there will be no peace apart from him who is called "the prince of peace," [48] "the king of kings, and lord of lords." [49]

In the eyes of the unprejudiced the extraordinary fruitfulness of the Church in all good things is a fact that cannot be denied.

---

48. Isaiah 9, 6.
49. Deut. 10, 17; I Tim. 6, 15; Apoc. 19, 16.

IV. ITS CATHOLIC UNITY

Although men desire unity, history shows that they have never attained it in the natural order. Indeed, history almost leads one to despair of any unity for it constantly reminds one of the economic, religious, racial, cultural, and ethical differences separating men. These differences have given birth to innumerable wars between nations, cities and individuals. And they still separate men today. In fact, unity now seems more hopeless than ever before. Though we had every reason to hope for real peace after the last war, we have never enjoyed it. At present, we are fighting a cold war with Russia. The United Nations appears to be a tragic failure. And who knows how many struggles go on within the various countries?

Perhaps you will say: "Thank God! I live in the U.S.A. At least, we are united." But even our unity is rather superficial. As a nation, we do not agree on any religion, philosophy or morality. Certainly, these are obstacles to unity. Needless to say, there is racial conflict within our borders. The struggle between labor and management appears to be almost class warfare. . . . No wonder men become cynical about unity!

In marked contrast to this universal disunity stands the Catholic Church. Throughout the centuries and throughout the world, it has succeeded in uniting hundreds of millions of people differing in every respect. It has united men of every age, nation and class on those points about which men most often disagree. It has united them in *faith, worship* and *government.*

This unity among Catholics is far greater than most people suppose. Catholics do not merely agree on generalities like "faith in Jesus as Lord and Saviour." But all the articles of Catholic belief are defined and clearly stated. And all Catholics believe them interiorly and profess them exteriorly, or else they cease to be Catholics. This *unity of faith* is maintained despite the fickleness of the human mind, the natural desire to exalt private judgment, and the natural reluctance to accept what cannot be fully understood.

Just as its faith is *one and unchanging,* so is its *worship.* Since Catholics believe that Christ established the manner in which God must be worshipped, they do not individually decide whether they should offer one form of sacrifice or another. The central, official and public worship of the Catholic Church is the Mass. This is essentially the same whether it is offered by its priests in Europe, Africa, Asia, Australia or America. Just as the sacrifice of the Mass is one, and the same, so are its sacraments, those special means of grace instituted by Christ for the sanctification of its members.

Of course, all Catholics do not follow the same rites. By a rite is meant the prayers and ceremonies used in the sacrifice of the Mass and in the administration of the sacraments. In fact, there are ten different rites used in the Church, if the several variations in the Latin rite are counted as only one. Of these, nine originated and are used principally in the East.[50] The Popes have recognized these rites as of equal dignity with those of Rome. While some of the languages used in these rites are now dead (e.g., Coptic, Ge'ez), others are vernacular (Rumanian, Arabic).[51] Moreover, the church laws of these Eastern Catholic churches differ somewhat from those of the Western church. In the administration of the sacraments, the majority of them use leavened altar-bread, give Communion in both species together, administer Confirmation immediately after Baptism by immersion, and permit marriage before ordination.[52] These different rites and church laws show the catholicity, the unity without rigid uniformity, and historic origins of the Catholic Church.[53]

Finally, all its members are *united under one head.* Although

50. Cf. the chart at the end of this chapter. Today there are over eight million Catholics of Eastern rites. Usually, they dislike the name Uniate, for it was coined as a term of contempt. They may be called, for example, "Catholics of the Greek rite" or simply "Greek Catholics," if they belong to the Greek rite.

51. As the chart shows, many of these rites are used in the United States. Catholics of the Latin rite may attend Mass and receive Communion in their churches. Usually, they call the Mass "the Divine Liturgy" or "the Offering."

52. Many of these rites and laws are older than ours. Pope Leo XIII decreed that any Western priest who would try to persuade an Eastern Catholic to adopt the Latin rite *ipso facto* incurs suspension. Cf. the encyclical, *Orientalium dignitas* (1894) of Leo XIII; the "motu proprio" *Dei providentis* (1917) of Benedict XV; the encyclical, *Ecclesiam Dei* of Pius XI; and the encyclicals, *Orientalis Ecclesiae* (April 9, 1944) and *Orientales Omnes Ecclesias* (Dec. 23, 1945). At a solemn papal Mass, the epistle and gospel are sung in Greek, as well as in Latin.

53. Cf. Donald Attwater, *The Christian Churches of the East,* Milwaukee (Bruce), 1947, I, 1–39. These Eastern Catholic churches descend in a direct

they may differ in race, culture, nationality and political ideals, they all recognize the Pope as the Successor of Peter, the Vicar of Christ on earth.

And yet the Church has no armored corps. Its members *freely* choose to belong to it. The Church offers them no earthly reward. In fact, it promises them only the cross. Hundreds of thousands of its members have suffered martyrdom. Untold millions have been persecuted. And yet they love the Church with a love more vehement than the hatred of all its enemies.

These men, women and children, who are loyal to the Church, are not fanatics. They are *ordinary people from every walk of life*—employers and employees, scientists and farmers, bankers and scrub women. There is no type of mind or way of life that does not feel at home in the Church. It is not the Church of the rich or the poor, the learned or the unlearned, the strong or the weak. It is big enough to include all these. In respect to *classes*, it is *perfectly catholic*.

During the last war, our servicemen came to appreciate *another aspect of its catholicity*. No matter where they went, they found that the Catholic religion had preceded them. Some were amazed, for example, to find that Guam is ninety-seven per cent Catholic. Others were inspired by the faith of the South Sea islanders. They discovered that men, whom they never knew existed, agreed with them perfectly in religion, philosophy and morality. Even in Japan, they discovered hundreds of thousands of Catholics in cities like Hiroshima and Nagasaki.

In every nation where there is any freedom of religion Catholic missionaries are at work. Even after thirty years of persecution, they still work underground in Russia. In geographic extent, or in numbers of adherents, there is no comparison between the Catholic Church and any Protestant sect. In fact, the Catholic Church has more members than all the Protestant sects combined.

Thus the Church belongs to no age, no race, no culture, no class, no place. It is universal—catholic in every respect.

How can this marvelous unity among men of every age, race, culture, and interest be explained? As we have seen, unity is not

---

line from the churches of St. Athanasius, St. Ignatius of Antioch, St. Cyril of Jerusalem, St. Cyril of Alexandria, St. Basil, St. Gregory Nazianzen, St. Gregory of Nyssa, and others—none of whom celebrated Mass in Latin or used the Roman Liturgy.

easily attained even in a small way. Yet the Catholic Church has united 300,000,000 men of every generation during the past two thousand years. It has united them in religion, philosophy and morality without any armed force. Today it is stronger than ever before.

How do you explain these facts so evident to all—this universal unity? We are convinced *no natural explanation* is at all adequate. Nothing short of the power of God can explain it! God alone can unite so many, so perfectly, so long! The Catholic Church, therefore, is God's Church.

V. ITS UNCONQUERED STABILITY

That the Roman Catholic Church is a miracle of the social order is also clear from its unconquered stability as an existing society. For it has endured and still endures in the face of an opposition, so deep, so widespread, and so persistent, that any society within the natural competence of men would have been destroyed long ago. Thomas Macauley, while failing to realize the miraculous character of the Church's survival, does recognize the extraordinary nature of the stability of the Catholic Church in contrast with other human institutions. He says:

There is not and there never was on this earth, a work of human policy so well deserving of examination as the Roman Catholic Church. The history of that Church joins together the two great ages of human civilisation. . . . The proudest royal houses are but of yesterday, when compared with the line of the Supreme Pontiffs. The line we trace back in unbroken series from the Pope who crowned Napoleon in the nineteenth century to the Pope who crowned Pepin in the eighth; and far beyond the time of Pepin the august dynasty extends. . . . The republic of Venice is gone, and the Papacy remains. The Papacy remains, not in decay, not a mere antique, but full of life and youthful vigor. The Catholic Church is still sending forth to the farthest ends of the world missionaries as zealous as those who landed in Kent with Augustine, and still confronting hostile Kings with the same spirit with which she confronted Attila. . . . Nor do we see any sign which indicates that the term of her long dominion is approaching. She saw the commencement of all ecclesiastical establishments that now exist in the world; and we feel no assurance that she is not destined to see the end of them all. . . . It is not strange that, in the year 1799, even sagacious observers should have thought that, at length, the hour of Rome was come. An infidel power ascendant, the Pope dying in captivity, the most illustrious prelates of France living in a foreign country on Protestant alms, the noblest edifices which the munificence of former ages had consecrated to the worship of God turned into temples of Victory, or into banqueting houses for political societies. . . . But the end was not yet. . . . Anarchy had had its day. A new order of things rose out of the confusion, new dynasties, new laws, new titles; and amidst them emerged the ancient religion. The Arabs have a fable that the Great Pyramid was built by antediluvian kings, and alone, of all the works of men, bore the weight of the flood. Such as this was the fate of the Papacy. It had been buried under the great inundation; but its deep foundations had remained unshaken; and, when the waters abated, it appeared alone midst the ruins of a world that had passed away. The republic of Holland was gone, and the empire of Germany, and the great Council of Venice, and the old Helvetian League, and the House of Bourbon, and the parliaments and aristocracy of France. Europe was full of young creations, a French empire, a kingdom of Italy, a confederation of the Rhine. Nor had the late events affected only territorial limits and political institutions. The distribution of property, the composition and spirit of society, had, through a great part of Catholic Europe undergone a complete change. But the unchangeable Church was still there.[54]

Pondering over these five aspects of the Church's life we can well understand why the fathers of the Vatican Council could say: "Through its wonderful growth, its peerless sanctity and inexhaustible fruitfulness in all good works, its catholic unity and unconquered stability, it (the Catholic Church) is a great and perpetual motive of credibility and an unassailable testimony of its own divine mission."

54. Thomas Macaulay, *Critical, Historical, and Miscellaneous Essays and Poems,* New York (Lavell), 1898, Vol. II, pp. 465–466, 498–499. Macaulay was a Protestant historian.

CHAPTER VIII

The Marks of the Church

THE second proof presented by the Roman Catholic Church in order to justify its claims is known as the proof from the marks of the Church. The Vatican Council proposes this proof in these words: "And, that we may be able to satisfy the obligation of embracing the true faith and of constantly persevering in it, God has instituted the Church through his only begotten Son, and has bestowed on it manifest notes of that institution, that it may be recognized by all men as the guardian and teacher of the revealed word; for to the Catholic Church alone belong all those many and admirable tokens which have been divinely established for the evident credibility of the Christian faith." [1]

That these notes or marks of the true Church are four in number, namely, unity, catholicity, holiness and apostolicity, is evident from the Creed of Constantinople, which says: "I believe . . . in one, holy, catholic, and apostolic Church." The proof from the marks of the Church can, therefore, be presented in argumentative fashion in this way. Our Lord declared that his Church should be one, catholic, holy, and apostolic. But the Catholic Church alone possesses these four notes or marks. Therefore the Catholic Church is the true Church of Christ.

I. OUR LORD'S INTENTION

Christ's Church was to be *one* Church. At the last supper Christ prayed: "Yet not for these alone (the Apostles) do I pray, but for

1. Session III, cap. 3—Denz. 1793.

those also who through their word are to believe in me, that all may be one, even as thou, Father, in me and I in thee; that they also may be one in us, that the world may believe that thou hast sent me. And the glory that thou hast given me, I have given to them, that they may be one, even as we are one: I in them and thou in me; that they may be perfected in unity, and that the world may know that thou hast sent me, and that thou hast loved them even as thou hast loved me." [2] St. Paul expresses Christ's will for the unity of his Church in a striking manner. Over and over again he likens the Church to a living body: "As the body is one and has many members, and all the members of the body, many as they are, form one body, so also is it with Christ. For in one Spirit we were baptized into one body, whether Jews or Gentiles, whether slaves or free." [3] He teaches that all the members of Christ's Church are as parts of a living organism. The unity so described entails a unity of government, faith, and worship.

Christ's Church was to be one in government.[4] For he compared his Church to "a sheepfold," "a city," "a kingdom." He spoke of his Church, never of his churches. St. Paul, echoing the desires of his master, says that the Church must be "one body and one Spirit." [5] In other words, just as in the living body there is only one governing will, so in the Church there must be but one governing authority.

Christ's Church was to be one in faith. For Christ commanded his apostles: "Teach ye all nations . . . teaching them to observe all things whatsoever I have commanded you." [6] In the Church, says St. Paul, there must be "one Lord, one faith, one baptism." [7] Just as in the living body there is but one mind, so also in Christ's Church there must be one faith. "Mark them,"

2. John 17, 20–23.

3. I Cor. 12, 12ff.

4. In the historical proof we have seen that Christ himself provided for this unity of government in his Church. Here, abstracting from this precise point—the reason for so doing will appear as we proceed, we only affirm that the unity which Christ willed for his Church was so intimate as to entail a unity in government, faith, and worship.

5. Ephes. 4, 4.

6. Matt. 28, 19–20.

7. Ephes. 4, 5.

he warns, "who cause dissensions and scandals contrary to the doctrine that you have learned, and avoid them. For such do not serve Christ our Lord." [8] And he exhorted the Romans: "May then the God of patience and of comfort grant you to be of one mind towards one another according to Jesus Christ; that, one in spirit, you may with one mouth glorify the God and Father of our Lord Jesus Christ." [9]

Christ's Church was to be one in worship. For worship is the external manifestation of faith. If then there was to be one faith, there must be oneness likewise in worship. That Christ himself provided for this oneness in worship is clear from the fact that he himself established the rites by which God was to be honored and men were to be sanctified, namely, the seven sacraments as revolving around the central act of divine worship, the holy sacrifice of the Mass.[10]

Christ's Church was to be catholic or universal. For Christ commanded his Apostles to preach his message to all men without any exception. He bade them preach the Gospel to "all nations" [11] and to "every creature." [12] These words show beyond a shadow of doubt that the mission of Christ on earth was to be extended by means of his Church to persons of every race and color, of every nation, of every social level. The Apostles obeyed this emphatic command of the master and, indeed, so successfully that St. Paul was able to apply to himself and his fellow-preachers the words of the Psalmist: "Their sound has gone forth into all the earth, and their words unto the ends of the whole world." [13] And, speaking to the Colossians, he says that the Gospel is believed "in the whole world." [14]

Christ's Church was to be holy. Christ placed before his followers a lofty goal, namely, an intimate, everlasting union with God himself in the kingdom of heaven. "Beloved, now we are

8. Rom. 16, 17–18.
9. Rom. 15, 6.
10. The fact that Christ himself instituted the seven sacraments and that he instituted the holy sacrifice of the Mass at the last supper will be discussed and vindicated in a later course.
11. Matt. 28, 19.
12. Mark 16, 15.
13. Rom. 9, 18.
14. Col. 1, 6.

the children of God," says St. John, "and it has not yet appeared what we shall be. We know that when he appears, we shall be like to him, for we shall see him just as he is." [15] St. Paul expresses this thought in these words: "We see now through a mirror in an obscure manner, but then (we shall see him) face to face. Now I know in part, but then I shall know even as I have been known." [16] Accordingly, Christ placed before his disciples an equally lofty ideal. "Be ye perfect, therefore, as also your heavenly Father is perfect." [17]

He made this ideal more precise in the sermon on the Mount. "Blessed are the poor in spirit, for theirs is the kingdom of heaven. Blessed are the meek, for they shall possess the earth. Blessed are they who mourn, for they shall be comforted. Blessed are they who hunger and thirst for justice, for they shall be satisfied. Blessed are the merciful, for they shall obtain mercy. Blessed are the clean of heart, for they shall see God. Blessed are the peace-makers, for they shall be called children of God. Blessed are they who suffer persecution for justice' sake, for theirs is the kingdom of heaven. Blessed are you when men reproach you, and persecute you, and, speaking falsely, say all manner of evil against you, for my sake. Rejoice and exult, because your reward is great in heaven; for so did they persecute the prophets who were before you." [18]

Yet Christ foretold that all the members of his Church would not live up to this lofty ideal. Among his immediate followers, there were some who were morally good; others, indifferent; others, positively wicked. Judas Iscariot was the traitor among Christ's intimate friends, an Apostle chosen from among his disciples by Christ himself. Others turned against him or abandoned him at crucial moments in his life or simply because of what they considered his hard doctrines. That Christ expected such human failings in the members of his Church is all too clear. He compared his Church, his kingdom, to a wheat field in which his enemy, the devil, had sown cockle. But he tells us what will be done. "Suffer both (the wheat and the weeds) to grow until the harvest, and in the time of the harvest I will say to the

15. I John 3, 2.
16. I Cor. 13, 12–13.
17. Matt. 5, 48.
18. Matt. 5, 3–12.

reaper: Gather up first the cockle, and bind it into bundles to burn, but the wheat gather ye into my barn." [19] And a little later on he said: "The kingdom of heaven is like to a net cast into the sea, and gathering together all kind of fishes, which, when it was filled, they drew out, and sitting by the shore, they chose out the good into vessels, but the bad they cast forth." [20] It is clear that, while Christ placed before his followers a very lofty ideal, he did not expect all the members of his Church to be holy, even in the lowliest sense of the word.

Christ's Church was to be apostolic. For Christ founded his Church upon a small band of men chosen by him from among his disciples. "Then he went up onto the mountain side, and called to him those whom it pleased him to call; so these came to him, and he appointed twelve, to be his companions, and to go out preaching at his command." [21] They became his chief concern for the few years of his life on earth. In fact, he spent most of his time instructing them. While he preached only to the lost sheep of Israel, they were to carry his message throughout the world. Repeatedly he stressed their role. They were to be "fishers of men," the "salt of the earth," and the reapers of an abundant harvest. To them did he entrust the secrets of the kingdom. For three long years he instructed and trained them. Then, just before his ascension into heaven, he sent them forth to preach his message to all mankind. "All power in heaven and on earth has been given to me. Go, therefore, and make disciples of all nations." [22] "You shall receive power when the Holy Spirit comes upon you and you are to be my witnesses in Jerusalem, and throughout Judea, in Samaria, yes, and to the ends of the earth." [23] The Church of Christ must, then, be apostolic in its doctrine.

It must likewise be apostolic in its means of sanctification. For Christ established certain rites for the glory of God and the sanctification of souls. They are the seven sacraments and the holy sacrifice of the Mass.[24] *Baptism:* "And he (Christ) said to them,

19. Matt. 13, 30.
20. Matt. 13, 47ff.
21. Mark 3, 13-15.
22. Matt. 28, 19.
23. Acts 1, 8.
24. Most Protestant sects recognize only two sacraments: baptism and the Lord's Supper.

Go out into all the world . . . he who believes and is baptized will be saved; he who refuses belief will be condemned." [25] *Confirmation:* "When the Apostles, who were in Jerusalem, had heard that Samaria had received the word of God, they sent unto them Peter and John; who, when they were come, prayed for them that they might receive the Holy Ghost, for he was not yet come upon any one of them, but they were only baptized in the name of the Lord Jesus. Then they laid their hands upon them, and they received the Holy Ghost." [26] *Penance:* "When he (Christ) had said this, he breathed upon them, and said to them, 'Receive the Holy Spirit; whose sins you shall forgive, they are forgiven them; and whose sins you shall retain, they are retained.' " [27] *The Blessed Eucharist as a sacrament:* "Amen, amen, I say unto you: except you eat the flesh of the Son of Man and drink his Blood, you shall not have life in you; he that eateth my flesh and drinketh my blood hath everlasting life, and I will raise him up in the last day, for my flesh is meat indeed and my blood is drink indeed; he that eateth my flesh and drinketh my blood, abideth in me and I in him." [28] *The Blessed Eucharist as a sacrifice:* "I have received of the Lord that which also I delivered unto you, that the Lord Jesus, the same night in which he was betrayed, took bread and giving thanks broke and said: 'Take ye and eat: this is my body which shall be delivered for you; this do for the commemoration of me.' In like manner also the chalice, after he had supped, saying: 'This chalice is the new testament in my blood: this do ye, as often as you shall drink for a commemoration of me.' For as often as you shall eat this bread and drink the chalice you shall show forth the death of the Lord until he come." [29] *Holy Orders:* "The Holy Ghost said to them, 'Separate me Paul and Barnabas for the work whereunto I have taken them.' Then they, fasting and praying and imposing hands, sent them away. So they being sent by the Holy Ghost went to Seleucia." [30] *Matrimony:* "The husband is the head of the wife, as Christ is the head of the Church . . . Husbands, love your wives, as Christ also loved

25. Mark 16, 16.
26. Acts 8, 14–17.
27. John 20, 22–23.
28. John 6, 54–57.
29. I Cor. 11, 23–26.
30. Acts 13, 3.

the Church and delivered himself up for it that he might sanctify it. This (marriage) is a great sacrament, but I speak in Christ and the Church." [31] *Extreme Unction:* "Is any man sick among you? Let him bring in the priests of the Church and let them pray over him, anointing him with oil in the name of the Lord, and the prayer of faith shall save the sick man; and the Lord shall raise him up; and, if he be in sins, they shall be forgiven him." [32] Here we have only indicated briefly [33] the rites established by Christ.[34]

II. THE CHURCH AND THE MARKS

Christ willed his Church to be one, catholic, holy and apostolic. Which Church possesses these notes or marks of the true Church of Christ? When we examined the testimony of history we put forward some of the evidence for our conviction that Christ himself established the apostolic Church as a visible society; that Christ himself gave authority to teach, govern, and sanctify all men to the Apostles and their successors, the bishops of his Church; that he bestowed supreme authority over the whole Church to St. Peter and his successors in the see of Rome. At the time, we saw that many Protestants reject the Church's claim to their allegiance. Usually they will admit quite readily that the Roman Catholic Church is historically continuous with the primitive Christian Church. How do they justify their defection from the Church? First of all, they eliminate any direct connection between Christ and the primitive or apostolic Church as a visible society. As proceeding from Christ the primitive Church was an invisible society. It was this invisible Church which was to be one, catholic, holy and apostolic. It was with this invisible gathering of the faithful that Christ promised to "remain all days even to the consummation of the world." Who established the primitive Church as a visible society? His Apostles and disciples did so after his ascension into heaven.

---

31. Ephes. 5, 23–32.
32. James 5, 14–15.
33. As we have noted already, the fact that Christ instituted these special means of grace will be vindicated in a later course.
34. In the historical proof for the Church's claim there is still another sense in which the Church was to be apostolic, namely, in authority. In other words, it should be able to trace its authority back to the apostolic Church which received that same authority from Christ himself.

Having severed the bond between Christ and the primitive Church as a visible society, they were now in a position to justify their severance of the bond between themselves and the Roman Catholic Church. On what grounds? The primitive Church, they said, since it truly embodied the invisible Church of Christ, was one, holy, catholic, and apostolic. But, they contended, this visible Church which had once lived in apostolic fervor became corrupted and fell away from its original excellence. They could never come to any agreement among themselves as to when this catastrophe had occurred. Conjectures of the sixteenth century "reformers" placed its defection at any conceivable time between the first Christian Pentecost and the Council of Constance (1414–1418). They were certain, at any rate, that the original Christian Church, which they identified quite readily with the Roman Catholic Church, had become corrupt; in fact it had become so corrupt that it was no longer a fitting visible embodiment of the invisible Church of Christ.

Acting on this assumption, they considered it not only a right but a duty to establish a new Church to replace the Roman Catholic Church. Since this new Church was to be the visible embodiment of the invisible Church of Christ and was to recapture the original purity and fervor of the primitive Church, it should manifest the characteristics or notes of the latter, its unity, catholicity, holiness and apostolicity. But things did not work out that way. The rejection of the authority of the Roman Catholic Church started an ever-increasing fragmentation of the new Protestant Church. Instead of one reformed and purified Church, churches began to multiply beyond measure. Thus the reformers were driven into the position that the visible Church was only a secondary, even if valuable, adjunct to the invisible Church of the true followers of Christ; that, in fact, membership in one visible Church was just as good as membership in another—that is, if one felt any need to belong to such an organization.

This position led to the abandonment of the traditional four notes of the Church. Now, any visible Church became acceptable if it fulfilled two basic requirements, namely, if within such a society the word of God was taught sincerely and if the sacraments were properly administered. It was agreed that both of these notes were to be found in all the Protestant churches, but not in the Roman Catholic Church. But this position created still further difficulties. The first problem was the diversity of doctrine among the Protestant sects. This lead to a further retreat. A distinction began to be drawn between two grades of revealed truth. The "sincerity" that the reformers demanded in the preaching of the Gospel within any acceptable visible Church only involved accuracy with reference to "fundamental" doctrines, as they called them. Error about secondary doctrines was of little moment. Again, the second note of the true Church, namely, the proper administration of the sacraments, created its own difficulty. This problem was eventually solved by eliminating all but two of the sacraments, namely, baptism and the Lord's Supper.

The Roman Catholic Church still points to the four notes or marks, namely, unity, catholicity, holiness and apostolicity, as the distinguishing features of the true Church of Christ. And the Roman Catholic Church, as the embodiment of the invisible Church, the mystical Body of Christ, claims to possess these identifying marks.[35] That the Roman Catholic Church is one—one in government, faith, and worship—is clear from the preceding chapter. That the Roman Catholic Church is holy—holy both in its doctrines and in its results—has also been shown therein. That the Roman Catholic Church is catholic or universal is obvious. In its fold are peoples of every race, nation and social position and it strives unceasingly to fulfil Christ's command to bring his message to all nations, to every creature. Finally, the Roman Catholic Church is apostolic both in its doctrines and in its sacraments. The Church has guarded with infinite care the deposit of divine revelation confided to the Apostles by Christ himself. It encourages the faithful not only to know what it teaches but to trace these doctrines back to their sources in divine revelation. It challenges those outside the Church to an unprejudiced examination of these same doctrines. As to the seven sacraments and the holy sacrifice of the Mass, it offers more than abundant evidence that these were the special means instituted by Christ for the worship of

35. We are pretending, for the sake of argument, that the Protestant position in question is true, namely, that Christ did not found his Church as a visible society, that the notes of unity, catholicity, holiness and apostolicity, belong to the invisible Church which he established. One could rightly expect that the visible Church in which this invisible body of the faithful would become embodied would clearly manifest the distinguishing marks of the invisible Church. The only visible Church that does so is the Roman Catholic Church.

God and the salvation of souls; that these were the visible signs of invisible grace employed in the primitive Christian Church and on down through the centuries.

III. NO SALVATION OUTSIDE THE CHURCH

Nothing about the Catholic Church irritates some non-Catholics as much as its claim to be the one true Church of Christ. They like to repeat that one religion is as good as another or that it is not what you believe, it is how you live that counts.

Any Christian, however, who believes that the Son of God became man should not say that one religion is as good as another. For the pagan world into which Christ was born was crowded with oriental religions. Now if all religions were equally good, there would have been no need of another religion. Thus the incarnation, life, passion, death, and resurrection of Christ would have been useless.

Often secularists say that all religions are equally good and helpful because all have the same purpose. However, the fact that they all have the same end does not make them equal for they may not attain it. Although all automobiles, for example, have the same purpose, most men would prefer a new Lincoln to a worn-out Ford. Now the purpose of the Christian religion is to teach the complete and unadulterated doctrine of Christ. To do this equally well, all Christian religions would have to teach the same doctrine. Since they teach different doctrines,[36] they obviously cannot be equally good and helpful.

Moreover, the often repeated statement, "it is not what you believe, it is what you do that counts," should not be uttered by a sincere Christian.[37] For Christ himself said: "He who believes and is baptized will be saved; he who refuses belief will be con-

36. As we have mentioned, the so-called Christian churches contradict one another on many important points. For example, some believe that Christ is the Son of God equal to the Father in all things, while others do not; some believe that Christ condemned divorce, though others do not; some believe the Mass is the highest form of worship, while others consider it idolatry. In fact, of the hundreds of religious sects in this country, no two agree perfectly on teaching and practice. Certainly, Christ himself did not teach contradictory things.

37. To say God does not care what form of Christianity men profess is exactly equivalent to stating that he does not care whether they believe what is true or false.

demned" (Mark 16, 16). And St. Paul stated: "It is impossible to please God without faith" (Hebrews 11, 6).

Because Catholics are certain that their Church is the one true Church, they do not necessarily think that all non-Catholics are going to hell. Ordinarily, Catholics are willing to believe in the good faith of those outside the Church and consequently to hope for their salvation. Today no Catholic questions the fact that many Protestants live by high Christian ideals and have an unaffected love for Christ. In regard to these people, they recall the principle stated by Pius IX:

Those who are hampered by invincible ignorance about our holy religion, and, keeping the natural law, with its commands that are written by God in every human heart, and being ready to obey him, live honorably and uprightly, can, with the power of Divine light and grace helping them, attain eternal life. For God, who clearly sees, searches out, and knows the minds, hearts, thoughts, and dispositions of all, in his great goodness and mercy does not by any means suffer a man to be punished with eternal torments, who is not guilty of voluntary fault.[38]

Of course this principle does not apply to fallen-away Catholics who, having possessed a knowledge of their faith, abandon Catholicism in favor of agnosticism or some other religion.[39] While it is normal to assume that a Catholic who falls into heresy is in danger of hell fire, it is unreasonable to hold that one born and bred in heresy, who does not "see his way" to accept the Catholic faith is in the same danger. All his habits of thought, all the prejudices of his environment, all the influences of his friends and teachers weigh against his chances of becoming a Catholic. And ordinarily he is not responsible for those circumstances of environment and education which have made him a heretic. As Msgr. Knox says:

So long, therefore, as he does not come in contact with the Catholic system at all, or does not come across it in such a way as to be effectively challenged by its claims, he has not refused grace. So long as he takes all reasonable pains to study those claims in a fairminded spirit, and still, through some defect of outlook, of temperament, of intellectual apparatus, finds himself drawn no nearer to the truth, he has not refused grace. His ignorance is, so far as we can tell, of the invincible kind; he remains what he is "in good faith." If he falls into grave sin he has, of course, no access to sacramental absolution; but it is still possible for

38. Denzinger, *op. cit.*, no. 1677.
39. *Ibid.*, no. 1794.

him to make that perfect act of contrition which claims forgiveness. We have no fears for such heretics as this.[40]

The attitude of mind, however, which says, "I am not qualified to judge the truth about the Catholic Church," is an attitude of intellectual indolence masquerading as intellectual humility. The man who "thinks there is some truth in it," yet makes no effort to find out how much, is not in good faith. The man who does not look into the Church for fear lest he be converted, or who is "too busy," when he really dreads the troubles that conversion to the Church would entail, is not in good faith. Of course, God alone can judge the individual soul. No theologian can determine whether a non-Catholic is in good or bad faith, whether he is worthy of praise or condemnation in the eyes of God.[41] Theologians state objective truths. God alone knows the consciences of men.

40. Knox, *op. cit.*, pp. 238–239.
41. Pius IX said: "We must hold as certain that invincible ignorance is not a sin in the sight of God. Who will dare to arrogate to himself the right of determining the exact limits of such ignorance when he considers the infinitely varied and unfathomable influence of social environment, character, and so many other circumstances upon which it depends?" Allocution, "Singulari Quadam," December 29, 1854.

PART II

THE

TEACHING AUTHORITY

OF THE CHURCH

In the first part of the course we have sought to vindicate the claim that the Roman Catholic Church was given authority to teach, govern, and to sanctify all men in the name of Christ. Now we turn to its teaching authority. Here we meet up with two prob-lems. First of all, there is the question of infallibility. Did Jesus Christ bestow an *infallible* teaching authority upon his Church so that it cannot err in matters of faith and morals? If he did so, then we must ask: upon whom did he bestow this infallible teach-ing authority? As Roman Catholics we believe that Christ did endow his Church with an infallible teaching authority and that he granted the supreme infallible teaching authority to St. Peter and his successors, the bishops of Rome. Here, this position of ours must be vindicated.

The second problem is this: how does the Church actually exer-cise her infallible teaching authority? She does so in two distinct ways: First there is the solemn magisterium. This occurs when the Pope speaks *ex cathedra,* that is to say, when he, as head of the Church, teaches the universal church on matters of faith or morals, or when an ecumenical council, together with and subject to the

Pope speaks definitively to the whole Church on matters of faith or morals. Secondly, there is the ordinary magisterium. This occurs in the day-to-day instruction given in the Church by the bishops throughout the world as united under the supreme leadership of the Roman Pontiff. Here we must examine this twofold exercise of the Church's teaching authority.

CHAPTER IX

The Infallibility of the Pope

MANY non-Catholics do not understand this doctrine.[1] They seem to think that it means the Pope can make unerring pronouncements on any subject whatsoever. They ask, for example, if the Pope can foretell the outcome of the fourth race at Arlington. Unfortunately, they never realize how modest the claim really is. In his Preface to *St. Joan*, George Bernard Shaw says:

Perhaps I had better inform my Protestant readers that the famous dogma of Papal Infallibility is by far the most modest pretension of the king in existence. Compared to our infallible democracies, our infallible medical councils, our infallible astronomers, our infallible judges, and our infallible parliaments, the Pope is on his knees in the dust confessing his ignorance before the throne of God. . . .[2]

As Catholics, we do not believe that the Pope can teach on any subject that strikes his fancy. Nor do we think that infallibility renders him impeccable.[3] Infallibility does not put truth into his

1. Most non-Catholics do not recognize any teaching authority in the church because they think Christ founded an invisible church. The high-church Episcopalians and the Separated Eastern Churches who admit Christ founded a visible church believe in the existence of an infallible teaching authority in the church. According to them, the organ of that infallible authority is a council of bishops.

2. Shaw, *St. Joan*, New York (Bretano's), 1924, Preface xlix.

3. Some historians have charged five or six Popes with immorality. But no historian accuses any of these Popes of teaching false doctrine. In fact, an immoral person may teach what is good and true. A drunkard may urge his son never to touch a drop. Needless to say, he is a poor teacher by his exam-

mind. A Pope may be quite ignorant and a poor theologian. It does not mean that he receives new revelations from God. Like anyone else, the Pope has to acquire knowledge of God's revelation by diligent study, for what he does not know he cannot teach.

Indeed, Catholics carefully distinguish between infallibility and inspiration. The latter connotes a positive divine help given to a person.[4] Infallibility simply means that Providence will see to it that the Pope does not officially teach error. Thus we say that the Pope, when he defines a doctrine is guided, not inspired. As Ronald A. Knox says: "The difference between inspiration and guidance is the difference between a schoolmaster who should control the hand of a pupil while he wrote, and that of a schoolmaster who should stand by, ready to intervene if he saw him about to go wrong." [5]

Consequently, the Pope uses every possible precaution before he defines any doctrine infallibly. He makes sure that Scripture and Tradition have been carefully studied. He considers the opinions of all theologians. Finally, he sees to it that the doctrine is stated in the most precise terminology. If the Pope did not take all these precautions, he would be guilty of the sin of presumption.

Of course, the Pope may not teach at all. He may keep silence even when it would profit the Church if he did speak. But if he does speak in such a way as to commit the Church, then what he says will not be false. In other words, Catholics believe that *when the Pope, acting as head of the Church, teaches the whole Church on some point of faith or morals, God sees to it that he does not teach error.*[6] Before we are sure that the Pope teaches infallibly,

---

ple. But no one claims that the Pope teaches infallibly by his example. Fortunately the great majority of Popes have been virtuous men. Seventy-nine Popes have been canonized.

4. Catholics believe, for example, that the human authors of Sacred Scripture were divinely inspired. God prompted them to write, guided their choice of materials, and caused them to think the things he wanted written.

5. Knox, *The Church on Earth,* New York (Macmillan), 1929, p. 40.

6. The definition of the Vatican Council literally translated states: "The Roman Pontiff, when he speaks *ex cathedra*—that is, when as pastor and teacher of all Christians, he defines by virtue of his supreme apostolic authority a doctrine of faith or morals to be held by the whole Church—is endowed, through the divine assistance promised to him in blessed Peter, with that infallibility with which the divine Redeemer willed his Church to be

therefore, we must verify three conditions. First of all, the Pope must speak officially, or *ex cathedra,* that is from the chair of Peter as the supreme ruler and teacher of the whole Church. Secondly, the doctrine which he promulgates must be a point of faith or morals. Thirdly, his pronouncement must be addressed to the whole Church.

The belief of Catholics in the infallibility of the Pope follows from their belief in the supremacy of the Pope and the infallibility of the Church. For if the Pope has supreme and final jurisdiction in matters of faith and morals, and if the Church is infallible, then the Pope is infallible. This is evident, for if God always cares for the Church so that it does not lead men into error, then the last court of appeal in the Church must be preserved from error. Thus, the infallibility of the Church makes all the difference in the world between the Papacy and the Supreme Court of this country. No one claims the Supreme Court is infallible because no one holds that the United States is infallible. Since this nation is not infallible, the Supreme Court may hand down a wrong decision. But if the Church is infallible, the Holy See, the final court of appeal in the Church, cannot make an error in matters of faith or morals. It is important, therefore, that we discuss the reasons why Catholics believe in the infallibility of the Church before we consider the reasons why they believe in the infallibility of the Pope.

I. THE INFALLIBILITY OF THE CHURCH

As we have seen, Christ came down from heaven to teach all men the truths necessary for salvation. Since he did not intend to remain upon this earth, he founded a visible society, his

---

fortified; and, therefore, the definitions of the Roman Pontiff are irreformable of themselves, and not from the consent of the Church."

Infallible papal decrees are *exceptional* and usually mean that there has been some doubt as to the precise teaching of the Church on a matter of faith or morals. Ordinarily, the Pope does not speak infallibly in his encyclicals or allocutions. Nevertheless we should give this teaching an interior, religious assent. This obligation springs from the obedience we owe him as our ecclesiastical superior and from prudence which counsels us to respect the opinions of so great an authority who is assisted by eminent scholars. Should it ever happen that learned Catholics think that they have serious reasons for doubting some points in his ordinary teaching they should privately and respectfully submit their views to him.

Church, to carry out his mission even to the consummation of the world. And he placed all men under an obligation to accept its message or be condemned. "Go out over the world, and preach the gospel to the whole of creation; he who believes and is baptized will be saved; he who refuses belief will be condemned" (Mark 16, 16).

The Church is his great legacy to mankind.[7] Under his guidance, it has continued to preach his message and offer his sacraments to all men for the past nineteen hundred years. As Catholics, we believe that Christ made his Church infallible; that he will never allow the whole Church to fall into error in matters of faith and morals. Let us now investigate the reasons for this belief. First of all, we should consider the antecedent probability of this doctrine. Secondly, we will investigate its foundation in Scripture and Tradition.

A. Antecedent Probability

It seems antecedently probable that Christ would insure his Church against errors in faith and morals. Otherwise his principal work would appear to be imperfect and incomplete, for within a few centuries the mistakes of the leaders of the Church might frustrate the whole purpose of his coming.[8] Such an imperfect work would seem unworthy of the Son of God.

Moreover, "he who wills the ends, wills the means." Without doubt, Christ wanted men of every age to know with certainty all that he revealed. Thus he must have willed the means of preserving that revelation unimpaired.[9] But if the Church were fallible, men of the twentieth century would never know what Christ's revelation means, for some men in every age would surely question the decisions of a fallible Church. And after nineteen hundred years of disputation we would be lost in the turmoil of conflicting opinions. With even human foresight Christ should

7. Some people speak as if the New Testament is his great legacy to mankind. They forget that it was written by official teachers of the Church after the death of Christ. It was not guaranteed by our Lord personally but by the Church which declared it to be inspired.

8. If such a fallible Church erred, Christ would be "forcing" men to accept falsehood under penalty of going to hell. (Mark 16, 16) This is absurd.

9. Obviously, the Bible alone could not serve as an infallible guide because the Bible always requires an interpreter.

have foreseen such a catastrophe. Thus it seems antecedently probable that Christ would protect his revelation from being nullified through error since he could easily do so.[10]

But these are *a priori* arguments. We must turn to Sacred Scripture and tradition for the actual proof of the Church's claim to infallibility.

B. Proofs from Scripture and Tradition

In every century, the Catholic Church seems to have had an unwavering confidence that its Divine Founder was constantly with it to protect it from error. Certainly, it has that confidence today. And very few will question its primitive character. Apparently, it springs from the very words of our Lord as they were understood by the Apostles and their successors. When our Lord told the Apostles of his approaching death, he promised to send them the Spirit of Truth. "It will be for him, the truth-giving Spirit, when he comes, to guide you into all truth . . . he will make plain to you what is still to come" (John 16, 13).

After his resurrection, our Lord once again promised the Apostles that the Holy Spirit would aid them: "Enough for you, that the Holy Spirit will come upon you, and you will receive strength from him; you are to be my witnesses in Jerusalem and throughout Judaea, in Samaria, yes, and to the ends of the earth" (Acts 1, 8).

This special divine assistance was not to be a mere transitory gift, but would continue until the end of the world. "And behold I am with you all through the days that are coming, until the consummation of the world" (Matt. 28, 20).

Obviously, our Lord knew that many centuries would roll by before the end of the world. By this statement [11] he was promising

10. Some non-Catholics do not seem to realize that infallibility is a far less thing than inspiration. Although they readily admit the authors of the Bible were inspired, they shy away from any mention of infallibility.

11. This statement of our Lord has three significant points: first of all, the presence of Christ with his church, "And behold I am with you"; secondly, his continual presence without even a day's absence, "all through the days that are coming"; thirdly, his presence to the end of time, "until the consummation of the world." Thus the true church must have existed from the beginning without any lapse and will last until the end of time. All that is necessary, then, is to find this church founded by Christ. Since he is always with it, we may have perfect confidence that it will not lead us into error.

to be not only with the Apostles but with their successors continually until the end of time. Since the bishops of the Catholic Church are the successors of the Apostles, they are assured of his divine assistance in teaching. This special divine assistance must, at least, mean that they will not fall into error when they are teaching the word of God.

Thus St. Paul tells the Ephesians that their faith is built upon the foundation of the Apostles and prophets, Jesus Christ being himself the chief corner stone (Ephesians 2, 20). By faith, St. Paul evidently means their intellectual belief, for in no other way do the Apostles and prophets act as media between Christ and the individual Christian. Under divine inspiration, St. Paul points out the Church as the principle and source of truth: "So much I tell thee by letter . . . so that, if I am slow in coming, thou mayest be in no doubt over the conduct that is expected of thee in God's household. By that I mean the Church of the living God, the pillar and foundation upon which the truth rests" (I Tim. 3, 14–15).

The confidence of all the Apostles in the ever present guidance of the Holy Spirit became evident at the Council of Jerusalem. There the Apostles assume that a decision of the Church, even though it follows a stormy discussion, is the decision of the Holy Spirit. Thus the decree of the Council begins with the words: "It is the Holy Spirit's pleasure and ours . . ." (Acts 15, 28).

This confidence of the leaders of the Church in the guidance of the Holy Spirit is manifested in the works of the Fathers. It underlies all their appeals to general councils. It explains their demand that everyone must accept as true what has been taught by the Church. In their eyes, a man who denies what the Church teaches, commits an inexcusable error. Guided by the Holy Spirit, the Church always teaches the truth. Thus St. Irenaeus (125–202) declares: "The successors of the Apostles have received a sure gift (charisma) of truth according to the will of the Father." [12]

Again, he says: "Where the gifts (charisma) of the Lord are placed there we must learn the truth, namely, from those who have succeeded the apostles in the Church. . . . These preserve our faith." [13]

St. Ephraem (373) asserts: "The heavenly spouse has established the Church and made her firm in the true faith." [14]

12. St. Irenaeus, *op. cit.,* IV, 26, 2.
13. *Ibid.,* IV, 26, 5.
14. St. Ephraem, *De Instaur. Eccl.,* II, 1.

And St. Cyprian (210–258) says: "It is of her that we are born; with her milk we are nourished; her breath is our life. The spouse of Christ cannot become adulterate; she is undefiled and chaste. She owns but one home; with spotless purity she guards the sanctity of one chamber." [15]

In his masterful way, St. Augustine sums up the convictions of all the Fathers when he declares: "Unless the Lord dwelt in the Church, as she is now, the most careful speculation would fall into error; but of this Church it is said: She is the holy temple of God." [16]

As St. Augustine points out, the abiding presence of our Lord with his Church is necessary to keep it from error. Since our Lord left behind no syllable of writing, he committed entirely to his Church the task of representing him, and not misrepresenting him to the world. If he merely depended upon the careful speculation of his followers, the Church would have certainly fallen into error. Compare, for example, modern Lutheranism with Luther or modern Anglicanism with Cranmer and you will see at a glance how changes creep in. In his divine wisdom, our Lord safeguarded his message from this peril by remaining with the Church to insure it against error.[17]

Although it is possible to give many more quotations from the Fathers, it seems unnecessary. The unanimity of their belief in the Church's infallibility has never been questioned. In fact, no one who admits that Christ founded the Church as a society denies that it is infallible. As we have seen, reason alone indicates that its infallibility is antecedently probable. And the words of our Lord as interpreted by St. Paul and the Fathers of the Church leave no room for reasonable doubt. The Church is infallible because the Holy Spirit remains with it even to the consummation of the world. By means of his Church, Christ offers men of every generation his complete and unadulterated message.[18]

15. St. Cyprian, *De Unitate Ecclesiae,* 5, 6.

16. St. Augustine, *On Psalm IX,* 12 (PL., 36, 122).

17. Cf. Knox, *The Belief of Catholics,* New York (Sheed & Ward), 1940, p. 154.

18. Protestants claim to take their guidance immediately from a living Christ. But what is the guidance he gives us, and where are we to find it? Protestants have never and never will answer that question satisfactorily. As Ronald A. Knox says: "For the Catholic, as for the Protestant, sanctification is the direct work of Christ; it is Christ, not the Church, who gives us (as Priest and Victim) his Body and Blood in Communion. It is Christ who for-

II. THE INFALLIBILITY OF THE POPE

The infallibility of the Pope follows from the infallibility of the Church. Since the Pope has supreme and final jurisdiction in matters of faith and morals, he is the court of last appeal in the Church. Therefore, since the Church is infallible the Pope must be infallible, just as the United States Supreme Court would be infallible if God made this nation infallible.

In his splendid work, *The Early Papacy*, Adrian Fortescue says:

If the Pope were to pronounce heresy, refusing his communion to all who did not agree with him, one of two things would follow. Either the Church would be out of communion with her primate, or she would be committed to heresy. Either means bankruptcy of the whole Catholic system; so God cannot allow either to happen. God cannot allow it to happen, that is all the Vatican Council says. There are many things that we are confident God cannot allow to happen. He cannot allow anything that would ruin his Church. He cannot allow all bishops suddenly to die without having ordained a successor, because that would be the end of the priesthood. Here we have another case of something God cannot allow to happen—unless he means to abandon his Church and make Christ's promises vain. How could God prevent a Pope from declaring heresy *ex cathedra?* That we must leave to God. His providence is almighty; if he intends a thing not to occur, it will not occur. Suppose God promised that a certain kingdom should never go to war, and suppose its king had the power of making war. Then we should be quite sure that, somehow, God would manage that the king never used this power.[19]

Indeed, divine protection against error may be given to any man. So far as we know, God's providence may have determined that Bishop Sheen will never make a theological mistake in a sermon. If so, he is infallible in that respect. But there is no proof of anything of that kind. There is proof, however, in the case of

---

gives us our sins, sometimes when we submit them to the Church in confession, sometimes before. The Catholic, no less than the Protestant, hopes to be saved through the merits of Christ's Blood shed for him, and for no other consideration. The Church, then, in the order of worship, does not come between Christ and the individual soul. But in the order of intellectual conviction, the Church does, if you will, come between Christ and the individual mind. It is through the Church that the Catholic finds out what he is to believe and why he is to believe it." *(Ibid.,* pp. 131–132).

19. Fortescue, *op. cit.,* pp. 23–24.

the Pope, because he is the final court of appeal for the Church that Christ promised shall not fail.

Perhaps Providence will take care that no bishop shall teach heresy in his diocesan letters because, if he did so, it would be extremely unfortunate. But we have no guarantee here. The error of a bishop can be corrected by his superior. The Pope has no superior on earth in matters of faith and morals. Therefore God must see to it that the Pope does not teach heresy when he commits the whole Church. If the consultation of theologians or any other means are necessary to protect the Pope from error, God will see to it that these means are used. But the Pope will not officially teach heresy whatever happens. As Fortescue says: "If you say that a man will not die in a certain year, you do not mean that he will not die, if nothing happens to cause his death. You mean that nothing will happen to cause his death." [20]

Certainly, the Pope as final court of appeal in the infallible Church is infallible. Since we proved from Scripture and tradition that the Church is infallible, it seems unnecessary to offer a detailed proof from those sources for the infallibility of the Pope. Nevertheless we will consider briefly some of the arguments theologians use in speaking of the infallibility of the Pope. These arguments are based on Scripture, tradition, and the official teaching of the Church.

A. Scripture

As we have seen, our Lord designated St. Peter as the rock on which the Church is built.[21] He promised that the "gates of hell shall not prevail against it." Now suppose Peter were to lead the whole Church into error. The Son of God would have been mistaken. The powers of hell would have prevailed. Obviously, this supposition is foolish. Therefore it seems reasonable to expect that our Lord will at least keep Peter from leading the Church into error.

Moreover, our Lord gave Peter and his successors the "keys of the kingdom of heaven." He promised that whatever Peter binds or looses on earth he will ratify in heaven. In other words, our Lord will approve what Peter does. Since our Lord would never approve untruths, we may be sure that Peter will never teach them.

20. *Ibid.*, p. 25.
21. Cf. p. 240.

On another occasion, our Lord tells Peter that he has prayed for him that his faith may not fail for he is to be the support of his brethren.[22] This is the only record we have of Christ offering prayer for an individual. It is because of the role Peter plays. The whole Church depends upon him as its principle (its rock) of stability and union. Without a doubt the prayer of Christ was answered. Peter will ever live and rule in his successors to support his brethren in the true faith.

After his resurrection, Christ makes Peter the shepherd of all his lambs and sheep.[23] He is to feed them with the words and sacraments of Christ. Surely our Lord will insure Peter and his successors against error when they teach his flock. Otherwise his whole work might be frustrated.

It is possible to enlarge upon each one of these points. But it seems unnecessary. The words of our Lord can be understood naturally supposing that he promised a special divine assistance to Peter and his successors. This special divine assistance should at least keep them from teaching error. If a person does not admit that, he has to find a novel interpretation for each passage. And he will be at a loss to explain the attitude of the Fathers and Councils towards the successors of St. Peter.

B. The Fathers and Councils

By their words and acts, the Fathers and early Councils of the Church indicate their belief in the infallibility of the Pope.[24] Of course, we do not expect to find that belief stated as clearly and precisely in the first centuries as it is today.[25] Like the doctrine of the Trinity, its scope and limitations were not clearly defined until men denied it. Since no one questioned the infallibility of the Pope before the sixteenth century, no one in the early Church

22. Cf. p. 247.

23. Cf. p. 248.

24. In the first part of this chapter and in the last chapter, we used many quotations from the Fathers and early Councils in speaking of the infallibility of the Church and the supremacy of the Pope. Here we presuppose a knowledge of those quotations for some of them offer additional testimony that Christians have always believed at least implicitly in the infallibility of the Pope.

25. In his book, *The Faith of Our Fathers,* Cardinal Gibbons explained clearly how dogmas have developed through the centuries. Cf. pp. 31–35, 156–157.

wrote a treatise on it. Belief in it, however, was manifested in several ways.

Often we hear a Father protesting that his faith is that of the Roman See. Although he might say this of any Catholic see, the numerous references from the East and West to Rome indicate it is the final standard of right belief. In fact, some Fathers point out Rome as the standard for all. Others say that God will never allow the Church of Rome to err in faith. Let us examine some of their statements.

1. ST. IRENAEUS

First of all, we should recall the memorable words of St. Irenaeus (125–202). In refuting the Gnostic heretics Irenaeus uses the Roman Church as the criterion of orthodoxy. He writes:

Since it would take too long in a book such as this to enumerate the succession of all churches (from the apostles), we point out the Tradition which has been received from the apostles and the faith which has been preached to all by the greatest, the oldest, and the universally known church established at Rome by the two most glorious apostles, Peter and Paul, through a succession of bishops down to our own times. Thus we refute all heretics. . . . For because of its pre-eminent authority, every church, that is, the faithful everywhere, must agree with this church, in which by universal consent, the apostolic tradition has been preserved intact.[26]

The phrase, "every Church must agree with," may also be translated "must go to the Roman Church." If Irenaeus actually meant to say "agree with," then the Roman Church is obviously the criterion of orthodoxy for all Churches. Two noted Protestant scholars, Stiern and Harnack, favor this translation. Harnack says: "*Convenire* is probably to be understood in its derived meaning (agree with): the literal and therefore obvious sense 'every church must go to the Roman Church' is not admissible." [27]

Of course, it does not make a great deal of difference which translation is used.[28] Although the translation, "go to the Roman

---

26. St. Irenaeus, *Against Heretics*, III, 3, 3. Apparently, Irenaeus uses the word, "oldest," here in the sense of "greatest authority" as he does in II, 5, 4. Certainly, he knew that Rome was not the oldest church in years for he says that Antioch was founded earlier (III, 12, 14). Origen also calls the Church of Rome the oldest. Cf. Eusebius, *History of the Church*, VI, 14, 10.

27. Harnack, *op. cit.*, II, 157, n. 3.

28. A Catholic scholar, Funk, preferred the latter translation.

Church," somewhat obscures the meaning of the passage, it does not change it. The Churches are to go to the Roman Church in which the teaching of the Apostles is preserved unimpaired.

Some non-Catholic writers have interpreted this passage to mean that people from all nations go to the great city of Rome and there they learn what is believed in all the different nations. It is, however, the exact opposite of what St. Irenaeus says. He does not mention the greatness of the city but he speaks of the mightier rule of the Church of Rome. He does not say that strangers go to the city but every Church must agree with (or, go to) the Roman Church. So long as they are in agreement with Rome, they have the true tradition of the apostles.

2. St. Cyprian

In the third century, St. Cyprian (210–258), bishop of Carthage in Africa felt confident that the Roman Church would never err. He declared that the African schismatics "had not considered that the Romans are those whose faith is praised by the apostle, to whom perfidy cannot have access." [29]

3. Synod of Antioch

This confidence in the Roman Church was also evident at Antioch where a hundred and fifty-three Eastern bishops held a synod in 379. At its conclusion they publicly proclaimed their perfect agreement in faith with Rome. "Here ends this letter or exposition of the Roman synod held under Pope Damasus, and sent to the East, to which the whole Eastern Church, having held a synod at Antioch, agrees in the same faith; and all thus agreeing profess the faith explained above, each one by his own signature." [30]

4. Pope Damasus I

Everywhere the faith of Rome was the criterion of orthodoxy. A decision of the Pope put an end to controversy. Thus the historian, Sozomenus, relates how Pope Damasus I (366–384) stopped the heresy which made the Holy Spirit inferior to God the Father and the Son (in 380).

29. *Ep.*, LIX, 14.
30. PL., 13, 353.

When this question was discussed and grew from day to day from love of debate, the Bishop of the city of Rome, having heard of the controversy, wrote to the Churches of the East that they must confess the consubstantial Trinity equal in honor and glory, as do the Western bishops. When he did this all were quiet, as the controversy was ended by the judgment of the Roman Church; and this question at last seemed to be ended.[31]

5. St. Jerome

In a letter to Pope Damasus, St. Jerome states his faith clearly:

I speak with the successor of the fisherman and the disciple of the cross. I, following no one as my chief but Christ, am joined in communion with thy holiness, that is, with the See of Peter. On this rock I know that the Church is built. Whoever eats the lamb outside this house is profane. Whoever is not in the ark of Noah will perish when the deluge comes.[32]

6. Synod of Milan

When heretics at Milan refused to believe the bishops of that area, a Synod at Milan (389) referred them to Rome as the final standard of right belief. "But if they (the heretics) will not believe the teaching of the bishops . . . let them believe the apostles' creed, which the Roman Catholic Church keeps and preserves incorrupt." [33]

7. Pope Innocent I

Apparently, appeals to Rome were quite common for after Pope Innocent I (401–417) answered a question of faith submitted to him by a Synod at Mileve (416) in Africa, he concludes:

Whenever a question of faith is raised I hold that all our brothers and fellow-bishops should refer it to Peter only, that is, to the heir of this name and honor, as you have done. For he can help all Churches throughout the whole world.[34]

8. St. Augustine

Later in referring to this decision St. Augustine said: "Already two synods (Mileve and Carthage) have sent to the Apostolic See

31. Sozomenus, *Historia Ecclesiae,* VI, 22 (PG., 67, 1346).
32. *Ep.* XV, *Ad Damasum,* 2 (PL., 22, 355–356).
33. Ambrosi, *Ep.* XLII, 5.
34. *Ep.,* XXX, 2 (PL., 20, 590).

concerning this affair. The rescript has come from there; the cause is finished. Would that the error were finished too." [35]

This statement by Augustine gave rise to the well known proverb, *Roma locuta est, causa finita est* (Rome has spoken, the case is settled).

9. POPE ZOSIMUS

Innocent's successor, Zosimus (417–418), sums up the teaching of all the Fathers of the Church in these words: "The tradition of the Fathers gives so much authority to the Apostolic See that no one dare contradict its judgment. . . . So great is our authority that no one may go back on our verdict." [36]

10. ST. PETER CHRYSOLOGUS

St. Peter Chrysologus (406–450) of Ravenna urges the heretic Eutyches to "hear obediently what is written by the most blessed Pope of the Roman city; because St. Peter who lives and rules on his own throne, gives the faith to those who seek it." [37]

11. THE COUNCIL OF CHALCEDON

Previously, we quoted the cry that went up from all the bishops at Chalcedon (451) after the dogmatic letter of Pope St. Leo I had been read. "This is the faith of the fathers; this is the faith of the apostles. We all believe so. The orthodox believe so. Anathema to him who does not so believe. Peter has spoken thus through Leo." [38]

Through sixteen more centuries Peter has spoken through a Leo, an Innocent, a Benedict. Today Peter speaks through a Pope John XXIII. Pope John will certainly die but the voice of Peter will not die with him. As Fortescue says: "For twenty centuries more, if the world last so long, Peter will live in his successors and will speak, when need arises through them; till at the end the last Pope hands back to his master the heavy burden of those keys that he first received on the shore of the Lake of Galilee." [39]

The six hundred and thirty Eastern bishops of Chalcedon ex-

35. Contra duas Epist. Pelag., II, 3, 5 (PL., 758).
36. *Ep. XII, ad Aurelium,* 1 (PL., 20, 676).
37. *Ad Eutychen, inter Ep. Leonis I,* XXV, 2 (PL., 54, 741).
38. Hefele, *op. cit.,* III, p. 317.
39. Fortescue, *op. cit.,* pp. 60–61.

pressed the universal belief of Christendom in the fifth century. Like their predecessors, they regarded the Pope as the successor of Peter, the guarantor of orthodoxy. Indeed, they respected the Pope as if he were St. Peter himself.

Although the Fathers do not use the same terms as we do, in speaking of the Pope, their faith was substantially the same. This faith has always been based on the words of our Lord to St. Peter as they were understood by the apostles and their successors. In fact, any other interpretation of them faces insurmountable obstacles. First of all, the "interpreter" would have to explain why he does not take the words in their obvious, literal sense as the Fathers do. Secondly, he would have to offer a plausible interpretation of each passage. Thirdly, he would have to explain why the Fathers respect the Pope as if he were St. Peter himself and regard Rome as the criterion of orthodoxy. Finally, he would have to explain how the Pope acquired this astounding prerogative within a century or two.

Perhaps one or two of his "explanations" might sound plausible. But it would take unlimited faith to accept all of them. It is very easy to say "I do not believe," but to give another reasonable interpretation to the words of Scripture and the Fathers is a practical impossibility.

C. The Infallible Church

As Catholics, we are convinced that the Church of Christ lives still and will live to the end of the world. Because the Holy Spirit is with the Church, it is infallible in matters of faith and morals. In the twentieth century we have the same confidence in the Church as Catholics did in the first century, for the Church was not more guided by the Holy Spirit then than it is today.

Since Christ has given the Church its authority, we can trust it as we trust Christ. "Who heareth you, heareth me." The principal reason, therefore, why Catholics believe in the infallibility of the Pope or any other dogma is because the Church teaches it. From the Church, we learn all that Christ has revealed.

Of course, theologians do not stop there. They endeavor to prove that each doctrine taught by the Church was revealed by Christ and has been believed from the beginning. This requires a good deal of research. Without a doubt such theological research confirms our beliefs. But it never becomes the main reason for them. Primarily, a theologian believes in any doctrine taught by the Church for the same reason as an illiterate Catholic does, that is, because the infallible Church teaches it.

Because the infallibility of the Pope follows from the infallibility of the Church and because it may be deduced from the words of our Lord to St. Peter, it would hardly seem to require special definition by the Church. But since some people in the nineteenth century were confused about it, the Vatican Council stated clearly what is meant by the infallibility of the Pope. The definition of the Council literally translated reads:

The Roman Pontiff, when he speaks *ex cathedra*,—that is, when as pastor and teacher of all Christians, he defines by virtue of his supreme apostolic authority a doctrine of faith and morals to be held by the whole Church—is endowed, through the divine assistance promised to him in blessed Peter, with that infallibility with which the Divine Redeemer willed his Church to be fortified; and, therefore, the definitions of the Roman Pontiff are irreformable of themselves, and not from the consent of the Church.[40]

Without a doubt, this was an official teaching of the infallible Church for it was issued by the bishops of the whole Church, the successors of the apostles. Therefore anyone who believes the Church is infallible must admit that the Pope is infallible. As we have seen, this was not a new doctrine. The Council merely expressed more clearly and explicitly what Christians have always believed.

D. Alleged Failures

In the past, some non-Catholic authors have questioned the infallibility of the Pope because they said four Popes have erred. Paul V and Urban VIII were supposed to have erred in condemning Galileo. Popes Liberius and Honorius were said to have fallen into heresy. Lest anyone be confused by these accusations which are still being repeated, we shall consider briefly the cases in question.

1. GALILEO (1564–1642)

Before his conversion to the Catholic Church Arnold Lunn wrote: "No instructed critic would quote the condemnation of

40 Denzinger, *op. cit.*, 1839.

Galileo as an argument against the Vatican definition of Papal Infallibility." [41]

The reason is obvious. Galileo was not condemned by any Pope personally but by the Roman Congregations of the Holy Office and the Index. These Congregations are committees of learned men who assist the Pope in his work. But their decisions have never been regarded as infallible. Therefore, the Galileo case is no argument against papal infallibility. Indeed, Cardinal Bellarmine (1542–1641), who was a member of the Congregation of the Holy Office at the time, did not even regard its decision as irreversible.

More often today non-Catholics refer to the Galileo case as if it proves that the Catholic Church is hostile to scientific progress and freedom of research. Of course, this is not an objection to the infallibility of the Pope but a misrepresentation of the attitude of the Church. They like to picture Galileo as a martyr who suffered because he proposed a new scientific theory when he taught that the sun is immovable and that the earth rotates on its axis. They forget that Cardinal Nicholas of Cusa (1401–1464) and Canon Copernicus [42] (1473–1543) had proposed the same theory many years before Galileo without any difficulty.[43] Galileo's trouble was not due to his scientific theory but due to the fact that he imprudently rejected the traditional interpretation of some texts of

41. Ronald Knox and Arnold Lunn, *Difficulties*, London (Eyre and Spottiswoode), 1932, p. 130. Hilaire Belloc has a clear and concise treatment of this question in *The Catholic Church and History*. He states: "The whole attack on the Church in connection with Galileo turns upon these two misunderstandings, of which the first is unessential, but the second capital: First, that a proved scientific fact was at issue; secondly, that this proved scientific fact was denied, because it was novel, and was denied by that authority which alone throughout the centuries had been held competent to establish points of doctrine, the Papacy and the councils of the Church over which it spiritually presides. The first is wrong and the second is wrong. The Copernican theory was not novel in Galileo's time; it was still only a theory. His condemnation accuses him of returning to the *oldest* conception (Pythagorean). He was not condemned by the Church, and the instance of his condemnation, such as it was, by the appointed committee, was his persistence in teaching as a proved fact what was still only hypothesis." *Ibid.*, pp. 50–51.

42. The work of Copernicus, *De Revolutionibus Orbium Caelestium*, owed its publication to the financial support of two Cardinals. It was dedicated to Pope Paul III.

43. Aristarchus of Samos (lived about 250 B.C.) taught this theory.

the Bible in defending the Copernican theory against the attacks of other scientists.

After the scientists began to fight about the interpretation of Scripture, the Roman Congregations intervened. The question was how to interpret those passages in the Bible which seem to say that the sun moves.[44] These passages had all along been taken in their literal meaning, for it has always been a principle of biblical interpretation to take texts literally unless it is quite clear that they should be taken figuratively. This was the rule set forth by St. Augustine and sanctioned by Pope Leo XIII. Until 1687 the Copernican theory was an unproved hypothesis. In fact, the great majority of scientists taught the theory of Ptolemy. Unfortunately, the Congregation sided with the majority of scientists. After Newton proved (1687) that the Copernican theory was true, Catholic theologians changed their interpretation. Obviously, it was not a matter of great importance.[45] When the author of those books of the Bible spoke of the sun rising and setting, he was speaking not as a scientist but as an ordinary man describing things as they appeared. Even today, men still speak of the sun rising and setting. In his encyclical, *Providentissimus Deus,* Pope Leo XIII removed the danger of any similar error in the future.

When non-Catholics mention the Galileo case, Catholics should ask them why they have to go back to the sixteenth century to show that the Church is opposed to scientific progress. Apparently, the evidence is very sparse. Certainly, they can find no evidence in modern times. The fact that great Catholic universities today are doing everything in their power to further scientific progress and research proves their thesis is false.

2. POPE LIBERIUS (351–366)

When Pope Liberius refused to sign an Arian formulary of faith, he was exiled (355) by the Emperor Constantius. Two years later he was permitted to return to Rome. Scholars still dispute whether or not he signed the formulary.

Scholars who maintain that he did sign it have never proved

44. I Paralipomenon, 16, 30; Ecclesiastes, 1, 5–6; Josue, 10, 13.

45. Einstein said that it would not have mattered a pin's point whether it was said that the earth goes round the sun, or the sun round the earth. Cf. Einstein and Infeld, *The Evolution of Physics,* London (Cambridge University Press), 1938, p. 224.

that the formulary contained anything heretical. Many of the Arian formularies were quite orthodox. But even if Pope Liberius signed an heretical formulary, he certainly did not teach heresy *ex cathedra.* Thus there is no question about papal infallibility in this case. Moreover, if Pope Liberius signed it, he did so as a prisoner under duress. Ronald A. Knox says: "I was always taught (as a Protestant) that Liberius acted under *force majeure,* and that clearly invalidates his expressions of opinion, which he withdrew when at liberty. Nobody claims for the Pope a gift of invincible fortitude." [46]

3. POPE HONORIUS (625–638)

In the midst of the Monothelite heresy, Pope Honorius wrote two letters, one to Sergius, a Monothelite, another to Sophronius, the champion of orthodoxy, in which he forbade further discussion and declared that "there is but one will in Christ." [47] As a result, Honorius was later condemned as a heretic by the General Council of Constantinople (680–681).

In this case again there is no question of papal infallibility. First of all, Honorius did not intend to define any doctrine *ex cathedra* in his letters, for he said, "It doth not behove us to settle the question whether the number of operations in Christ is one or two." He merely wished to put an end to the controversy which he wrongly considered to be a "war of words." Secondly, Honorius asserted there was but one will in Christ because he thought that Sophronius was teaching "that there were two conflicting wills in Christ." St. Maximus, who was the leading scholar of the Eastern Church after the death of Sophronius, exonerated Honorius from all charges of heresy. The Council condemned Honorius because some thought he had favored the Monothelite heresy by silencing both parties. In those days anyone whose actions were thought to favor heresy was regarded as a heretic. Pope Leo II confirmed the decree inasmuch as Honorius had been negligent "in extinguishing the rising flame of heresy."

The fault of Honorius was in not pronouncing a decision at all. He thought the controversy should be left unsettled for the sake

46. Knox and Lunn, *op. cit.,* p. 138.

47. Mansi, XI, 538. The Monothelites taught that the human will of Christ was absorbed in the divine will. If this were true, Christ would not be a true man.

of peace in the Church. After the event, it is easy to see that he was wrong. But nobody ever claimed the Pope was infallible in not defining a doctrine.

4. THE OBJECTIONS INSIDE OUT

It is easy to turn these objections inside out. How few and far-fetched are the alleged failures of infallibility? If someone proposed the theory that the Supreme Court was infallible, a person could discover any number of cases where the Court has reversed its decision. But as Ronald A. Knox says:

Here have these Popes been, fulminating anathema after anathema for centuries—certain in all human probability to contradict themselves or one another over and over again. Instead of which you get this measly crop of two or three alleged failures! I don't say that proves infallibility; that would be claiming too much. But surely it suggests there has always been a tradition in the Church—call it an instinct if you like—that what has been laid down by a previous Pope is of itself irreformable. And that is the Vatican doctrine against which these criticisms are really directed. One Pope who yielded, when he was much in the position of Tikhon with the Bolshevists; one, who thought it would be nice if the question of two Wills (much complicated because nobody had yet invented the blessed words "form" and "content") were left an open question—and then you had to fish round wildly and even dig out poor old Galileo to make up a party! [48]

III. CONCLUSION

In this chapter we have considered some of the reasons why Catholics believe in two important truths, the infallibility of the Church and the infallibility of the Pope. In regard to the infallibility of the Church, reason alone indicates that the Son of God would most likely make his Church infallible. The words of our Lord leave no room for doubt about it. On several occasions, he promised to send the Holy Spirit to guide his Church even to the consummation of the world. These solemn promises of our Lord explain why the Fathers of the Church believed in the infallibility of the Church. In the twentieth century Catholics have the same confidence in the Church as the Fathers did in the first centuries, for the Church was not more guided by the Holy Spirit then than it is today.

The infallibility of the Pope follows from the infallibility of

48. Knox and Lunn, *op. cit.*, pp. 138–139.

the Church. Since the Pope is the last court of appeal in an infallible Church, he must be infallible. This reason for believing in the infallibility of the Pope is corroborated by a study of Sacred Scripture. When the words of our Lord to St. Peter are taken in their obvious, literal meaning, it seems reasonable to expect that our Lord will at least keep Peter and his successors from leading the whole Church into error. Indeed, only this interpretation of his words accounts for the universal respect in the early Church for the Church of Rome. Many Fathers regard it as the criterion of orthodoxy. They respect the Pope because, as they put it, St. Peter speaks through him. Others say that the Church of Rome will never err. Because no one questioned the infallibility of the Pope in the first centuries, no one wrote a treatise on it. But by their words and acts, the Fathers and Councils manifest their belief in it.

Although the Fathers and Councils do not use the same terms as we do in speaking of the infallibility of the Pope, their belief was substantially the same. All their statements in respect to Rome can be understood naturally supposing that they believed in the infallibility of the Pope. If a person does not admit that, he has to find a difficult, often a tortuous interpretation of each statement. Thus when the Vatican Council stated clearly and precisely the scope and limitations of papal infallibility, it was merely defining a divinely revealed truth which had been accepted from the beginning in the Church.

Indeed, this official teaching of the infallible Church is still another reason for believing in the infallibility of the Pope. After the Vatican Council, a person can no longer deny the latter without denying the former. Thus all the reasons that induce us to believe in the infallibility of the Church, should lead us to believe also in the infallibility of the Pope.

THE WEIGHT OF EVIDENCE

Supplementary reading from Selden P. Delany, *Why Rome?* New York (The Dial Press), pp. 229–231.

It is characteristic of my type of mind that I postpone decisions as long as possible, and avoid making investigations the result of which is likely to be upsetting. I must confess that I had never read Pope Leo XIII's Bull which declared Anglican orders invalid until I began working on this chapter. Long ago I read the reply to the Bull made by the Anglican archbishops, together with many other defenses of Anglican orders. I wish now I had read the Bull, "Apostolicae Curae," thirty years ago. It might have made a vast difference in my subsequent life.

At the time when I began writing this book, I made a resolution that I would make no change in my ecclesiastical position until I had completed my argument. I can always work things out better in writing than by abstract reasoning. In writing I can proceed step by step, as in climbing a mountain. To a mountain climber the whole ascent looks impossible from the valley. But one can always take the step, and with the step there is that much gained. Because of my dislike of hurting those who had trusted me, I wanted to remain where I was as long as I could do so conscientiously. If only the customary Anglican argument against Rome might continue to appeal to me, I would hold my ground, even though disillusioned and disheartened.

One by one these arguments have broken in my hands. I came to see that St. Peter had undeniably been given by our Lord the position of supremacy in the apostolic college. As I read over once more the history of the early Church I became convinced that the Petrine tradition was carried on by the Bishops of Rome, and that on this ground their supremacy was everywhere recognized. I discovered that the Church in Rome from the very beginning became the regulative norm for the whole Church, in doctrine, in discipline, in the orders of the ministry, and in the formation of the Canon of Scripture. I learned that the general councils became ecumenical only when confirmed by the Bishop of Rome. I had to admit that the infallibility of the Catholic Church necessarily carried with it the infallibility of her chief Bishop. Finally, I was driven to the conclusion that for one hundred years after the Reformation no valid orders were conferred in the Church of England, and that therefore she lost the apostolic succession. That meant that I was not a priest, and never had been.

After coming to such a conclusion, there was only one course open for me. Immediately after the close of the Diocesan Convention, I called upon Father Ford, the Catholic Chaplain of Columbia University, and told him of my decision. Through his kind offices an interview was arranged with Cardinal Hayes. His Eminence received me most graciously, and after listening patiently to my story, told me the steps that I should take. I then resigned from my parish, wrote to Bishop Manning renouncing the ministry of the Protestant Episcopal Church, and left for a ten-day retreat in the Benedictine Priory at Portsmouth, R. I. There my old friend, Father Sargent (now Dom Leonard), gave me instructions preparatory to my reception into the Catholic Church. I was received by Monsignor McMahon in the Church of Our Lady of Lourdes, on the Feast of St. John the Baptist.

CHAPTER X

The Teaching Authority
in Action

THE Church teaches the content of divine revelation infallibly in two distinct ways: ordinarily or solemnly. The reason should be apparent from all that has been said up to the present. Christ bestowed authority to teach, govern and sanctify all mankind upon the apostles and their successors, the bishops of his Church. He bestowed supreme authority over the whole Church in this threefold task upon St. Peter and his successors, the bishops of Rome. The twofold manner in which the Church exercises its infallible teaching authority flows directly from the hierarchical and monarchic nature of the Church as founded by Christ himself. In one case the Church is said to exercise its *ordinary* "magisterium," or teaching power; in the other, its *solemn* "magisterium."

I. THE ORDINARY MAGISTERIUM

The ordinary magisterium or teaching office of the Church is exercised through the day-to-day instruction given to the faithful throughout the world by the competent authorities in the Church. These are the bishops, the successors of the Apostles. They carry out their teaching office personally as well as through their priests and other competent delegates. Thus the Pope and the other bishops of the Church, in union with him and subject to him, make up what is called the *ecclesia docens,* the teaching Church. The other members of the Church, that is to say, all who are subject to the bishops, constitute the so-called *ecclesia discens,* the Church which learns.

The individual bishop is not infallible in his statements on faith and morals; it is possible for him to err even on these matters. However, the episcopal college, as a body and as united to the supreme bishop, the Pope, does possess infallible teaching authority. When they as a whole, though each in his own diocese, teach a doctrine as contained in divine revelation, then there is no possibility of error. This conclusion flows necessarily from the infallibility of the Church.

The doctrines taught by the ordinary magisterium of the Church are made manifest in: 1) the official or liturgical prayers of the Church; 2) the symbols or formularies or creeds, 3) the approved cathechisms and theological manuals, 4) the pastoral instructions of the bishops and certain papal documents.

The liturgical prayers are the petitions which the Church, the mystical body of Christ, makes to God for those things which we hope to possess through God's merciful omnipotence. But the things which we hope to obtain are precisely those which have been made known to us through the doctrines which we accept by divine faith. Since the liturgical prayers are the official prayers of the universal Church, their doctrinal content is clearly the work of the ordinary magisterium of the Church.

The symbols, formularies or creeds, likewise, manifest what is taught by the ordinary magisterium of the Church. From her earliest days the Church has expressed her basic beliefs in such forms. They are many: for example, the Apostles' Creed, the Nicene Creed, the Creed of Constantinople, the Creed of Toledo, the professions of faith of the Council of Trent, St. Pius X's Oath against Modernism, etc.

Catechisms and other books of Christian doctrine which have been approved by the bishops of the Church for teaching the content of divine revelation to the faithful manifest, to the extent that they are unanimous, the doctrines taught infallibily by the ordinary magisterium of the Church.

The doctrines taught *universally* in the pastoral instructions of bishops, in the diocesan, provincial and plenary councils and in certain allocutions and letters of the Roman Pontiff must likewise be considered as the fruit of the ordinary magisterium of the Church and, therefore, as infallibly true.

II. THE SOLEMN MAGISTERIUM

The magisterium or infallible teaching authority of the Church may also be exercised in a solemn manner and this indeed in two ways. The Roman Pontiff may speak *ex cathedra*, using the fulness of his power in teaching the universal Church on matters of faith and morals. Or, an ecumenical council, in union with and subject to the Roman Pontiff, may speak definitively to the universal Church on these same matters.

A. The Roman Pontiff

As the bishop of Rome, the Pope is the successor of St. Peter and the vicar of Christ on earth. By virtue of this office he has all the powers bestowed upon St. Peter and his successors, the authority to rule over the whole Church, his fellow bishops as well as the faithful. Thus the Pope is the supreme teacher and the primary guardian of the deposit of the faith. All the teaching authority inherent in the Church is centered in his person; he is, as it were, the mouthpiece of its infallible teaching power. This authority he exercises in two ways: positively, by defining what is true, and negatively, by condemning what is false.

An excellent example of the way in which a positive statement of the truth is presented to the faithful is found in the encyclical "Ineffabilis Deus," of December 8, 1854, in which Pope Pius IX defined the doctrine of the Immaculate Conception. The various aspects of a solemn definition are brought out clearly in the heart of this encyclical. The *purpose* of the declaration is stated: "For the honor of the holy and undivided Trinity, for the honor and glory of the Virgin Mother of God, for the exaltation of the Catholic faith and the growth of the Christian religion . . ." The *power* which the Pope is exercising is also stated here: ". . . by the authority of our Lord Jesus Christ, of the Holy Apostles Peter and Paul and by our own authority . . ." The *nature* of the papal decision is likewise affirmed: ". . . we declare, pronounce, and define that the doctrine which holds that the most blessed virgin Mary was at the first instant of her conception, by a singular grace and privilege of almighty God preserved free from all stain of original sin because of the merits of Jesus Christ the Saviour of the human race, is revealed by God and therefore is to be believed by all the faithful firmly and constantly." Finally the consequences of the denial of the doctrine are stated: ". . . Therefore, should any person presume, which God forbid, to think in their hearts otherwise than as we have defined, let them know and realize that they are condemned by their own judgment, that they have suffered shipwreck about the faith and that they have fallen from the unity of the Church. Moreover, if they dare to manifest what they think by word, in writing or in any other way externally, they are subject to the penalties prescribed by law for that very fact."

The Pope may use his infallible teaching authority negatively in the condemnation of error. He does so by attaching a theological censure either to a false doctrine or to the form in which a true doctrine is expressed. The most important and strongest censures are those which are pronounced against false doctrines. Of these the most serious is the citing of a doctrine as *heretical*. When the Pope condemns a statement as heretical, he defines that its contradictory is true. In other words, a statement is qualified as heresy only when it involves a direct and immediate contradiction to a truth taught by the ordinary or solemn magisterium of the Church. The next important censure of a statement is the qualification *proximate to heresy*. Such a statement denies a proposition which, at the present moment in the development of the doctrine of the Church, has not actually been defined but is ready to be defined, for the preparatory theological investigation of the doctrine has already been completed. The censure *savoring of heresy* indicates that a statement is dangerously ambiguous. Such a statement could be taken in an orthodox manner but, all things being taken into consideration, could just as easily be interpreted in an heretical sense.

When a statement does not directly deny the doctrine taught by the Church as divinely revealed but offers an incorrect explanation of the dogmatic formula in which that doctrine is expressed it is censured as *erroneous*. A milder censure of this type is *rash* or *temerarious:* it is used against the denial of a theological conclusion which, because it is solidly founded, has gained wide acceptance in the Church.

Over and above these censures for doctrinal inaccuracies, there are others which are aimed at the form in which the doctrine is expressed. Such are *captious* (misleading), *offensive to pious ears, ill sounding,* and so on.

The Pope exercises his teaching office in many different ways. Usually he does so through letters and through documents known as encyclicals, bulls, pontifical constitutions. At times he teaches orally through "allocutions" given to those whom he wishes to instruct. Or he may speak through the various congregations,—agencies like the Holy Office, the Biblical Commission, the Congregation of Rites, and so on,—which assist him in the direction of the affairs of the Church. Quite obviously his infallible teaching cannot be delegated to these agencies. But even when he speaks directly to the Church, by letter or by means of an allocution, he does not always use the fulness of his infallible teaching authority. For he can teach, even officially, in such a way as not to demand a definitive acceptance of the doctrine from all the faithful throughout the world.[1]

B. *The Ecumenical Council*

The second organ of the solemn magisterium of the Church is the general or ecumenical council, that is to say, of all the bishops who, in union with the Pope and subject to his authority, constitute the *ecclesia docens*. In such a council the hierarchy acts as corporate unit and, doing so, can define infallibly when it teaches the universal Church on matters of faith and morals.

In order that a general council may fulfill the requirements of an ecumenical council, it must be called together by the Pope; it must be presided over by him, either personally or through his appointed delegates; and, finally and above all, its proceedings must be approved by the Pope. If this last requirement is lacking the decisions of the council cannot be regarded as the solemn teaching of the Church. Furthermore, the bishops of the Church throughout the world are invited and enough of them do take part in the discussions and in the voting processes so that the ensuing definitions can be said to express the mind of the episcopal college.

Twenty councils are recognized as ecumenical. In temporal sequence and under the Roman Pontiff reigning at the time, they are:

1. The Pope may be a theologian and nothing prevents him from acting as such if and when he pleases. In doing so, he is not exercising his papal teaching authority. His writings in this capacity depend, in their value, upon his competence as a theologian.

1. Nicea, 325, Pope St. Sylvester.
2. First Constantinople, 381, Pope St. Damasus.
3. Ephesus, 431, Pope St. Celestine I.
4. Chalcedon, 451, Pope St. Leo I.
5. Second Constantinople, 553, Pope Vigilius.
6. Third Constantinople, 680–81, Pope St. Agatho.
7. Second Nicea, 787, Pope Adrian I.
8. Fourth Constantinople, 869–70, Pope Adrian II.
9. First Lateran, 1123, Pope Callistus II.
10. Second Lateran, 1139, Pope Innocent II.
11. Third Lateran, 1179, Pope Alexander III.
12. Fourth Lateran, 1215, Pope Innocent III.
13. First Lyons, 1245, Pope Innocent IV.
14. Second Lyons, 1274, Pope St. Gregory X.
15. Vienne, 1311–12, Pope Clement V.
16. Constance, 1414–18, Pope Martin V.
17. Florence, 1438–45, Pope Eugenius IV.
18. Fifth Lateran, 1512–17, Pope Leo X.
19. Trent, 1545–63, Popes Paul III, Julius III, and Pius IV.
20. Vatican, 1870–?, Pope Pius IX.[2]

Not all of these councils recognized by the Church as ecumenical councils actually possessed all the requirements noted above. For example, the First and Second Councils of Constantinople were, in themselves, regional rather than ecumenical councils; the bishops of the western Church were not even invited. They were given the status of ecumenical councils by the Roman Pontiff who accepted their decisions as expressive of the beliefs of the universal hierarchy of Christ's infallible Church. Moreover, not all of the decisions of all twenty councils are valid, because the Roman Pontiff can withhold, and has actually done so on occasion, his ratification of a certain conciliar decision. This happened, for example, in the case of the eighth canon of the council of Chalcedon.

Although only the bishops of the Church take part in an ecumenical council by divine right, it has been the custom for centuries to invite others not belonging to the episcopal college. Among those invited are cardinals who are not bishops, abbots who have a territorial jurisdiction like that of a bishop in his

2. The Vatican Council has not yet been officially closed.

diocese, vicars apostolic and prefects apostolic. Moreover, the superiors-general of the great religious communities of the Church can also attend and exercise the voting privilege in such a council.

The doctrinal decisions of such ecumenical councils, like those of the Roman Pontiff, are presented positively or negatively. Sometimes the positive teaching on the content of divine revelation is expressed in a symbol or creed, as was the case in the first councils of Nicea and Constantinople. Usually it is expressed in instructions given to all the faithful. The negative teaching consists in the condemnation of heretical teachings, and the anathematization of the proponents of such teachings.

Against the whole idea of these ecumenical councils a number of objections could be, and have been, presented. First of all, there is no essential difference between a papal and a conciliar definition. Secondly, Christ, the founder of the Church, did not make them a matter of precept; no such command is to be found in Scripture or Tradition. Again, the holding of such ecumenical councils is fraught with difficulties: the long journeys by the bishops and the time lost from their pastoral duties, the great expenses involved, the opposition which civil governments sometimes offer, and so on. In answer to these objections, the Church affirms that, even if such ecumenical councils are not absolutely necessary, they are very useful. First of all, by their erudition, prudence and experience the bishops are of great assistance to the Roman Pontiff in determining doctrinal truth and in using the means to establish those laws which are best for the universal Church, all the circumstances of time and place being taken into consideration. Again, they are an efficacious means of settling any differences within the Church in a safe and expeditious manner. Finally, while an ecumenical council presided over by the Pope has no greater intrinsic authority than the Pope, acting officially as the head of the Church and as the Vicar of Christ on earth, yet the external and human authority of the pronouncements is enhanced by the great solemnity surrounding an ecumenical council.

III. CONCLUSION

It is clear, from all that has been said, that there is an element of truth in the two opinions which admit that Christ founded a visible Church, that He bestowed infallible teaching authority upon it but which disagree with us upon the question: who exercises this infallible teaching authority? [3] The opinion of the Separated Eastern Churches and the high-church Episcopalians has its element of truth: the bishops of the Church, as a college, *do* possess infallible teaching authority but we would add this qualification, namely, only *if* they are in communion with the supreme bishop, the Roman Pontiff. It is quite obvious, then, that the bishops of the Roman Catholic Church could not, in conscience, sit down in an ecumenical council with the bishops of the Separated Eastern Churches and the high-church Episcopalian bishops who, at best, concede only a primacy of honor to the Roman Pontiff.

On the other hand, the second opinion which would attribute supreme spiritual authority in the Church to the faithful as a body, or to their representatives, would—or, at least, should [4]— admit that this body possesses infallible teaching authority. There is a certain element of truth even in this opinion. We distinguish between the *active* infallibility of the teachers, the *ecclesia docens,* and the *passive* infallibility of the taught, the *ecclesia discens.* It is the teaching of the Church that the faithful as a whole possess passive infallibility. This teaching is based on the belief that the Holy Spirit, the soul of the Mystical Body, moves the teachers to teach only what is true and the faithful to accept only what is true. Thus, the agreement of the faithful—if it is certain and clear, if it is explicitly manifested, at least in some public and constant practice or custom, and if it is morally unanimous—is a sure sign of the truth of a doctrine.

3. See above, p. 68, footnote 1.

4. This conclusion follows from our discussion on the infallibility of the Church. See above, pp. 62–63.

PART III

THE SOURCES

Our third and last problem is this: from what sources does the Church derive its doctrines? One could answer the question very simply by saying: from tradition. For, while there has been a progressive increase in the body of revealed truths throughout Old Testament times and while this increase continued under the influence of the Holy Ghost even after our Lord's ascension into heaven, it ended forever with the death of St. John, the last of the apostles. "For the Holy Spirit," says the Vatican Council,[1] "was not promised to the successors of Peter, that by His revelation they might make known new doctrine, but that by His assistance they might inviolably keep and faithfully expound the revelation or deposit of faith delivered through the apostles."

At the last supper Our Lord said to his apostles: "These things I have spoken to you. But the Advocate, the Holy Spirit, whom the Father will send in my name, he will teach you all things, and bring to your mind whatever I have said to you . . . Many things yet I have to say to you, but you cannot bear them now. But when he, the Spirit of truth, has come, he will teach you all the truth."[2] Upon the successors of the apostles the obligation was imposed of guarding this body of truth as a sacred trust. "O Timothy," warns St. Paul, "guard the trust and keep free from profane novelties in speech and the contradictions of so-called knowledge, which some have professed and have fallen away from

1. Vatican Council, Session 4, Chapter 4, D. 1836.
2. John 14, 26; 16, 12–13.

the faith." [3] "For I know whom I have believed, and I am certain that he is able to guard the trust committed to me against that day. Hold to the form of sound teaching which thou hast heard from me, in the faith and love which are in Christ Jesus." [4] "Beloved, while I was making every endeavor to write to you about our common salvation, I found it necessary to write to you to contend earnestly for the faith once for all delivered to the saints." [5]

While it can be said quite truthfully, then, that the Church derives its doctrines from tradition alone, it would be more correct to say that there are two sources of divine revelation. The Vatican Council referred to them in these words: "This supernatural revelation . . . is contained *in the written books,* and *in the unwritten traditions* which have come down to us. Having been received by the apostles from the mouth of Christ himself, or from the apostles themselves by dictation of the Holy Spirit, they have been transmitted, as it were, from hand to hand." [6] In this final stage of our investigation into the foundations of our faith we will examine these two sources, the written books and the unwritten traditions, from which the Church derives its doctrines.

3. I Tim. 6, 20–21.
4. 2 Tim. 1, 12–14.
5. Jude 3.
6. Vatican Council, Session 3, Chapter 2, D. 1787.

CHAPTER XI

Holy Scripture and Tradition

THE proximate rule of faith for a Roman Catholic is the teaching authority of the Church established by Jesus Christ. But the ultimate rule of faith for a Roman Catholic is the teaching authority of God. Why do I believe the mystery of the Blessed Trinity? Because the Church teaches it. But why does the Church teach it? Because this doctrine is contained in God's revelation to mankind. But where do I find God's revealed word? In Holy Scripture, the written word, and in Tradition, the unwritten word.

I. HOLY SCRIPTURE

Holy Scripture is known to all as the Bible. The Bible is divided into the Old Testament and the New Testament.[1] The Old Testament is by far the larger part of the Bible, covering, in 46 books, the time from the beginning of the world down to the Christian era. These books are of three kinds. Some are historical, such as the Pentateuch (the first five), Ruth, Kings, Tobias, etc.; these treat the history of God's chosen people, and of certain special personages. Other books are didactical, such as Job, Psalms, Proverbs, etc.; these deal with ethical or moral instruc-

1. A testament here signifies a pact or covenant between God and man. The Old Testament was a covenant between God and the Hebrew nation. It was concluded through their representative, Moses, on Mount Sinai. The New Testament is a covenant between God and man which was concluded through the representative of mankind, Jesus Christ.

tion. Others, finally, are prophetic, such as Isaias, Jeremias, Ezechiel, Daniel, etc.; these treat mainly of the coming Messias and the messianic age. These three types of books are arranged in this same order: the historical books come first; they are followed by the didactical books, and the prophetic books are put in the last place.[2]

The New Testament comprises twenty-seven books. There are four apostolic accounts of the life of Christ: Matthew and John were apostles; Mark wrote for St. Peter and Luke for St. Paul. Besides these four Gospels, there is the account of apostolic times, the Acts of the Apostles, then the letters of the apostles, twenty-one letters of epistles in all, and, finally, the Apocalypse, the only prophetic book of the New Testament. The sequence, as is obvious, is the same as in the Old Testament: first, the five historical books; then, twenty-one didactical books; and, finally, one prophetic book.

Now the Catholic Church teaches that all the books of the Bible were *inspired* by God. In saying this, the Church means that they were written under a special divine influence. In other words, in the production of these books God was the principal cause, while the human authors acted as instrumental causes. To understand what this statement implies we must get some idea of these two types of causality. A principal cause is one that moves another cause, called the instrumental cause, towards the production of an effect which surpasses the natural powers of the instrumental cause. In the production of an ordinary book, for example, an author uses, as instrumental causes, a pen, a pencil, a typewriter, or even a secretary. In this case the book is attributed to the human author as to the principal cause. But the books of the Bible present a message which God Himself wished to communicate to mankind. It is clearly beyond the natural power of any human being to act as the principal cause in the expression of a divine message. God, therefore, was the principal cause in the production of the books of the Bible; their human authors acted as instrumental causes under his influence.

It is important to distinguish clearly between revelation, inspiration, and infallibility, since each implies a special divine influence. When we say that the Popes are infallible we simply

2. The only exceptions are the two historical books, the First and Second Machabees, which are placed at the very end of the Old Testament.

mean that, *if* and *when* a Pope, as head of the Church, teaches the whole Church on some point of faith or morals, God will see to it that he will not teach error. Thus we say that a Pope, when he defines a doctrine, is guided, not inspired. As Ronald A. Knox says: "The difference between inspiration and guidance is the difference between a schoolmaster who should control the hand of a pupil while he wrote, and that of a schoolmaster who should stand by, ready to intervene if he saw him about to go wrong." [3] Inspiration implies a positive divine influence whereas infallibility, of itself alone, only implies a negative divine influence. Divine revelation is quite distinct from both infallibility and inspiration. It involves an actual communication of truths, previously unknown to us, by God Himself. Now inspiration does not necessarily presuppose a divine revelation. For the human writer who is inspired by God need not necessarily have received by way of a divine revelation the truths which he writes down acting as God's instrument. He may set down truths which he has come to know by purely natural means. For example, the writers of the historical books of the Bible recounted events which they had seen themselves or about which they could have learned from actual eyewitnesses. The same holds true of infallible guidance; it does not necessarily presuppose a divine revelation. God could see to it that a writer would not teach error in the communication of knowledge that he had acquired by natural means.

That the books of the Bible were inspired by God is clear from Holy Scripture itself. For the inspiration of the Old Testament several arguments can be drawn from the books themselves. First of all, the writers were prophets, in the sense that they spoke in God's name and were his interpreters.[4] Some felt a divine impulse to speak which they could not resist.[5] Others foretold future events and their predictions actually were fulfilled.[6] Secondly, the prophets were often commanded by God to write down their utterances. Finally, the writings of the prophets were given such significant names as "The book of Jahweh," "The Book of the Law of Jahweh," "The Law of Jahweh," or "The Sacred Books." There are two passages in the New Testament which explicitly

3. Knox, *The Church on Earth,* New York (Macmillan), 1929, p. 40.
4. Cf. Exodus, 3ff.
5. Cf. Jeremiah 20, 9.
6. Cf. Isaias, Jeremiah, Daniel, etc.

refer to the Old Testament as inspired. "All Scripture," says St. Paul, "is inspired by God and useful for teaching, for reproving, for correcting, for instructing injustice; that the man of God may be perfect, equipped for every good work." [7] This passage speaks of the fact of inspiration, of an inspiration that extends to the origin of the Old Testament, as well as to the New Testament. "This, then," says St. Peter, "you must understand first of all, that no prophecy of Scripture is made by private interpretation. For not by will of man was prophecy brought at any time; but holy men of God spoke as they were moved by the Holy Spirit." [8] This passage explains more fully the nature of inspiration. The words of the prophets are not the products of their own minds nor can mere human interpretation explain them; their words are of divine origin.

While the New Testament has no explicit indications of its own inspiration, two texts can be cited for it. "Therefore, beloved," says St. Peter, "while you look for these things, endeavor to be found by him without spot and blameless, in peace. And regard the long-suffering of our Lord as salvation. Just as our most dear brother Paul also, according to the wisdom given him, has written to you, as indeed he did in all his epistles, speaking in them of these things. In these epistles there are certain things difficult to understand, which the unlearned and the unstable distort, just as they do the rest of the Scriptures also, to their own destruction." [9] The phrase "according to the wisdom given him" seems to refer to the charism of inspiration given to St. Paul. "For the Scripture says, 'Thou shalt not muzzle the ox that treads out the grain,' and 'The laborer is worthy of his wages.'" [10] The phrase "For the Scripture says" seems to refer to both of the texts cited, Deuteronomy 25, 4 and Luke 10, 7.

The Fathers of the Church clearly teach the inspiration of the Bible. They speak of these books as containing *indisputable truth*,[11] as *inspired by God*,[12] as *having God as their author*.[13]

7. 2 Tim. 3, 16.

8. 2 Pet. 1, 20–21.

9. 2 Pet. 3, 14–16. This was written about A.D. 66–67, when the first three Gospels and nearly all of St. Paul's Epistles were already in circulation.

10. 1 Tim. 5, 18.

11. St. Justin, St. Irenaeus, St. John Chrysostom, etc.

12. St. Ignatius of Antioch, St. Cyril of Alexandria, St. Gregory of Nyssa, etc.

13. St. Cyril of Jerusalem, St. Gregory the Great, etc.

They say that God *dictated* the Bible and *spoke* to us through its books,[14] that God used the sacred writers *as his instruments*.[15]

II. TRADITION

Tradition is distinguished from Holy Scripture as the spoken word from the written word. Protestant Christians [16] recognize only one source of divine revelation, the Bible; the Catholic Church recognizes Tradition as a source distinct from Holy Scripture.

That everything Christ said and did is not recorded in the New Testament is clear from the New Testament itself. St. Paul says to the Thessalonians: "So, then, brethren, stand firm, and hold the teachings that you have learned, whether by word or by letter of ours." [17] As a matter of fact, the Apostles do not usually refer the faithful to the books written by themselves. At Christ's command, they appointed ministers who were to be the custodians of the deposit of faith handed on to them, who were to be teachers through the Holy Spirit who was given them and who will remain in them; they admonish the faithful to hold firm to those things that they have learned by hearing. St. Paul's exhortation to Timothy is: "O Timothy, guard the trust and keep free from profane novelties in speech and the contradictions of so-called knowledge, which some have professed and have fallen away." [18] Again, writing to Timothy, he says: "Hold to the form of sound teaching which thou hast heard from me, in the faith and love which are in Christ Jesus. Guard the good trust through the Holy Spirit, who dwells in us." [19] And again he says: "Therefore, my child, be strengthened in the grace which is in Christ Jesus, and the things that thou hast heard from me through many witnesses, commend to trustworthy men who shall be competent in turn to teach others." [20] And again: "If anyone

14. St. Irenaeus, St. Jerome, St. Augustine, etc.
15. St. Justin Martyr, St. Jerome, St. Gregory the Great, etc.
16. The high-church Episcopalians and the Orthodox Churches are exceptions. All other Protestants, at least in theory, reject tradition; for them the Bible alone is the rule of faith. Moreover, while Conservative Protestants defend the inspiration of the Bible, Liberal Protestants deny it.
17. 2 Thess. 2, 14.
18. 1 Tim. 6, 20.
19. 2 Tim. 1, 13–14.
20. 2 Tim. 2, 2.

preach a gospel to you other than that which you have received, let him be anathema." [21]

St. John, as he completes his Gospel, says: "But there are many other things which Jesus did; which, if they were written every one, the world itself, I think, would not be able to contain the books that should be written." [22] We know that Christ gave the Apostles many instructions after his resurrection from the dead, during the forty days that preceded his ascension into heaven. And then the Church went on following his instructions. Thus, from what the Church did, we can learn what Christ told it to do. After all, the primitive Church was functioning for some decades before the first Gospel was written, and almost four hundred years before all the inspired books of the New Testament were collected together into one book.

In the course of time those things that had been handed down by word of mouth were eventually written down. We find them recorded in the writings of the *Fathers* of the Church. The Fathers of the Church are all those ancient, holy, orthodox writers who have been approved by the Church, the guardian of both Scripture and Tradition. They are called *ancient*, because the title is restricted to men who lived in the early ages of the Church, in the infancy of the Church. Theologians commonly name St. John of Damascus (d. 754) the last of the Fathers in the East and St. Isidore of Seville (d. 636) the last in the West. Many of the Fathers were bishops; Ephraem the Syrian (d. 373) was a deacon; Justin Martyr (d. 165) and Prosper of Aquitaine (d. 463) were laymen. They are called *holy*, because all of them were conspicuous for the sanctity of their lives. They are called *orthodox*, because they have been unswerving witnesses of the Catholic faith. Those ancient writers, like Origen (d. 254), Tertullian (d. 220), Clement of Alexandria (d. 215), and others, who were lacking either in eminent holiness or complete orthodoxy, are not numbered among the Fathers of the Church; they are referred to as "ecclesiastical writers."

We must confess that there is much ignorance among Catholics with regard to this important source of divine revelation which is called Tradition. Few indeed have read much, if any, of the magnificent Christian literature of these early days of the Church.

21. Gal. 1, 9.
22. John 21, 25.

And yet it is far-reaching in its scope. In the standard collection of the writings of the Fathers by Migne, we have 217 large volumes in Latin, and 161 large volumes in Greek.[23] These writings include magnificent sermons, letters, theological treatises and discussions by such renowned men as Augustine, Ignatius of Antioch, Cyril of Jerusalem, Gregory the Great, Gregory of Nyssa, Ambrose, and many others.[24]

To give a brief example of the kind of information that can be found in Tradition, rather than in Holy Scripture, take the following passage from the "Teaching (didache) of the Twelve Apostles," a Greek document written shortly after St. John's Gospel, and only rediscovered a few decades ago. "Meet together on the Lord's Day (Sunday—as opposed to the Jewish Sabbath) and break bread and celebrate the Eucharist, having confessed your transgressions so that your sacrifice may be pure. Let no one who is at variance with his neighbor join you until he is reconciled, that your sacrifice may not be defiled. For this is that sacrifice that was spoken of by the Lord, 'In every place and time offer me a pure sacrifice.' " (*Didache*, Chap. 14). Here we find mention of a communal worship on Sunday, of the celebration of Mass and of the forgiveness of sins through confession; we are given information on the life of the Church in these early days. In fact, the writings of the Fathers of the Church are a mine of information that supplements and completes Holy Scripture.

III. THE DEVELOPMENT OF DOCTRINE

For a Roman Catholic, the proximate rule of faith is the teaching authority of the Church established by Christ; the ultimate rule of faith is the teaching authority of God as manifested to us in Holy Scripture and Tradition. Our last problem is this: are all the truths taught by the Church contained in Holy Scripture and Tradition in exactly the same way? They are not. It is the failure to understand this point and its consequences that is the cause of ill-feeling on the part of Protestant Christians. Whenever the Church solemnly defines a doctrine, as it does from time to time, a cry of protest is raised that it is making up "new" doc-

23. The larger part of the patristic writings is in these two languages. But many important texts have come down to us in Syriac, Coptic, and Armenian.

24. Migne's collection of writings actually extends much beyond the patristic period properly so called.

trines, doctrines not contained in divine revelation. It is important, then, to get a clear picture of how the Church derives its teachings from divine revelation.

Some of the truths taught by the Church are derived *wholly* from divine revelation. Of these, some are contained therein explicitly. That Christ conferred authority upon His apostles to forgive sins is explicitly stated in the text: "Whose sins you shall forgive they are forgiven them." [25] Other truths are contained in divine revelation only implicitly. Such, for example, is the doctrine of the Immaculate Conception, the doctrine which states that Mary, the Mother of the incarnate Son of God, was, by a unique privilege, preserved free from the stain of original sin at the moment of her conception. There are other truths that are not derived wholly from divine revelation but rather partly from divine revelation and partly from reason. In other words, the truth flows from two premises, one divinely revealed and the other known naturally. The fact that Christ's human intellect possessed infused knowledge while he was on earth is a truth of this kind. The premise from divine revelation is this: Christ merited for us from the very beginning as man. The premise from reason is this: In order to merit, to have a right to a reward, one must know what one is doing and do it freely. Therefore, if Christ began to merit for us at the very moment of his coming into the world, i.e., before he could gain knowledge through experience, his human intellect must have had infused knowledge, knowledge "poured into" his mind by God.

Is there any such thing, then, as a development of doctrine in the Church? There is and there is not. A development of doctrine in the sense of an addition of *new* doctrines properly so called? Not at all! Divine revelation ceased, as substantially complete, with the death of St. John, the last of the Apostles. But that in no way eliminates *all* development of doctrine. First of all, those truths which are derived wholly from divine revelation wherein they are found explicitly are subject to more careful formulation, to a development, not in the doctrine itself but in its expression. One of the reasons for this increased precision of terminology in which the doctrine is expressed arises from the need to combat heresy. One of the favorite tactics of heretics has been to use orthodox terms in an unorthodox meaning. For example, the

25. John 20, 23.

Church had always taught that there was only one will in Christ, in the sense of a moral unity between his human will and the divine will; that his human will was always in complete conformity with the divine will. The Monothelites taught that there was only one will in Christ in an entirely different sense; they denied that he possessed a human will.[26]

Secondly, those truths which are derived wholly from divine revelation wherein they are contained only implicitly become explicit in the course of time. The early Christians believed in the doctrine of the Immaculate Conception implicitly; they believed that Mary was, by a special privilege in view of the divine Maternity, preserved free from all sin. As the Church penetrated more deeply into the doctrine of original sin as contained in divine revelation, it became clear that if Mary had been preserved free from *all* sin, then she must have been preserved from the stain of original sin. But a major difficulty then arose. This notion seemed to be incompatible with the doctrine of the Church that *all* the descendants of Adam and Eve, without exception, have to be redeemed through the merits of Christ. After centuries of debate on this and other problems, Duns Scotus, the famous Franciscan theologian, presented an answer which was accepted by the Church. The two doctrines are not incompatible. Mary was redeemed through the merits of her divine Son but in a manner different from the ordinary, a more perfect manner. Mary's redemption was by anticipation; she was preserved from contracting the stain of original sin which she normally would have contracted at her conception. Her redemption then was preventive, rather than curative. Christ, Our Redeemer *cures* us from the effects of original sin; he prevented his mother from contracting the sin. Both of these actions are redemptive, so he is still the universal Redeemer. From then on the doctrine of the Immaculate Conception moved slowly but steadily on towards its solemn definition by the Church. When the Council of Trent proclaimed the universality of original sin in its decrees of 1546, it made an explicit exception for the Mother of God, without formally defining, however, that she was conceived without the stain of original sin. It was not until December 8, 1854, that Pius IX solemnly defined this doctrine.

Thirdly and lastly, those truths which are derived partly from

26. See above, pp. 199–200.

divine revelation and partly from reason (such truths are said to be contained only "virtually" in divine revelation) become actually known in the course of time. There are two sources of development here. These truths are conclusions from two premises, one drawn from divine revelation, one known with certainty by human reason, and both these sources offer occasion for a development of doctrine. On the one hand, as the implicit truths of divine revelation become explicit in the course of time, they can be linked up with truths known with certainty by human reason. On the other hand, there is a slow but real progress in Catholic philosophical thought, a progress which permits of an ever-deepening penetration into the necessary consequences of the revealed truths, into those truths that are only virtually contained in divine revelation.

This idea of the development of doctrine within the Church brings us back to the idea that there is, in a sense, only one source of Christian doctrine, namely, tradition. In its fullest and richest sense, tradition can only be the total deposit of faith that Christ entrusted to the living Church which he founded two thousand years ago. And precisely because his Church is a living Church, the truth within it is also a living truth. Just as the mind of man naturally seeks an ever deeper and more complete understanding of reality, so also does the mind of the living Church, moved by the Holy Spirit, pursue an increasingly more penetrating and comprehensive understanding of the deposit of faith.[27]

27. Many Conservative Protestants find this "a hard saying." Over and above their denial that Christ founded his Church as a visible society and that he conferred infallible teaching authority upon it, two other obstacles stand in the way of an acceptance of any doctrinal development. First of all, the Bible is their sole rule of faith. Secondly, they show a strong tendency to accept only those truths that are contained explicitly in the Bible. Nor can we rule out their traditional suspicion of human reason: Conservative Protestants have always protested against the intrusion of philosophy into theology.

Philosophical Presuppositions

JUST as professors of Cartography must presuppose some knowledge of Geometry, so also must professors of Theology presuppose some knowledge of Philosophy, of that science which seeks an explanation of all things in their ultimate causes as known by unaided human reason. However, a brief review of some of the philosophical notions may be helpful.

I. HUMAN REASON AND GOD

A. God's Existence

In his greatest work, the *Summa Theologica*, St. Thomas presents five proofs for the existence of God.[1] Although they begin with the observation of different sensible facts, they are closely related. In fact, they perfect and complement one another. In every respect they are reasonable. Indeed, they are so perfectly reasonable that for centuries no one has been able to improve upon them. Here we will consider only one of the proofs. We do not have time for more. Before we study this proof, however, we should recall Pascal's famous wager.

1. PASCAL'S WAGER ARGUMENT

Pascal addresses his argument to the typical man of the world who regards making money and amusing himself, not as a means to the end, but the real purpose of existence. Even if he refuses

1. Otto Karrer, *Religions of Mankind*, New York (Sheed & Ward), 1936, pp. 131–133, 135–136.

to consider his ultimate destiny, Pascal maintains such a man cannot avoid wagering about it. In practice, he must stake everything on one of two propositions, either A) that there is a purpose in life (God made us for life with him); or B) there is not. Man cannot refuse to wager for by doing so he implies that there is no purpose in life.[2]

Under one disguise or another, human selfishness is always urging man to stake everything on "B." Pascal tries to show that it is far more reasonable—even from the viewpoint of self-interest —to stake all on "A." If you bet everything on "B" and "A" is the truth, you lose an eternal good. But if you stake all on "A" and "B" is the truth, you lose only a few temporal pleas· ures.[3]

Pascal describes the thoughts of the typical man in these words:

2. "This is the momentous truth, and there is none more disturbing to the consciousness of the world today, nor possibly indeed, to the consciousness of all ages. The problem of his destiny is so propounded to man that, whatever he may do, he cannot remain in suspense about it, he cannot be neutral. Suppose that a man is drowning; if I hesitate to save him, I have decided against it. If I remain indifferent when brought face to face with truth, I decide against it, 'for he who thinks that he can remain neutral is a sceptic *par excellence;* this neutrality is the very essence of the sect.' If I remain indifferent with regard to death and the hereafter, I am acting as if I had not an immortal soul; I am deciding against. It is not then a voluntary choice; we must wager, and he who does not wager *for* God wagers *against* Him. He who does not renounce self, renounces God. There is one point settled; you have to wager one way or another." Chevalier, *Pascal,* London (Longmans, Green & Co.), 1930, pp. 245–246.

3. "And what do you risk by taking the chance? What evil can happen to you? You will have lived uprightly; you will have renounced corrupt pleasures, but you will have gained others of inestimable value, and you will not have risked your eternal life. Perhaps you will object: it is uncertain whether I shall win, and it is certain that I am taking a risk. But every gambler stakes a certainty to gain an uncertainty, and it is not unreasonable to act thus. All men do so; all are working for an uncertainty as long as they do not know the reason for it; it is thus with sea voyages, commerce, battles. If we did not work for an uncertainty, we should do nothing at all. Religion is not certain, you say. I agree with you. But there is more certainty in religion than in the knowledge that tomorrow will dawn for us; nevertheless we are all working as if tomorrow were a certainty, and this is sensible, and what we ought to do, according to the rule of chances that has been demonstrated. Now if it is not a sin against reason to risk the finite with certainty to gain the uncertain finite, ought we not to risk the finite with certainty when the stake is infinity? *Ibid.,* 247–248.

I know not whence I came or whether I go. I only know that on quitting this world, I shall fall forever either into nothingness or into the hands of an angry God. . . . And yet I conclude that I should pass all the days of my life without bothering to inquire into what must happen to me. Perhaps I might find some solution to my doubts, but I do not want to take the trouble. . . . I intend to go forward without looking ahead and without fear towards this great event, facing death carelessly, still uncertain as to the eternity of my future state.

Pascal adds: "Truly it is a glory to religion that it has such unreasonable men among its enemies." [4]

In other words, Pascal thinks it is not merely a moral tragedy but an intellectual blunder to wager on "B," that is, to refuse to recognize a purpose in life. He feels sure the typical man would soon have faith if he renounces pleasure.[5] At least, he should search for the truth. "According to the doctrine of chance, you should search earnestly for the truth; for if you die without worshipping the True Cause, you are lost. 'But,' you say, 'if God had wished me to worship him, he would have left me signs of his will.' Indeed, God has done so; but you ignore them." [6]

2. THE PROOF FROM CONTINGENCY

The proof from the contingent character of our own selves and of the creatures that surround us runs like this:

Every existing thing must either

a) exist of itself (then it is called self-existent), or

b) have received its existence from another (then it is called "contingent" or "dependent" because it depends for its existence on another.)

From experience we know many things that have received their existence from some other being. Although they now exist, they once did not. They are contingent.

Evidently, any such being could not be the cause of its own existence. Otherwise it would have to exist before itself. In other words, some other thing must have existed in order that it may exist.

Now if you consider two such contingent beings it is clear that the one (A) might have conferred existence on the other (B), or

4. Pascal, *Pensees*, III, 194.
5. Cf. *ibid.*, III, 240.
6. *Ibid.*, III, 236.

vice versa, but either one could not have conferred existence on both. Otherwise it would have existed before itself.

The same reasoning applies to *any* number of contingent beings. If you wish to explain their existence, you have to search outside them. No one of them can possibly confer existence on all. Otherwise it would have to exist before itself.

Thus you do not explain fully the existence of A by saying that it has received existence from B, for the question immediately comes to mind—where does B get its existence? Nor does it fully explain the existence of A to say that it has received its existence from a billion or more contingent beings. That is only putting off the all-important question. For what we are interested in is not the existence of any one contingent being but the very existence of existence; the source of the existence of the *totality* of contingent beings. Indeed, the greater the number of contingent beings, the greater the problem.

Ultimately, you must make a choice. Either the existence of all things springs from nothing or there is a self-existent being whom men call God.[7] Obviously, the first answer is foolish. Common sense alone tells us that "something doesn't come from nothing." If a person told you his new Buick "popped out" of nowhere, as he was walking down the street, you would laugh at him. Either he takes you for a fool or he is a fool. The same may be said of those who maintain that all things come from nothing.

Of course, it is possible to avoid any answer by mumbling, "I don't know." But, as Chesterton said, that "is to give up the riddle, and to give it up, not because you cannot find the answer, but because you have found the answer, and have found it unpalatable."

A rough analogy may clarify this point. Suppose a person asked you to explain why a box car on a railroad track begins to move. And you reply, "Why! that's simple. It's moved by the next box car." Obviously, that is not a satisfactory answer. Without doubt he will ask you to explain the motion of the second car. If you attribute its motion to the third car you still are not giving him an adequate explanation. Increasing the number of cars does not account for the movement. In fact, it does not make any difference how many box cars there are—they may ex-

7. In other words, if anything exists, then self-existent Being must exist; if self-existent Being does not exist, nothing can exist.

tend from New York to San Francisco and back again—you do not explain how one begins to move until you come to some engine or propelling force. Indeed, the greater the number of box cars moving, the greater the necessity for a powerful motive force. Thus you cannot fully explain the existence of any contingent being by pointing to the next contingent being or to any series of them. For the greater the number of contingent beings, the greater the need for some self-existent being to explain them. As we said, this self-existent being men call God.

Evidently, it always existed; it has existence of itself. And just as it is foolish to inquire why a circle is round for it is round of its very nature, so it is foolish to inquire why the self-existent being exists, for it exists of its very nature.[8]

B. God's Nature and Attributes

What can reason tell us about this Supreme Being, this God? Our mind, St. Thomas replies, cannot be led by sense so far as to see the essence of God; because the sensible effects of God do not equal the power of God as their cause. Hence from the knowledge of sensible things the whole power of God cannot be known; nor therefore can his essence be seen. But because they are his effects and depend on their cause, we can be led from them so far as to know of God *whether he exists,* and to know of him what must necessarily belong to him, as the first cause of all things, exceeding all things caused by him.[9]

In other words we build up a complex mental picture of God

8. "In the hands of St. Thomas the argument does not simply assert that the proposition 'Necessary Being exists' is a logical consequence of the proposition 'Contingent being exists,' but maintains that contingent being derives its own existence from Necessary Being; in other words, that we are not concerned just with logical relations between propositions, but with metaphysical or ontological relations between existent beings.

"What is necessary, in short, if we are to pass from a belief in the existence or finite beings to a belief in the existence of God is not so much that we should thoroughly instruct ourselves in the laws and procedures of formal logic as that we should thoroughly acquaint ourselves with finite beings and learn to know them as they really are . . .

"But their real value is in stimulating the mind to examine finite beings with such attention and understandings that it grasps them in their true ontological nature as dependent upon God, and so grasps God's existence as their Creator." F. L. Mascall, *He Who Is,* New York (Longmans, Green), 1943, p. 73 and p. 80.

9. St. Thomas, *Summa Theologica,* I, q. 12, a. 12.

by going from creatures as his effects to God as their cause. We do this in three ways. First of all, we attribute to him all the perfections possessed by his creatures which do not involve any imperfection. Secondly, we assert that they exist in God in a preeminent, infinite manner, whereas no creature, no matter how perfect, possesses them except in a limited, finite manner. Thirdly, we deny that the imperfections of creatures exist in God. This, in general, is the threefold process by which we are able to build up a complex picture of God. Using it, we come to a very imperfect knowledge of the Godhead, but some knowledge, no matter how imperfect, is better than none.

But, you may well ask, to what concept of God does this process lead? Let us examine some of the conclusions to which we must come.

The cause of my personality, for example, cannot have less personality than I have. He can only lack my limitations. Since we can know and love, God must know and love in a way immeasurably higher. In other words, God is personal for a person is "a being who knows and loves."

Secondly, reason tells us that God is *simple*. By simple is meant "not composed." If God were composed, there would have to be a composer. But this is impossible since God is the First Cause. Therefore he is simple. (Note that any material thing necessarily owes its existence to another.)

Thirdly, God is *spiritual*. This means he is an "active, intelligent, immaterial being—without extension." Since matter has parts and is not simple, God is not material. Yet he must be an Active, Intelligent Being for he is the First Cause of all things. Therefore, God is a Spirit.

Fourthly, reason tells us God is infinite. This means he is unlimited. In created things, existence (a perfection) is always limited by the nature (the capacity) in which it is received. But God, unlike contingent beings, does not receive existence. Since he is self-existent, his nature is to exist. Thus his existence has no principle of limitation so that he is truly infinite.[10] This implies that he possesses every perfection in its highest form.

10. "Consider how immeasurable a difference this makes between God and all contingent beings. They may exist or may not. God must exist. He cannot non-exist. Their nature is to be able to exist. God's nature is to exist. They can have existence. God *is* existence." F. J. Sheed, *Theology and Sanity*, New York (Sheed & Ward), 1946, p. 34.

In the fifth place, God is one. If there were two infinities, one would be outside the power of the other and hence neither would be infinite. They would, as it were, bump shoulders. Obviously, it is impossible that each one should independently possess *all* perfections.

In the sixth place, God is immutable. Immutable means changeless, or unchanging. Since God has all perfections (infinite), he cannot acquire any more. And if he were to lose a perfection, he would no longer be God. Therefore God is immutable.

In the seventh place, reason informs us that God is eternal. Eternity does not mean unlimited time, but the plentitude of existence. Since God is infinite, he is eternal—possessing the plentitude of existence.

Since God is infinite, all conceivable perfections are found in him in their purest, highest and most intense degree. He is all-good, all-beautiful, all-truth. He is omnipotent, omnipresent and omniscient.

Of course, we do not mean that God possesses these perfections just as we do. He is not a sort of super-man. These perfections are found in him in an infinitely higher manner. In some incomprehensible way all perfections are identical with his nature. These questions will be discussed at length in Natural Theology and Dogma. In Apologetics we merely wish to indicate how a man *can* reason to the attributes of God; what reason tells us about God.

C. Common Objections

Some men are atheists or agnostics for moral reasons. They wish to salve their consciences for they live as if there were no God. Often they are vociferous about their atheism like small boys who whistle in the dark to conceal their fears. Others are troubled by the common objections against the existence of God. Sometimes all they have heard about God are these objections. And to a man who does not think about them they may seem quite unanswerable. As Belloc says:

Those who have replied and do reply "No God," have the immediate certitudes in their favor. One might draw a comparison here between the man who affirms that the earth is flat, against the man who affirms that the earth is round. The first man, who says it is flat, has on the face of it a solid case, and a case apparently more agreeable to the most immediate evidence than the second. The earth certainly seems flat as we go about on it.

In the same way there seems at first sight to be no God, so far as human reason is concerned.[11]

1. MISLEADING IMAGE OF GOD

When some people think of God, they picture him as a venerable old man with a beard. Even though they are not conscious of its influence, this misleading image of God colors all their judgments about him just as illustrations in a novel often affect our ideas of characters in the book. As a result, they tend to think of God either as an equal or as an extra.[12]

Often they speak of God as if he were another man to whom they could offer suggestions. Or they admit his existence as if it was the "proper thing" to do. But they think no more about him. He is ignored as a remote and impotent figurehead. In other words, they become practical atheists. No doubt, this misleading image of God is not the sole cause of their ignorance. But it is a contributing factor in many cases. This false concept of God should be dispelled by the proofs for his existence.

2. THE PROBLEM OF EVIL

The fact of evil in the world leads some to deny the existence of God. They have heard it said that God is infinitely good. Yet they feel there is much needless suffering in the world. At times they are appalled by the vast amount of pain, disease, and destruction which does not seem to serve any purpose. Above all, they feel that, if God is infinitely *just*, he should bestow good or ill fortune according to our merits here and now. This, however, is not the case. As a result, they conclude that the postulate of God is false.

Because they tend to think of God as an equal, the problem of evil seems insoluble. Unfortunately they lack intellectual humility. While they live in a moment of time and witness a fragment of reality, they feel competent to judge the whole scheme of things. Unconsciously, they make themselves equal to God, at least, in knowledge. Usually they judge things without regard to a future life. No wonder they deny God.

11. Hilaire Belloc, *The Question and the Answer*, Milwaukee (Bruce), 1932, pp. 23–24.

12. Cf. Sheed, *Theology and Sanity*, New York (Sheed & Ward), 1946, pp. 27–29.

Moreover, they make a gratuitous assumption when they suppose the purpose of an all-good God must be to give us present delights and spare us present pain at all costs. Surely we would not praise a father who makes this his supreme principle in the treatment of his children. How much more unworthy would such conduct be of a God who is all-good and all-wise? Indeed, a God who would gratify all our indiscrimate wishes would not be all-good. And once you grant that some suffering is not inconsistent with divine goodness, who is to determine the limits? As A. E. Taylor says: "There is no limit to the amount of suffering on the part of individuals which we might not see to be compatible with the wisdom and goodness of our Creator, if we knew, as we do not, what is won by it in the end for the sufferer and for others. If it should be the price of 'eternal life'?" [13]

In other words, the fact of evil in this world should not lead men to deny the existence of God. Until we know the whole scheme of things, we are in no position to judge. Nor may we assume that a good God must bestow happiness and unhappiness in this world according to our merits. The answer to this difficult problem of evil, of course, is found in the revelation of Christ; but it cannot even be outlined here.[14]

3. SCIENCE VERSUS GOD

Some people are under the impression that "science" has killed God. Most scientists are amused by the idea for the very nature of the methods of experimental science precludes them from considering religious questions at all. Basically, all "scientific problems" are of one type. Some hypothesis is proposed concerning the existence of a certain uniformity in space-time processes. Now scientists think that if the suggested "law" is a true one, certain definite effects will follow under given conditions, whereas if it is false, these effects will not follow. If the effects are not perceived, when experiments are conducted under the specified conditions, then the hypothesis is disproved. If they are perceived, they hypothesis is not necesarily proved, but it is not yet disproved. In other words, it remains a legitimate scientific hypothesis until it is proved false by exactly ascertained fact.

13. Taylor, *op. cit.*, p. 166.
14. Cf. M. J. Scheeben, *The Mysteries of Christianity*, St. Louis (Herder), 1946, pp. 243–313.

According to these principles, a scientist who wishes to disprove the existence of God must be in a position to say, "if God exists, certain space-time events must occur, which we know do not occur." But no scientist can say that. There is no space-time event of which a scientist can say, "this event must be perceived under certain conditions if there is a God." Thus, experimental scientists as scientists are not qualified to discuss any religious question. As scientists, they are exclusively concerned with the detection of uniformities of sequence in the course of events. They discover that whenever certain definitely measurable events occur, some other measurable event will also be found to happen. Obviously, they can tell us nothing about the existence of God.[15]

Unfortunately some scientists have felt omniscient. And many pseudo-scientists, who write popular "scientific" articles and books, have posed as scientists. Inspired by the "scientific spirit" these men spoke with infallible authority on every department of social activity from Sociology to Architecture and from Architecture to Law.[16] In every field, they attacked Christian civilization and the Catholic Church. If the Church answered them, they accused it of obstructing science. Without doubt, these scientists and pseudo-scientists have deceived and continue to deceive many.[17]

15. Cf. Taylor, op. cit., pp. 8–10. J. Arthur Thomson wrote: "There is no possible way in which science could disprove God. . . . We must not try to look out of two windows at once! We must not mix our concepts. . . . There is no alternative—'God or Darwinism'; no alternative—'Man as a child of God or man as the highest mammal'; no alternative—'divine creation or cosmic evolution.' For all of these express confusion of thought. The alternative is—'science only or science and the vision of God.'" Concerning Evolution, New Haven (Yale Univ. Press), 1925, pp. 230–232.

16. Some years ago many people thought that scientists had destroyed the value of Sacred Scripture when they emphasized what Catholic theologians had known for centuries, that the author of the Book of Genesis did not know the principles of astronomy, geology, paleontology, etc. No doubt, this was a shock to those people who regarded the Bible as the infallible source of all truth. But it was nothing new to Catholic scholars. As Catholic scriptural scholars had reiterated, the author of Genesis did not intend to give a scientific account of creation but merely a popular account to teach basic religious truths.

17. Belloc says: "It is no good protesting that the True Scientist is nothing of all this: that he does no more than patiently observe, never affirms a thing to be proved unitl it is, humbly rejects any claim to talk on things that are

In recent years, however, their influence is diminishing. Many people have become conscious of their self-contradictions, their extravagances, their arrogance, and the imperfection of their method.[18] The explosion of the first atomic bombs awakened many more to the realization that no "scientific" principles can save us from the destruction with which science threatens us. Moreover, intelligent men are beginning to see again that experimental science and knowledge are not co-extensive; that experimental science is a highly specialized and limited field of knowledge. Now when scientists claim that no methods except those of the experimental laboratory will lead to truth, someone may ask how scientists can test the truth of that assertion in a laboratory.

II. REASON AND RELIGION

The natural virtue of religion is discussed in Moral Philosophy or Ethics, in other words, in that part of Philosophy which studies the rules of conduct laid down by right reason for men.[19] Apologetics must presuppose such knowledge. However, a brief review of the leading ideas may be helpful, before we discuss the reliability of unaided reason as a guide in religion and the theory of evolution as an explanation for the origin and development of religion.

A. Reason Tells Us Some Duties Towards God

From what reason tells us about God it is easy to figure out some of our duties toward him. Reason, for example, informs us that we are absolutely dependent upon God for our existence. Of ourselves we have no title, no right to it. Each moment we receive it from him. Our body, our soul, our whole being depend upon his sustaining power. If he ceased to will us even for an instant, we would lapse into nothingness. Thus reason leads us to acknowledge God's supreme dominion and our own dependence upon him. And that is the heart of all religion, for the virtue of religion is defined as *a habit of mind by which man acknowledges the su-*

---

beyond him. Obviously the ideal scientist would behave so. But the human scientist, belonging as he does to a fallen race, didn't behave so." *Survivals and New Arrivals,* New York (Macmillan), 1929, p. 94.

18. Cf. *ibid.,* p. 96.

19. Moral Theology, on the other hand, studies the rules of conduct laid down in divine revelation for the fallen and redeemed sons of God.

preme dominion of God and his own dependence upon him.[20] Of course, religion may also be considered objectively and defined as the complex of truths and duties by which human life is ordered to God.

Thus reason alone leads man to practice religion for it points out his duties towards God. Since God who is a Personal Being is our Supreme Lord we ought to pay him the respect and honor (adoration) that is his due. Because he is all-good and all-powerful we should not hesitate to ask him for the many favors we all desire. Since he has been so generous to us we naturally wish to show our gratitude; to please him in any way we can. In his presence, we are conscious of our own sinfulness. Naturally we wish to do penance.

Evidently we may please God by prayer, sacrifice, and a good life. Prayer is the elevation of man's heart and mind to God. It is conversing with God, talking to him, and listening to him. Since we are continually in God's presence, it seems foolish not to speak to him. Sacrifice is simply a form of prayer that ordinarily involves a victim. A life pleasing to God is a life in accord with the end or purpose for which he made us. Fortunately, God has endowed man with a natural guide, a conscience, that ordinarily dictates what is in accord with right reason and what is not; what is pleasing to God and what is not. It points out his duties towards God and towards his fellow men. By the principle of the divine ownership of all things reason clarifies our duties towards ourselves and our neighbors.

Ordinarily, we express our interior convictions and feelings exteriorly. Indeed, it is so natural for us to show them outwardly that we have to make an effort to conceal them. Since there is no reason to hide our religious convictions we should express them by interior and exterior acts.

So far we have considered man only as an individual. Man,

20. "For only a God who is, in St. Anselm's phrase, 'something than which nothing greater can be thought,' or, as St. Thomas put it, 'subsistent Being itself,' can be the adequate object of Christian devotion, which has always believed itself to reach its climax in the sheer adoration in which the creature, knowing its own entire insufficiency and its relative nothingness, casts itself in complete abasement before the majesty and holiness of a God whom it recognizes as being altogether complete without it and yet as conferring upon it its very existence and tending it with the most gentle and intimate love." Mascall, *op. cit.*, p. 196.

however, is a social animal. He belongs to one or more societies (domestic, political, economic, ecclesiastical). As a member of society, he has certain duties towards God. Since each society (a moral person) is a creature of God, it is absolutely dependent upon him. It needs his protection and blessing. Thus the members of the society should perceive their obligation to honor, petition, and thank God as a group. By "religion" people ordinarily mean these *public and social forms of expressing religious convictions.*

Thus if we have a true notion of God, it is easy to figure out our duties towards him. For reason perceives a natural bond or relationship between God and us which is closer than the bond or relationship between a child and its parent; a relationship which no human declaration of independence can sever. On account of this relationship we are *obliged* to worship him. Reason likewise bids us to petition and thank God. It makes us conscious of these obligations both as individuals and as members of society, and of our responsibilities towards ourselves and our fellow men. In other words, reason alone leads us to practice religion.[21]

B. The Reliability of Reason Alone as a Guide in Religion

So far we have "glorified" the role of reason. We have pointed out what reason alone *might* do. What it *has done* is another question. To discover what reason unaided by divine revelation can actually do, we must study the religions existing *prior* to Christ for, needless to say, our reasoning at the present day is aided and perfected by the guidance of divine revelation.

In practice, reason has proved a reliable guide in so far as it has led men to acknowledge *the existence* of a *Supreme Being* (or Beings) who is concerned with them. As a result, man has always been naturally religious. As far as the light of history reaches, we find men, apparently without any revelation, acknowledging the existence of a God or Gods.[22] Everywhere they have offered some form of external, social worship through prayer and

21. Natural religion is the worship prescribed by reason unaided by revelation. When the truths and duties are learned from a divine revelation, the religion is called supernatural.

22. Cf. Karrer, *Religions of Mankind,* New York (Sheed & Ward), 1938, pp. 16, 73, and 100. Dawson, *Progress and Religion,* New York (Sheed & Ward), 1937, p. 88.

sacrifice; a worship that is based on a doctrinal and moral code. Atheists have always been a very small minority. They are like boys who whistle in the dark; men who "protest" too much.

It has been difficult, however, for man without the aid of revelation to form *correct notions about* the *nature* of God. In this regard reason has proved an *unreliable* guide. Although almost all men have admitted his existence, they have differed widely as to their notions about him. Indeed, the vast majority were lost in error. As a result, their worship and morals were more or less degraded. Any history of religions will verify this.[23]

Thus practically all the great pagan religions were polytheistic. Although they acknowledged the existence of a Supreme Being, they did not realize that he is One. The Hindus worshipped not only Brahma, but also Vishnu, Siva, and Krishna. The Japanese adored Amaterasu, Goddess of the Sun, and also many lesser gods and goddesses. The Babylonians adored Marduk, Nabu, Ishtar and many others.

Similarly, most men failed to recognize the spiritual nature of God. They imagined him to be material. Consequently, they adored every sort of idol. Even when pagan Greece and Rome were at their zenith in culture, they did not realize that God is a spirit. Moreover, they had a perverted notion of his other attributes. The Romans, for example, "created" a god as patron for every kind of vice.[24]

Naturally, superstition, puerility and obscenity found a place in their worship, for there is an intimate connection between man's concept of God and the worship he offers him. Also, moral conduct was at a low ebb. Since the gods themselves were immoral, vice paraded as virtue. Even Plato favored a community of wives

23. We are so used to thinking of God in a Christian sense that we imagine it is the most common conception in the world. "If men believe in God," we ask, "what other kind of God would they believe in?" "But," as C. S. Lewis remarks, "the answer of history is, 'Almost any other kind.' We mistake our privileges for our instincts; just as one meets ladies who believe their own refined manners to be natural to them. They don't remember being taught." *Miracles,* London (The Centenary Press), 1947, p. 139.

24. In India today, there are over two million married "women," and one hundred thousand widows under ten years of age. Prostitution flourishes in the Hindu Temples. About one-fourth of the Hindus are pariahs. A pious Hindu would prefer to be reborn a pig than a pariah. Cf. Karrer, *op. cit.,* pp. 25–26.

in his ideal state. Aristotle regarded slaves as mere beasts who could be tortured and put to death by their owners. If the leading philosophers of Greece were so badly mistaken, it is not surprising that ordinary men were wrong.

In truth, the vast majority of mankind seemed totally and hopelessly at sea. Although reason under ideal conditions could lead them to a true concept of God, a true worship, and good morals, it never did in practice. Reason alone, therefore, proved an unreliable guide.

Some of the *causes* of *reason's failure* are apparent. First of all, to figure out all the attributes of God by reason without the aid of revelation would require a good deal of ability and a lot of time. Most men did not have the ability to think consistently, nor the time, for they had to earn a living.

Secondly, the human mind is rather inert and lazy—hesitating before such a tremendous task. Thinking hurts. Most men preferred to take somebody's opinion. Or else they give free rein to their imaginations. And in this matter imagination is the mother of error and superstition.

Thirdly, when a man did reason out some truths about God he never felt certain. It did not take much to change him.

Finally, errors and prejudices hampered him. If you were brought up to believe in forty-nine gods, it would be hard to conclude that there is only one. If we were taught to picture God as an enormous giant of a man, it would be difficult to realize that he is a spirit. Besides, most men were not anxious to know the truth. As a result of original sin, their passions and feelings influenced their thinking. Often they used reason to justify their immorality for "if you don't live as you think, you'll think as you live." The very idea of a personal God who will reward or punish them for their deeds was abhorrent to them.[25]

25. "The truth about divine things which is attainable by reason is fittingly proposed to man as an object of belief. Three disadvantages would result if this truth were left solely to the inquiry of reason. One is that few men would have knowledge of God, . . . for three reasons. Some indeed on account of an indisposition of temperament, by reason of which many are naturally indisposed to knowledge. . . . Some are hindered by the needs of household affairs. . . . And some are hindered by laziness. . . . First, because this truth is so profound. . . . Secondly, because many things are required beforehand. . . . Thirdly, because at the time of youth, the mind, when tossed about by the various movements of the passions, is not fit for the knowledge of so

After such consideration a person is no longer surprised at the great variety of natural religions. Obviously, the religion of an individual, tribe, or nation was affected by any number of factors. All of them help to make *reason alone* an *unrealiable* guide. Evidently, men are rational but not too rational in religion unless they are guided by a better light than reason.

C. Evolution in Religion

After Darwin proposed the theory of evolution, some "armchair scientists" imagined that it applied in every field. And so they attempted to describe the evolution of religion as a progressive development from the less perfect to the more perfect forms of religion. In their opinion, the early primitives believed in magicism, animism and totemism because these seemed farthest removed from monotheism and a high moral standard of conduct. The later primitives showed a marked improvement in so far as they were merely polytheistic and less immoral. And as the centuries rolled by, men became less polytheistic and better morally until at the present stage of evolution most men are monotheistic and have a high standard of morality. Among the innumerable natural religions they "discovered" examples to fit their theories. As a result, they fooled a lot of people.

Unfortunately, they were more anxious to confirm their theories than to ascertain the truth. This was soon apparent, for archaeologists who had spent their lives studying the early primitives declared that most of them did not believe in magicism, animism, or totemism. In fact, the majority of them were monotheistic and had rather high moral standards. Probably, they were still guided by a primitive revelation given to Adam and Eve.

According to the archaeologists, magicism, animism, and totemism were *degenerate* forms of religion spreading among the *later* primitives. In fact, magic does not play an important role in religion until the time of the Egyptian and Babylonian empires. By the time of Christ, most nations were polytheistic or pantheistic and very immoral. Certainly, Greece and Rome were. If

---

sublime a truth. . . . The third disadvantage is that much falsehood is mingled with the investigations of human reason, on account of the weakness of our intellect in forming its judgments, and by reason of the admixture of phantasms." St. Thomas, Contra Gent., lib. 1, c. 4.

there had been any religious "progress," it was in the wrong direction.

Moreover, some Christian scholars like Schmidt [26] instead of theorizing in armchairs went out and lived among peoples who still have a primitive culture. After careful study, they found that the Pygmy tribes of Africa, the Bushmen of Australia, the natives of Tierra del Fuego, and the Arctic peoples are monotheistic. Although some of them honor a number of superior beings, they worship one as supreme. This is clear from the names and attributes they reserve for him. Some of them recognize his spiritual nature; others adore him as creator; still others regard him as a person.

Thus as far as we know today the early primitives were mostly monotheistic and had better moral standards than Hollywood. There is *no* factual proof of any evolution in religion. Of course, we will continue to read about it in "sensational" magazines and Sunday supplements.

26. Cf. W. Schmidt, *The Origin and Growth of Religion,* New York (Dial Press), 1931.

Supplementary Readings

THE EXISTENCE OF GOD [1]

The existence of God can be proved in five ways.

The first and more manifest way is the argument from motion. It is certain, and evident to our senses, that in the world some things are in motion. Now whatever is moved is moved by another, for nothing can be moved except it is in potentiality to that towards which it is moved; whereas a thing moves inasmuch as it is in act. For motion is nothing else than the reduction of something from potentiality to actuality. But nothing can be reduced from potentiality to actuality, except by something in a state of actuality. Thus that which is actually hot, as fire, makes wood, which is potentially hot, to be actually hot, and thereby moves and changes it. Now it is not possible that the same thing should be at once in actuality and potentiality in the same respect, but only in different respects. For what is actually hot cannot simultaneously be potentially hot; but it is simultaneously potentially cold. It is therefore impossible that in the same respect and in the same way a thing should be both mover and moved, i.e., that it should move itself. Therefore, whatever is moved must be moved by another. If that by which it is moved be itself moved, then this also must needs be moved by another, and that by another again. But this cannot go on to infinity, because then there would be no first mover, and, consequently, no other mover, seeing that subsequent movers move only inasmuch as they are moved by the first mover; as the staff moves only because it is moved by the hand. Therefore it is necessary to arrive at a first mover, moved by no other; and this everyone understands to be God.

The second way is from the nature of efficient cause. In the world of sensible things we find there is an order of efficient causes. There is no case known (neither is it, indeed, possible) in which a thing is found to be the efficient cause of itself; for so it would be prior to itself, which is impossible. Now in efficient causes it is not possible to go on

1. St. Thomas Aquinas, *Summa Theologica*, I, q. 2, a. 3.

242

to infinity, because in all efficient causes following in order, the first is the cause of the intermediate cause, and the intermediate is the cause of the ultimate cause, whether the intermediate cause be several, or one only. Now to take away the cause is to take away the effect. Therefore, if there be no first cause among efficient causes, there will be no ultimate nor any intermediate cause. But if in efficient causes it is possible to go on to infinity, there will be no first efficient cause, neither will there be an ultimate effect, nor any intermediate efficient causes; all of which is plainly false. Therefore it is necessary to admit a first efficient cause, to which everyone gives the name of God.

The third way is taken from contingency and necessity, and runs thus. We find in nature things that are possible to be and not to be, since they are found to be generated, and to be corrupted, and consequently, it is possible for them to be and not to be. But it is impossible for the totality of existent being to be of this type. Therefore, if everything can not-be, then at one time there was nothing in existence, because that which does not exist begins to exist only through something already existing. Therefore, if at one time nothing was in existence, it would have been impossible for anything to have begun to exist; and thus even now nothing would be in existence—which is absurd. Therefore, not all beings are merely possible, but there must exist something the existence of which is necessary. But every necessary thing either has its necessity caused by another, or not. Now it is impossible to go on to infinity in necessary things which have their necessity caused by another, as has been already proved in regard to efficient causes. Therefore we cannot but admit the existence of some being having of itself its own necessity, and not receiving it from another, but rather causing in others their necessity. This all men speak of as God.

The fourth way is taken from the gradation to be found in things. Among beings there are some more and some less good, true, noble, and the like. But "more" or "less" are predicated of different things according as they resemble in their different ways something which is the maximum, as a thing is said to be hotter according as it more nearly resembles that which is hottest; so that there is something which is truest, something best, something noblest, and consequently, something which is most being, for those things that are greatest in truth are greatest in being, as it is written in Metaph. ii. Now the maximum in any genus is the cause of all in that genus, as fire which is the maximum of heat, is the cause of all hot things, as is said in the same book. Therefore there must also be something which is to all beings the cause of their being, goodness, and every other perfection; and this being we call God.

The fifth way is taken from the governance of the world. We see that things which lack intelligence, such as natural bodies, act for an end, and this is evident from their acting always, or nearly always, in the same way, so as to obtain the best result. Hence it is plain that they achieve their end, not fortuitously, but designedly. Now whatever lacks intelligence cannot move towards an end, unless it be directed by some being endowed with knowledge and intelligence; as the arrow is directed by the archer. Therefore some intelligent being exists by whom all natural beings are directed to their end; and this being we call God.

BOYS' PHILOSOPHIES [1]

I have been asked to tell you what Christians believe, and I am going to begin by telling you one thing that Christians don't need to believe. If you are a Christian you don't have to believe that all the other religions are simply wrong all through. If you are an atheist you do have to believe that the main point in all the religions of the whole world is simply one huge mistake. If you are a Christian, you are free to think that all these religions, even the queerest ones, contain at least some hint of the truth. When I was an atheist I had to try to persuade myself that the whole human race were pretty good fools until about one hundred years ago; when I became a Christian I was able to take a more liberal view. But of course, being a Christian does mean thinking that where Christianity differs from other religions, Christianity is right and they are wrong. Like in arithmetic—there's only one right answer to a sum, and all other answers are wrong; but some of the wrong answers are much nearer being right than others.

The first big division of humanity is into the majority, who believe in some kind of God or gods, and the minority who don't. On this point, Christianity lines up with the majority—lines up with ancient Greeks and Romans, modern savages, Stoics, Platonists, Hindoos, Mohammedans, etc., against the modern Western European materialist. There are all sorts of different reasons for believing in God, and here I'll mention only one. It is this. Supposing there was no intelligence behind the universe, no creative mind. In that case nobody designed my brain for the purpose of thinking. It is merely that when the atoms inside my skull happen for physical or chemical reasons to arrange themselves in a certain way, this gives me, as a by-product, the sensation I call thought. But if so, how can I trust my own thinking to be true? It's like upsetting a milk-jug and hoping that the way the splash arranges itself will give you a map of London. But if I can't trust my own thinking, of course I can't trust the arguments leading to atheism, and therefore have no reason to be an atheist, or anything else. Unless I believe in God, I can't believe in thought: so I can never use thought to disbelieve in God.

Now I go on to the next big division. People who all believe in God can be divided according to the sort of God they believe in. There are two very different ideas on this subject. One of them is the idea that He is beyond good and evil. We call one thing good and another thing bad. But according to some people that's merely our human point of view. These people would say that the wiser you become the less you'd want to call anything good or bad, and the more clearly you'd see that everything is good in one way and bad in another, and that nothing could have been different. Consequently, these people think that long before you got anywhere near the divine point of view the distinction would have disappeared altogether. We call a cancer bad, they'd say, because it kills a man; but you might just as well call a successful

1. C. S. Lewis, *The Case for Christianity*, New York (Macmillan Co.), 1948, pp. 31–36.

surgeon bad because he kills a cancer. It all depends on the point of view. The other and opposite idea is that God is quite definitely "good" or "righteous," a God who takes sides, who loves love and hates hatred, who wants us to believe in one way and not in another. The first of these views—the one that thinks God beyond good and evil— is called Pantheism. It was held by the great Prussian philosopher Hegel and, as far as I can understand them, by the Hindoos. The other view is held by Jews, Mohammedans and Christians.

And with this big difference between Pantheism and the Christian idea of God, there usually goes another. Pantheists usually believe that God, so to speak, animates the universe as you animate your body: that the universe almost is God, so that if it didn't exist He wouldn't exist either, and anything you find in the universe is a part of God. The Christian idea is quite different. They think God made the universe— like a man making a picture or composing a tune. A painter isn't a picture, and he doesn't die if his picture is destroyed. You may say, "He's put a lot of himself into it," but that only means that all its beauty and interest has come out of his head. His skill isn't in the picture in the same way that it's in his head, or even in his hands. I expect you see how this difference between Pantheists and Christians hangs together with the other one. If you don't take the distinction between good and bad very seriously, then it's easy to say that anything you find in this world is a part of God. But, of course, if you think some things really bad, and God really good, then you can't talk like that. You must believe that God is separate from the world and that some of the things we see in it are contrary to His will. Confronted with a cancer or a slum the Pantheists can say, "If you could only see it from the divine point of view, you would realize that this also is God." The Christian replies, "Don't talk damned nonsense." For Christianity is a fighting religion. It thinks God made the world— that space and time, heat and cold, and all the colors and tastes, and all the animals and vegetables, are things that God "made up out of His head" as a man makes up a story. But it also thinks that a great many things have gone wrong with the world that God made and that God insists, and insists very loudly, on our putting them right again.

And of course, that raises a very big question. If a good God made the world why has it gone wrong? And for many years I simply wouldn't listen to the Christian answers to this question, because I kept on feeling "whatever you say, and however clever your arguments are, isn't it much simpler and easier to say that the world was not made by an intelligent power? Aren't all your arguments simply a complicated attempt to avoid the obvious?" But then that threw me back into those difficulties about atheism which I spoke of a moment ago. And soon I saw another difficulty.

My argument against God was that the universe seemed so cruel and unjust. But how had I got this idea of just and unjust? A man doesn't call a line crooked unless he has some idea of a straight line. What was I comparing this universe with when I called it unjust? If the whole show was bad and senseless from A to Z, so to speak, why did I, who was supposed to be part of the show, find myself in such violent reaction against it? A man feels wet when he falls into water, because man isn't a water animal: a fish wouldn't feel wet. Of course I could have given up my idea of justice by saying it was nothing but a private idea of my own. But if I did that then my argument against God collapsed too—for the argument depended on saying that the world was really unjust, not that it just didn't happen to please my private fancies. Thus in the vary act of trying to prove that God didn't exist—in other words, that the whole of reality was senseless—I found I was forced to assume that one part of reality—namely my idea of justice—was full of sense. Consequently atheism turns out to be too simple. If the whole universe has no meaning, we should never have found out that it has no meaning: just as if there were no light in the universe and therefore no creatures with eyes we should never know it was dark. Dark would be a word without meaning.

Very well then, atheism is too simple. And I'll tell you another view that is also too simple. It's the view I call Christianity-and-water, the view that just says there's a good God in Heaven and everything is all right—leaving out all the difficult and terrible doctrines about sin and hell and the devil, and the redemption. Both these are boys' philosophies.

It is no good asking for a simple religion. After all, real things aren't simple. They look simple, but they're not. The table I'm sitting at looks simple: but ask a scientist to tell you what it's really made of— all about the atoms and how the light waves rebound from them and hit my eye and what they do to the optic nerve and what it does to my brain—and, of course, you find that what we call "seeing a table" lands you in mysteries and complications which you can hardly get to the end of. A child, saying a child's prayer, looks simple. And if you're content to stop there, well and good. But if you're not—and the modern world usually isn't—if you want to go on and ask what's really happening—then you must be prepared for something difficult. If we ask for something more than simplicity, it's silly then to complain that the something more isn't simple.

THE RELIGION OF THE PRIMITIVE [1]

As the material collected by ethnologists proves, the primitive conceives God not only as the mighty, wise and benevolent creator or generator of life, but also as the "seer" who searches the heart, the Holy One who imposes commands and the Merciful One who pardons the guilty who ask His forgiveness. This picture of God is not confined to the Biblical account of man's origins, but is to be found in the traditions of primitive peoples all the world over, indeed of mankind as a whole, and influences man's practical thought and conduct to this day.

For Newman it was a fundamental principle that "as we have our initial knowledge of the universe through sense, so do we in the first instance begin to learn about its Lord and God from conscience." Every man, whether born into the blessings of higher culture or in the reed huts or pile dwellings of the primitive, bears in his heart a

1. Otto Karrer, *Religions of Mankind*, New York (Sheed & Ward), 1936, pp. 131–133, 135–136.

mysterious yet compelling clear command "Thou shalt." He did not give it to himself and he cannot get rid of it. We may agree with Scheler that it is innate in man as such. The apprehension of moral values is as native to him as his capacity for truth. We experience, and the primitive also experiences, goodness as a value, in fact, as the supreme value. We call conduct "good" when the choice which inspires it has decided in favor of the higher against the lower value, and we call a man good when the fundamental direction of his will is towards the good. Until a man possesses this moral sensibility he is no man. He is as little a man as a being incapable of intellectual knowledge and apprehension.

From this point of view the particular content of an individual's moral judgment is indifferent. We have not to enquire whether the primitive and the civilized man agree in all respects in their judgment of what is good or our duty, but simply whether we can discover in the former distinctively moral judgments of any description. The answer is not doubtful. The "formal" morality is to be found in the primitive equally with the member of an advanced civilization. He is conscious of a law in his heart, a voice speaking with authority which forbids certain actions and commands others. He regards it as wrong to do to another what he would not have done to himself, acknowledges a duty to be just, hospitable, ready to help his neighbor, grateful, respectful to elders, faithful in marriage. What is his reason? He has not made these laws, nor any man in authority over him, nor yet any human authority of the past. He is well aware of the distinction between the commands of man and those imposed by the inner voice of conscience.

The fact of conscience, however, this sense of right, the feeling of satisfaction when a man does right, of guilt when he does what he knows to be wrong, strikes the childlike primitive with "awe." Here too "awe" is the primary emotion. The man who retains the child's simplicity and does not attempt to explain his experience away by some forced interpretation, finds himself compelled to regard the obligation imposed from within as the echo of a supreme invisible will. And the tendency to personification characteristic of the primitive makes it impossible for him to be content with the abstract conception of a law or order. His experiences of conscience force upon the primitive the conclusion that there is a spiritual Being, a supreme and holy Lord, who has imposed a law upon him. No doubt he makes the mistake of conceiving the author of this "obligation" too anthropomorphically. But this is of minor significance. The important point is that the obligation is "the will of the absolute Being." Conscience is His voice. The tribal ordinances transmitted by education from generation to generation are the historic social precipitates of this aboriginal intuition of conscience. In short, as Newman sums it up, "the phenomena of Conscience, as a dictate, avail to impress the imagination with the picture of a Supreme Governor, a Judge, holy, just, powerful, allseeing, retributive." In other words, "they explain the origin of the moral conception of God."

Once conceived in the mind of the primitive, the notion of the "holy" God develops. It deepens, strengthens and enriches those original emotions from which itself arose. Awe becomes "reverence." For the Being who not only bestowed life in his goodness, but demands moral goodness, must Himself possess the most sublime purity. Man cannot but revere Him. It is a token of this reverence that He is mentioned with great awe, with trembling and in low tones. Indeed, to avoid profanation, the primitive even conceals his knowledge of Him by a secret name known only to the initiate. He has nothing but contempt for the strangers who speak of Him so lightly. With tears of heartfelt emotion he receives His laws delivered in His name by the elders of the tribe, and yields a willing obedience to the commands of One whom he may address as his lord and father. Surely we must believe that in this attitude the sentiments of the ancestors have survived, as they handed them on to their children.

This reverence is mingled with "love." For this Divine Being is good, perfectly good—because He commands goodness, and to practice the goodness which He commands produces an inner satisfaction, while at the same time bringing a blessing upon the tribe and shielding it from misfortune. We cannot therefore help loving the Supreme Being. For it is the nature of goodness to evoke love. The testimony of this is the powerful aspiration to be united to Him, and share mystically His bliss. The prayer of the primitive is a further witness. At initiation, above all, and by the grave of the dead, the primitive prays. Though some tribes are without the custom of daily prayer, all pray on solemn occasions or in the hours of need or peril. Primitive prayer resembles somewhat the conversation of a child with his father. There is little scope for premeditation. The prayer is the heartfelt utterance of a child's unreflecting confidence and trust, "Now He will look down upon us, our Father. Thanks, my Father. Thanks, thou kind old one." These and similar ejaculations are the customary prayers of the Yaman of Tierra del Fuego. . . .

The innocent child-man was, indeed, also acquainted with a righteous Deity. But he was purely the friend who rewarded good conduct and instilled peace into the soul. The man conscious of guilt discovers another aspect of His nature. He knows God as the angry and avenging Deity of retribution. This knowledge gives rise to the melancholy and gloomy features in the religions of mankind. Not only in this life is the wicked man punished by God, say the Andamanese; everyone is also judged at death. The same belief is held by the natives of Malacca, the Australians and the Negrillos. We may, if we like, dub it superstition when the primitive sees in the storm and lightning threatening signs of the Divine wrath. But what shall we say of the hecatombs of bloody sacrifice or the self-torture of crowds to which in all parts of the world men submit to appease their God? All these expressions of religious feeling though too often barbarities, claim our respect when we consider their fundamental motive. Most commonly, or at least very frequently, it is a sense of guilt which craves assurance of pardon. And in Newman's opinion "they who are not superstitious without the Gospel, will not be religious with it."

Among the surviving primitive peoples it is true, the Kamilaroi of Australia, for example, we occasionally find the belief that the wicked man, the kogil as the Kamilaroi term him, is beyond pardon. But the conviction predominant among the primitive peoples is "trust in a merciful God" who forgives the repentant sinner. This is the belief, amongst others, of the Andamanese, the Semang, the Senoi of Malacca, the Batak of Sumatra, the Dagari, Ewe and Mkulwe negroes, and the Eastern Malagasy. "I am guilty," the Ewe confesses to the Sky-god. "Lo, I bring thee the gift thou wilt have at my hands that thou mayest be wroth with me no longer. Therefore take me back into thy care as in the past." He will never sin against thee again," the priest pleads on behalf of his client. The Batak who falls ill, convinced that he has offended the tondi, the spirit of life, makes his confession: "Thus and thus" (the sins are specified) "have I sinned against Thee. I will amend. This offering is earnest money, the acknowledgment of my guilt." Here also the priest intercedes. "Have compassion upon him, impute it not to him." And in Dufaure Island a misfortune occasions an examination of conscience. "Ye are wroth with me. In your anger have ye taken our child from us. Be satisfied and bury your wrath . . ." "Be not wroth with me, hate me not, be merciful to me, have compassion on me," the Karens pray. After a detailed public confession and act of contrition the Mkulwe throw chips of wood and straws, symbols of their sins, into the air, with these words: "Now all my sins are blown away by the wind." In short, man believes in the mercy of God as he believes in His severity and holiness.

This conviction and confidence inspired by faith mankind has never wholly lost in the course of its history. Confession of sin in trust of pardon has been shown by Pettazzoni to be an almost universal feature of religion, as it has found expression throughout human history. "When shall I with joyful countenance behold Thy mercy?" prays the Indian penitent to Varuna. "I, thy bondservant, in bitter pains call upon Thee—but if Thou regardest a man with friendship he recovers," is the refrain taken up by the Babylonian.

It is the same with the Egyptians, Greeks and Buddhists. Though outside the Bible the expectation of deliverance is not completely or exclusively religious, it is part of the faith of humanity down the ages, and as A. Jeremias has shown, is in many respects comparable with the Messianic expectation of the Old Testament.

Select Bibliography

Adam, K. *The Spirit of Catholicism* (rev. ed.). New York: Macmillan 1946.
———. *The Son of God*. New York: Sheed & Ward, 1934.
———. *One and Holy*. New York: Sheed & Ward, 1951.
Albright, W. *From the Stone Age to Christianity* (2nd ed.). Baltimore: Johns Hopkins, 1946.
———. *Archeology and the Religion of Israel*. Baltimore: Johns Hopkins, 1942.
———. *The Archeology of Palestine and the Bible* (3rd ed.). New York: Revell, 1935.
Algermissen, K. *Christian Denominations*. St. Louis: Herder, 1945.
Allport, G. *The Individual and His Religion*. New York: Macmillan, 1950.
Amann, E. *The Church of the Early Centuries*. St. Louis: Herder, 1930.
Arendzen, J. *The Gospels: Fact, Myth, or Legend?* St. Louis: Herder, 1924.
———. *Prophets, Priests and Publicans*. London: Sands, 1926.
———. *Whom Do You Say?* (2nd ed.). New York: Sheed & Ward, 1941.
Attwater, D. *The Christian Churches of the East* (2 vols., rev. ed.). Milwaukee: Bruce, 1946.
Aubert, R. *Le Problème de L'Acte de Foi*. Louvain: Warny, 1945.
Bainvel, J. *Faith and the Act of Faith*. St. Louis: Herder, 1926.
———. *Is There Salvation Outside the Catholic Church?* St. Louis: Herder, 1917.
Barry, W. *The Coming Age and the Catholic Church*. London: Cassell, 1929.
Batiffol, P. *Cathedra Petri*. Paris: Cerf, 1938.
———. *Catholicism and Papacy*. London: Sands, 1926.
———. *The Credibility of the Gospel*. New York: Longmans, Green, 1912.
———. *Primitive Catholicism*. New York: Longmans, Green, 1911.
Bell, H. *Recent Discoveries of Biblical Papyri*. Oxford: Clarendon Press, 1937.
———, and Sheat, T. (eds.). *Fragments of an Unknown Gospel and Other Early Christian Papyri*. London: Trustees of the British Museum, 1935.
Belloc, H. *The Catholic Church and History*. New York: Macmillan, 1926.
———. *Essays of a Catholic*. New York: Macmillan, 1931.
———. *Europe and the Faith*. New York: Paulist Press, 1920.
———. *The Great Heresies*. New York: Sheed and Ward, 1938.
———. *The Question and the Answer*. Milwaukee: Bruce, 1932.
———. *Survivals and New Arrivals*. London: Macmillan, 1929.

Benson, R. *Christ in the Church*. St. Louis: Herder, 1911.

——. *Confessions of a Convert*. New York: Longmans, Green, 1913.

——. *Non-Catholic Denominations*. New York: Longmans, Green, 1910.

——. *Paradoxes of Catholicism*. New York: Longmans, Green, 1913.

Berdiaev, N. *The End of Our Time*. New York: Sheed & Ward, 1933.

Bettenson, H. (ed.). *Documents of the Christian Church*. New York: Oxford Univ. Press, 1943.

Bonsirven, J. *Juifs et Chrétiens*. Paris: Flammarion, 1936.

——. *On the Ruins of the Temple*. London: Burns, Oates & Washbourne, 1931.

Braun, F. *Où en est le Problème de Jésus?* Paris: Gabalda, 1932.

——. *L'Evangile devant les Temps Présents*. Paris: Desclée, 1938.

Brunhes, G. *Faith and its Rational Justification*. St. Louis: Herder, 1931.

Butler, E. *The Vatican Council* (2 vols.). New York: Longmans, Green, 1930.

Cayre, F. *Manual of Patrology* (2 vols.). Paris: Desclée, 1927.

Chapman, J. *Bishop Gore and the Catholic Claims*. New York: Longmans, 1905.

——. *The Four Gospels*. New York: Sheed & Ward, 1944.

——. *Studies on the Early Papacy*. New York: Benziger, 1928.

Chesterton, G. K. *Autobiography*. New York: Sheed & Ward, 1936.

——. *The Catholic Church and Conversion*. New York: Macmillan, 1926.

——. *The Everlasting Man*. New York: Dodd, Mead, 1937.

——. *Orthodoxy*. New York: Dodd, Mead, 1949.

——. *The Thing—Why I Am a Catholic*. New York: Dodd, Mead, 1930.

Chevalier, J. *Pascal*. New York: Longmans, Green, 1930.

Civardi, L. *A Manual of Catholic Action*. London: Sheed & Ward, 1935.

Claudel, P. *Letters to a Doubter*. New York: Boni, 1927.

——. *Ways and Crossways*. New York: Sheed & Ward, 1933.

Conway, B. *The Question Box* (New ed.). New York: Paulist Press, 1929.

Cyprian, St. *On the Unity of the Catholic Church*. New York: Macmillan, 1928.

D'Arcy, M. *Mirage and Truth*. New York: Macmillan, 1935.

——. *The Nature of Belief*. London: Sheed & Ward, 1931.

Dawson, C. *The Age of the Gods*. New York: Sheed & Ward, 1933.

——. *Beyond Politics*. New York: Sheed & Ward, 1939.

——. *Progress and Religion*. London: Sheed & Ward, 1929.

——. *Religion and Culture*. London: Sheed & Ward, 1948.

Delany, S. *Rome From Within*. Milwaukee: Bruce, 1935.

——. *Why Rome?* New York: Dial Press, 1930.

Denzinger, H. *Enchiridion symbolorum, definitionum et declarationem* (21-23 ed.). Friburgi Brisgoviae: Herder, 1937.

Dictionnaire Apologetique (6 vols. 4th ed.), edited by A. D'Ales. Paris: Beauchesne, 1911ff.

Dictionnaire de Theologie Catholique (15 vols.), edited by Vacant, Mangenot, and Amann. Paris: Letouzey, 1903ff.

Duchesne, L. *Early History of the Christian Church*. (4 vols. 4th ed.). New York: Longmans, Green, 1925.

Dunne, G. *Religion and American Democracy*. New York: America, 1949.

Dwight, T. *Thoughts of a Catholic Anatomist*. New York: Longmans, Green, 1927.

Eusebius. *The Ecclesiastical History* (2 vols.). New York: Putnam's, 1926-32.

Eymieu, A. *Two Arguments for Catholicism*. New York: Benziger, 1927.

Fanfani, A. *Catholicism, Protestantism, and Capitalism*. London: Sheed & Ward, 1935.

The Fathers of the Church, edited by Schopp and Deferrari. New York: Fathers of the Church, Inc., 1947ff.

Ancient Christian Writers, edited by Quasten and Plumpe. Westminster: Newman, 1946ff.

The Ante-Nicene Christian Library (24 vols.), edited by Roberts and Donaldson. Edinburgh: Clark, 1866–72.

The Ante-Nicene Fathers (10 vols.). American reprint of the Edinburgh ed., revised by Coxe. New York: Scribner's, 1925.

A Library of the Fathers (45 vols.), edited by Pusey, Keble and Newman. Oxford: Parker: Rivington, 1838–88.

A Select Library of Nicene and Post-Nicene Fathers of the Christian Church (28 vols.), edited by Schaff and Wace. New York: Scribner's, 1925.

Felder, H. *Christ and the Critics* (2 vols.). London: Burns, Oates & Washbourne, 1924.

Ferm, V. (ed.). *Religion in the Twentieth Century*. New York: The Philosophical Library, 1948.

Fillion, L. *The Life of Christ* (3 vols.). St. Louis: Herder, 1927–29.

——. *Les Miracles de Notre-Seigneur* (2 vols.). Paris, 1935.

Finlay, P. *The Church of Christ*. New York: Longmans, Green, 1922.

Fitzsimons, J. *The Christian in a Changing World*. South Bend: Fides, 1950.

Fortescue, A. *The Early Papacy*. London: Burns, Oates & Washbourne, 1920.

Gardeil, A. *La Crédibilité et L'Apologétique* (2nd ed.). Paris: Gabalda, 1912.

Garrigou-Lagrange, R. *De Revelatione* (2 vols., 4th ed.). Rome: Ferrari, 1945.

——. *Dieu, Son Existence et Sa Nature*. Paris: Beauchesne, 1923.

Gibbons, Card. *The Faith of Our Fathers*. Baltimore: Murphy, 1892.

Graham, A. *The Christ of Catholicism*. New York: Longmans, Green, 1947.

Grandmaison, L. *Jesus Christ, His Person, His Message, His Credentials* (3 vols.). London: Sheed & Ward, 1930–32.

Hastings, J. *A Dictionary of Christ and the Gospels* (2 vols.). New York: Scribners, 1906–08.

Hertzler, J. *Social Institutions*. Lincoln: University of Nebraska Press, 1946.

Hoffman, R. J. *Restoration*. New York: Sheed & Ward, 1934.

Huby, J. *The Church and the Gospels*. New York: Holt, 1931.

——. *Christus: Manuel d'Histoire des Religions*. Paris: Beauchesne, 1912.

Hugel, F. von. *Some Notes on Petrine Claims*. London: Sheed & Ward, 1930.

Hughes, P. *History of the Church* (4 vols.). New York: Sheed & Ward, 1934–36.

Janin, R. *Les Eglises Orientales et les Rites Orientaux*. Paris: Bloud & Gay, 1935.

Karrer, O. *Religions of Mankind*. London: Sheed & Ward, 1936.

Kenyon, F. *Our Bible and the Ancient Manuscripts* (4th ed.). New York: Harper, 1948.

King, A. *The Rites of Eastern Christendom* (2 vols.). Rome: Catholic Book Agency, 1947.

Knox, R. *The Belief of Catholics*. New York: Sheed & Ward, 1940.

——. *Broadcast Minds*. New York: Sheed & Ward, 1933.

——. *The Church on Earth*. New York: Macmillan, 1929.

——. *God and the Atom*. New York: Sheed & Ward, 1945.

——. *The New Testament in English*. New York: Sheed & Ward, 1947.

——, and Lunn, A. *Difficulties*. London: Eyre & Spottiswoode, 1932.

Koesters, L. *The Believer's Christ*. St. Louis: Herder, 1939.

——. *The Church: Its Divine Authority*. St. Louis: Herder, 1938.

Krull, V. *Christian Denominations*. (14th ed.). Chicago: Donohue, 1936.

Lagrange, M. *Christ and Renan.* London: Benziger, 1928.

——. *Introduction à L'Etude du Nouveau Testament.* Paris: Gabalda, 1933.

——. *The Meaning of Christianity.* New York: Longmans, Green, 1920.

——. *The Gospel of Jesus Christ* (2 vols.). Westminster: Newman, 1938.

Lattey, C. (ed.). *The Church.* Cambridge: Heffer, 1928.

——. *The Papacy.* Cambridge: Heffer, 1924.

——. *The Pre-Nicene Church.* London: Burns, Oates & Washbourne, 1935.

Lebreton, J. *The Life and Teaching of Jesus Christ Our Lord* (2 vols.). Milwaukee: Bruce, 1935.

——, and Zeiller, J. *The History of the Primitive Church* (2 vols.). New York: Macmillan, 1949.

Lelotte, F. *Fundamental Principles of Catholic Action.* Montreal: Fides, 1947.

Le Roy, A. *Religion of the Primitives.* New York: Macmillan, 1922.

Lewis, C. S. *Miracles.* London: Geoffrey Bles, 1947.

Luce, C. "The 'Real' Reason," *McCalls,* LXXIV (1947), 5, 6, 7.

Lunn, A. *Now I See.* New York: Sheed & Ward, 1934.

——. *The Third Day.* Westminster: Newman, 1945.

——. *Within That City.* London: Sheed & Ward, 1936.

——. and Joad, C. *Is Christianity True?* Philadelphia: Lippincott, 1933.

Mascall, E. *He Who Is.* London: Longmans, Green, 1943.

Maritain, J. *The Things That Are Not Caesar's.* London: Scribner's, 1931.

McNabb, V. *Infallibility.* St. Louis: Herder, 1927.

Messenger, E. (ed.). *Studies in Comparative Religion* (5 vols.). London: Catholic Truth Society, 1935.

Murray, J. "The Roman Catholic Church," *The Annals of the American Academy of Political and Social Science,* 256 (1948), 36–42.

Newman, J. *Apologia pro Vita Sua.* New York: Sheed & Ward, 1946.

——. *Certain Difficulties Felt by Anglicans in Catholic Teaching Considered* (2 vols.). London: Longmans, Green, 1901.

——. *The Church of the Fathers.* London: Burns & Oates, 1868.

——. *Essays and Sketches* (3 vols.). New York: Longmans, Green, 1948.

——. *Present Position of Catholics.* New York: Longmans, Green, 1935.

——. *Two Essays on Biblical and on Ecclesiastical Miracles.* London: Longmans, Green, 1907.

O'Brien, J. *The Faith of Millions.* Huntington: Our Sunday Visitor, 1938.

——. *Truths Men Live By.* New York: Macmillan, 1946.

O'Neill, J. *Catholicism and American Freedom.* New York: Harper, 1952.

Patrologia Graeca (162 vols.). Paris: Migne, 1857–66.

Patrologia Latina (221 vols.). Paris: Migne, 1844–55.

Phelan, M. *The Straight Path; or Marks of the True Church.* New York: Longmans, Green, 1935.

Pinard de la Boullaye, H. *L'Etude Comparée des Religions* (2 vols.). Paris: Beauchesne, 1922–25.

Pope, H. *The Catholic Church and the Bible.* New York: Macmillan, 1928.

Prat, F. *Jesus Christ* (2 vols.). Milwaukee: Bruce, 1950.

Ricciotti, G. *The Life of Christ.* Milwaukee: Bruce, 1947.

Ring, G. *Gods of the Gentiles.* Milwaukee: Bruce, 1929.

Salaville, P. *An Introduction to the Study of Eastern Liturgies.* London: Sands, 1938.

Schmidt, W. *The Origin and Growth of Religion.* New York: The Dial Press, 1931.

Schmidt, W. *Primitive Revelation.* St. Louis: Herder, 1939.

Sertillanges, A. *Le Miracle de L'Eglise.* Paris: Spes, 1933.

Sheed, F. *A Map of Life.* New York: Sheed & Ward, 1933.

————. *Theology and Sanity.* New York: Sheed & Ward, 1946.

Sheen, F. *Religion without God.* New York: Longmans, Green, 1928.

Steinmueller, J. *A Companion to Scripture Studies* (3 vols.). New York: Wagner, 1941–43.

Stoddard, J. *Rebuilding a Lost Faith.* New York: Kenedy, 1922.

Tawney, R. *Religion and the Rise of Capitalism.* New York: Harcourt, Brace, 1926.

Taylor, A. E. *Does God Exist?* New York: Macmillan, 1947.

Thomas, St. *Summa Theologica.* (Part I, QQ. I–XXVI.). London: Burns, Oates & Washbourne, 1920.

de Tonquédec, J. *Introduction à L'Etude du Merveilleux et du Miracle* (3rd ed.). Paris: Beauchesne, 1923.

Vassall-Phillips, O. *Catholic Christianity.* London: Washbourne, 1916.

Vermeersch, A. *Tolerance.* London: Washbourne, 1913.

Ward, L. *The Catholic Church and the Appeal to Reason.* New York: Macmillan, 1926.

Ward, M. and Sheed, F. *Catholic Evidence Training Outlines* (3rd ed.). London: Sheed & Ward, 1934.

Watkin, E. *The Bow in the Clouds.* New York: Macmillan, 1932.

————. *Some Thoughts on Catholic Apologetics.* St. Louis: Herder, 1915.

William, F. *The Life of Christ.* St. Louis: Herder, 1936.

Woodlock, T. *The Catholic Pattern.* New York: Simon & Schuster, 1942.

Index

Acts of the Apostles:
 historicity of, 62–63
Apostles:
 authority of, 114
 and resurrection of Christ, 96–98

Bible, *see* Scripture, Holy
Buddhism, 8-9

Catholic Church:
 apostolicity of, 175–176
 catholicity of, 164–165, 175
 founded by Christ, 108–146
 fruitfulness of, 159–161
 growth of, 149–153
 holiness of, 153–159
 ignorance of, 177
 infallibility of, 183–187
 stability of, 165–166
 unity of, 162–163, 175
Christ:
 claimed to be God, 30–41
 claimed to be Messiah, 27–28
 credibility of claims, 70–106
Censures, 207
Christ's Church:
 Protestant views of, 111–113
 Roman Catholic view of, 110–111
Communism, 12–13
Councils, General, 208–210

Deism, 45

Eastern Catholic Churches, 147
Epistles of St. Paul:
 historicity of, 62-63
Evidence:
 external, 50
 internal, 50

Fathers of Church:
 definition of: 60
 on infallibility of Pope, 190–195
 on primacy of Pope, 137–143

Genuineness of Gospels, 51–55
Gospels:
 apocryphal, 63
 critics, 44–49, 64–70
 date of composition of, 48–49
 genuineness of, 51–55
 integrity of, 56–62
 trustworthiness of, 55–56

Hallucination theory, 94–95, 103–106
Hinduism, 7–8
Historicity, *see* Gospels or Epistles
Holiness of Catholic Church, 153–159

Infallibility:
 how exercised, 204–211
 of the Church, 183–187
 of the Pope, 188–203
Indifferentism, 176–178
Inspiration of the Bible, 216–219

Intregrity of the Gospels, 56–62
Islam, 11–12

Jews, history of, 15–25

Magisterium of Church:
    ordinary, 204–205
    solemn, 206–210
Marks of the Church, 167–178
Messiah:
    Christ claimed to be, 27–28
    prophecies about, 70–72
    Jewish idea of, 25
Miracles of Chirst:
    apologetical fact of, 82
    historical fact of, 75–78
    supernatural fact of, 78–82

New Testament, 216

Old Testament, 15, 215–216
Orthodox Churches, 147

Paul, St.:
    authority of, 118–119
    reprimands St. Peter, 134 fn.
    see Epistles of,
Peter, St.:
    bestowal of primacy, 132–133
    exercise of primacy, 134–136
    promise of primacy, 125–132
Pharisees, 21–22
Philosophical presuppositions, 228–252
Pope:
    primacy of, 125–146
    infallibility of, 188–203

Proofs of God's existence:
    from contingency, 230–232
    in *Summa Theologica*, 245–246
    wager argument, 229–230
Prophecies:
    about Messiah, 70–72
    of Christ, 82–86
    fulfilled by Christ, 70–73
Prophets, 24–25

Reason as a guide, 240–243
Religion:
    definition of, 238–239
    evolution in religion, 243–244
Resurrection:
    Coma theory of, 86
    Deception theory of, 89–90
    Hallucination theory of, 94–95, 103–106
    vs. other "resurrections," 99–102
Resurrection appearances, 91–96

Sadducees, 22–23
Science vs. God, 236–238
Scripture, Holy:
    content of, 215–216
    inspiration of, 216–219
Shintoism, 11
Stability of Catholic Church, 165–166

Taoism, 9–10
Tests of Historicity, 49–50
Tradition:
    meaning of, 219
    and the Fathers, 220
Trustworthiness of Gospels, 55–56

Unity of the Catholic Church, 162–164